going up th

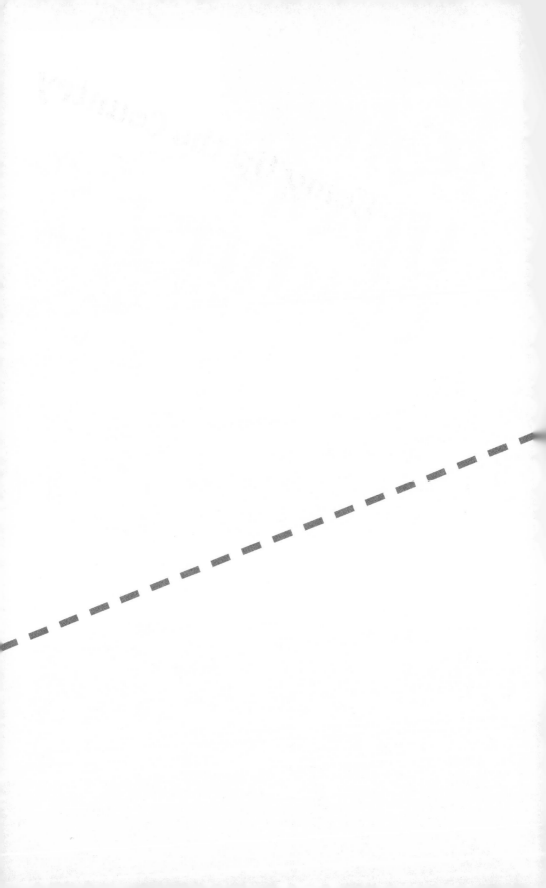

going Up the Country

When the Hippies, Dreamers, Freaks, and Radicals Moved to Vermont

YVONNE DALEY

Foreword by Tom Slayton

* * *

Wesleyan University Press

Middletown, Connecticut

Wesleyan University Press
Middletown, CT 06459
www.wesleyan.edu/wespress
© 2018 Yvonne Daley
All rights reserved
Manufactured in the United States of America
Designed by Eric M. Brooks
Typeset in Parkinson Electra by Passumpsic Publishing

First Wesleyan University Press edition 2020
Previously published by University Press of New England in 2018
ISBN for the Wesleyan edition: 978-0-8195-7971-3

The Library of Congress cataloged the previous edition as follows:

Names: Daley, Yvonne, author. | Slayton, Tom, 1941- writer of foreword.
Title: Going up the country : when the hippies, dreamers, freaks, and radi-
    cals moved to Vermont / Yvonne Daley ; foreword by Tom Slayton.
Description: Hanover : University Press of New England, [2018] | Includes
    bibliographical references and index. |
Identifiers: LCCN 2017053907 (print) | LCCN 2018032628 (ebook) |
    ISBN 9781512602838 (epub, mobi, & pdf) | ISBN 9781512600315 |
    ISBN 9781512600315 (pbk. : alk. paper) | ISBN 9781512602838 (ebook)
Subjects: LCSH: Counterculture—Vermont—History—20th century. |
    Hippies—Vermont.
Classification: LCC F55 (ebook) | LCC F55 .D35 2018 (print) | DDC 306/.1—dc23
LC record available at https://lccn.loc.gov/2017053907

5 4 3 2 1

Front cover image: Dressed up in the back yard. Photo by Peter Simon.
Simon wrote of this photo: "While living at Tree Frog Farm commune in
Vermont, our big 'dress up' celebration for the year would be the annual May
Day gathering of fellow communards in the southern Vermont and western
Massachusetts area. Here we are getting ready for the pilgrimage to our next-
door neighbor's commune, Total Loss Farm." Counterculture celebrations
throughout Vermont on May Day marked the ancient spring holiday while
also expressing solidarity with International Workers' Day.

In memory of

Philip Agnoletti

Davis Barrett

Lynne Sielaff Rheam

Sally Johnson

Harry Bender

Iris Ferraro

Barbara Herrigel Rawls

Peter Bourque

Patrick Farrow

Mark Skakel

Lou Buzone

Jim Nelson

Rod Clarke

Susan Green

Jane Skakel

counterculture | ˈkoun(t)ər ˌkəlcHər, noun:
a way of life and set of attitudes opposed to
or at variance with the prevailing social norm:
the idealists of the '60s counterculture.

NEW OXFORD AMERICAN DICTIONARY

* * *

God help us,
refugees in winter dress
skating home on thin ice
from the Apocalypse

VERANDAH PORCHE

* * *

How the sandpaper of life smooths us out.

CECILE BETIT

CONTENTS

Woods make people love one another & kind & obliging & good-natured.
They set much more by one another than in ye old settlements.
 REVEREND NATHAN PERKINS of Hartford, Connecticut, in his
 Narrative of a Tour through the State of Vermont in the Year 1789

When I was in high school, Vermont was perhaps the most politically conservative state in the Union. Now it may be the most liberal. The state legislature, once firmly moss-backed Republican, has become vigorously Democratic, with a peppering of Progressives. The state that in 1936 joined Maine and Maine alone in voting for Alf Landon over Franklin D. Roosevelt can now be counted on to cast its whopping three electoral votes for the Democratic presidential candidate, whoever he or she may be.

This transformation has affected virtually every aspect of our lives. In the 1950s, my town, Montpelier, had three or four restaurants, depending on how you counted. Today, by the same standard there are more than thirty. Several are run by the New England Culinary Institute, a professional cooking school started by graduates from nearby Goddard College. Local markets and chain supermarkets have been augmented by food co-operatives and natural food stores throughout the state. And our diets have been changed and enriched by the addition.

The same phenomenon has occurred in culture and entertainment. Instead of one movie theater in town, showing one movie for weeks at a time, we now have two movie houses showing six or more films that change often enough to keep us visually sated. One of these is a small art-film house that runs an annual film festival drawing viewers from across New England.

Not all the changes are positive. The number of dairy farms continues to dwindle, raising concern because they are the mainstay of Vermont agriculture. Yet Vermont's alternative-farming scene is flourishing, and produces an array of foodstuffs from locally grown wheat to organic vegetables and beef. Sheep, once the dominant farm beast in the Green Mountains, then just about abandoned as an enterprise forty years ago, are making a comeback.

It wasn't only the influx of the counterculture—communes and "hippies" and tie-dyed clothing or lack of clothing, drugs and all the rest of it—that changed Vermont. The interstate highways that in the 1970s linked Vermont to the outside world, and the amazing blossoming of new electronic media and the Internet also played major roles.

But the countercultural phenomenon, which Yvonne Daley skillfully recounts in this book, was an important part of that broad sweeping political and cultural change. To be sure, there was fear and some conflict when literally thousands of out-of-state young people began coming to Vermont to live —often in ways quite unlike their traditional Vermont neighbors. But there was also something else, something subtler and quite unexpected.

The largely unwritten story of the counterculture's "invasion" of Vermont was that the young nonconformist newcomers were, more often than not, helped and eventually welcomed by the native Vermonters they lived alongside. Chris Braithwaite, a Canadian newspaperman, moved to Glover in 1970 and lived communally with friends for a while on a farm they called Entropy Acres. Soon after, Braithwaite met a local farmer named Loudon Young, who was friendly and helpful. "He'd stop by and look at the stovepipe coming out of our wood stove and say something like, 'You really ought to clean that out once in a while,'" Braithwaite recalled, noting that Young had probably saved Entropy Acres from a serious chimney fire.

Braithwaite soon had an opportunity to return the favor. On July 4, 1971, one of Young's nephews set off a skyrocket that landed on the roof of a barn. That barn and another went up in flames, and though Young got his cattle out in time, he suddenly had to build a new barn to house them. Braithwaite pitched in to help, worked with Young to rebuild, and thereby cemented their friendship.

After a lot of hard work farming for very little financial reward, Braithwaite decided he'd had enough and began thinking about starting a local weekly newspaper. Young told him, "I don't think you've got a snowball's chance in hell," but shortly after the *Barton Chronicle* began publication in 1974, Young showed up at the paper's office with a neatly handwritten humorous column. "It was terrific," Braithwaite said. He ran it on the back page. "And Loudon just kept going. We became the paper people read backward." Young's column ran every week for years, and his young neighbor got an ongoing tutelage in upcountry Vermont lore and humor.

As Yvonne Daley points out, this sort of friendly relationship was repeated time after time across the state. There were some conflicts and confrontations, but more often there was understanding, and mutual assistance. Despite Vermont's original nervousness about an "invasion," for the most part, the newcomers were accepted and got along well, especially with their more traditional neighbors.

Why did this happen? I think there were a number of factors involved, many of which had to do with the way Vermont has been and is—its history, ethics, and folk culture. In the eighteenth century, Vermont was the frontier of America—the northern frontier. Life was tough here, and people needed one another to survive in a wilderness that literally howled. As the citified Reverend Nathan Perkins (who vigorously detested the newly formed state because of its bad roads, Deism, and rough-hewn crudity) noted with some amazement, people here depended on one another, and so were kinder and more considerate than in the large cities of southern New England. Newcomers were welcome because every new family was an additional bulwark against a hostile climate and rugged terrain. Vermonters needed each other then, and they need each other now.

The state today is statistically the most rural in the nation because some 65 percent of its people live in "rural" settings scattered across its exceptionally mountainous landscape. Consequently, over the last two centuries, the frontier ethic has become a rural ethic that endures. People are usually decent to their neighbors even when they disagree with them, and a primary reason for that is that Vermont is not only rural, but small—both in size and population. Vermont has something over 600,000 residents, which makes its total population about the same as a middle-sized American city. And with approximately 9,500 square miles within its borders, only five states are smaller geographically. Compounding this is the fact that for most of its history the state's bad roads and mountainous terrain meant that its 246 towns were often isolated, and the townsfolk had to live in close interdependence with one another.

It's really hard to be unpleasant to someone when you know that you're likely to meet them on the street the next day. Knowing your neighbors doesn't make either of you better people. But it does make you more considerate, especially if there aren't that many of them.

There is a negative side to smallness and rural isolation. Small villages can be ingrown and gossipy. The ten-cow hill farms of the past could produce blighted hopes and thwarted lives. But Vermonters have long loved their state because it represents an alternative way of living. Small towns, small schools, in small, rural valleys with small farms, and small churches, all overseen by a small state government—a world, that is, of limits willingly accepted—can create some of the very qualities the modern, predominately urban world lacks: closeness to nature, pleasure in simple work and activities, a sense of connection to your neighbors and community. In short, a meaningful life.

All this was, of course, precisely what many of the countercultural young people were seeking. And so they came, and often, they stayed. They wanted to get out of the rat race by building a different kind of life. They were willing to endure long winters, live simply, and do hard physical work. Consequently, after the initial strangeness of the newcomers wore off, their Vermont neighbors saw that they shared many values with them. Work was traded, friendships were made, and the counterculturists, over time, made lives in their newly adopted homes.

Verandah Porche was one of the founders of Total Loss Farm, a commune in the southern Vermont town of Guilford. She was a young poet who came there in 1968. She and a few others still live on the farm's eighty-plus acres of forest and gardens. And in the nearly fifty years since then, she has become a vital part of both the town—which she rightly regards as her hometown now—and the broader community of southeastern Vermont.

Porche conducts poetry workshops in local libraries, schools, hospitals, and other venues. She writes poems and articles celebrating the anniversaries, weddings, and deaths of her friends and neighbors in and around Guilford. And at Guilford's town meeting in March of 2017, she was elected to serve on the town's select board. She has, in short, become a valued part of Guilford's very vital community life. Vermont has, in effect, folded her in.

In 2011, to help celebrate the 250th anniversary of Guilford, she wrote a play, "Broad Brook Anthology," that anthologized the stories she had gathered from her neighbors. "It was a play of prose poems about their youth, schooling, mischief, courtship, and weddings," she recalled. "Afterwards, we had a lemonade social and all the actors got together with the people they portrayed."

"It was lovely," she recalled. "People still talk about it." The play, which she calls "my love poem to Guilford," will likely be performed again next year, when Total Loss Farm celebrates its 50th anniversary.

In *Going Up the Country*, Yvonne Daley touches on many aspects of the counterculture's arrival in Vermont. It's an important piece of our history because it documents one of the reasons Vermont changed dramatically during the latter twentieth century. Her book may also help to debunk a long-standing misperception of this state—as a land of taciturn farmers of predominately English extraction. That image has been false for more than a century. Waves of immigrants from French Canada, Italy, Sweden, Scotland, Germany, and, most recently, eastern Europe and the Middle East, have transformed the state's pedigree over and over again. Barre, Burlington, Rutland, Andover, Proctor, and other communities in the Green Mountains are ethnically rich. Black people have not only lived in Vermont since colonial times, they have many times been major actors in the state's history. The countercultural "invasion" of the 1970s was simply one more influx of immigrants, one that, like previous waves of newcomers, encountered some suspicion and resistance at first, but was accepted and ultimately welcomed. The experiences of Chris Braithwaite and Verandah Porche were repeated across the state.

And gradually, Vermont transformed those unconventional newcomers into Vermonters—even as the newcomers, in turn, transformed Vermont.

Going Up the Country

In Wildness is the preservation of the world.
HENRY DAVID THOREAU

Introduction

To have been a child at a time when words of wisdom and encouragement inspired one to think beyond one's own small needs and wants is a fortunate thing, while to have experienced the loss of one's champions—violently, suddenly—is a mighty shock, one that leaves the bereaved in bewilderment and with a penetrating sorrow. My generation was not the first to have witnessed this kind of diminution, but it was the first to do so from the safety of our "living" rooms as the killings were broadcast again and again on the new American marvel, the color TV. The murders of our heroes—President John Fitzgerald Kennedy, Attorney General Robert Kennedy, and Dr. Martin Luther King, Jr., the black preacher of nonviolence—have been rebroadcast so many times, you'd think they would no longer pain us, yet the sorrow is never diminished, and neither is the sense of lost possibility. I'd wager that our distrust of some aspects of government and our rejection of the status quo were born in those years in which these men were gunned down. For, despite the insularity and safety from suffering that our parents had tried so hard to provide, we felt cheated of the dreams these men embodied.

In other ways, there was a polarity to our lives that only began to reveal itself as our generation, the baby boomers, came of age. We walked to school in relative safety, played outdoors in any kind of weather, watched *American Bandstand* after school. There was canasta and lemonade on our front porches, sock hops and football games, class trips to Washington, and, for many, the opportunity to be the first in our families to go to college. But these and other sweet aspects of the era mask the darker sides of a country trying to ignore the horrors of war and poverty, one in which women were relegated to home and jobs, not professions; a time when you were measured by your last name, your occupation, where you worshiped, the color of your skin, the

1

cost of your car and home. From these contradictions, the counterculture, black power, and the women's liberation movement were born. Each in its own way and together left the nation polarized between those who passionately protested the status quo and those who would eagerly adopt the moniker popularized by President Nixon—"the silent majority"—to identify their adherence to traditional norms, mores, and values. For the people who had been through times much tougher than ours by any measure, our anger and rejection were incomprehensible.

Like so many of my generation, born at the end of World War II, I had missed the deprivation, rationing, and closeness to the casualties of war that defined my older siblings' childhood. Until my mid-teens, life was defined by Catholic school and church, an Irish/Italian neighborhood, the comfort of the middle class in the suburbs of Boston. Out there, somewhere, there were beatniks, un-American activities trials, racism, and deep misogyny, the Cold War and its fanaticisms, all of which I was fairly unaware of in the insulation of family, church, school, and neighborhood. And then, seemingly overnight, the world changed.

Suddenly, we were alive in it as each morning we woke to news of death: not just the deaths of our heroes, but soon the deaths of former classmates, of brothers and sisters, neighbors and strangers, dead in a foreign country fighting an ill-defined enemy; and the deaths and beatings of black people demanding the basic rights of citizenship and white college kids working for the black cause; so many adults and children, some much younger than us, murdered in church basements, on back roads in the South, at Kent State University, in Oakland, California. And, so, despite all our parents and our teachers and religious leaders had done to try to protect us, as with generations before, death came to define us.

And war as well.

Our fathers rarely spoke of their war but, in retrospect, we see that it was always present, as present in their silence as it was in their sudden angers and nightly cocktails. We grew up on military parades and trips to monuments to war, on TV shows where the settlers were the good guys and the American Indians the savages, on movies that celebrated valor and martyrdom, movies in which Americans were always victorious and the hero came home, but the names on the plaques in our city halls and the memorials in the town park were all for fathers and brothers who did not come home, who died, often young, to make us safe. These were other generations' wars, not ours, and even though in school we'd practiced how to survive a nuclear war, ducking and covering under our desks, by the time we'd read John Hersey's *Hiroshima*, required reading in many high school and college curricula, we knew survival after nuclear war would require more than acting like a turtle. Wouldn't putting all that effort into preventing war be a better approach for humankind? Thus, when it came to our generation's war and our unprepared brothers and friends being sent to battle in faraway jungles, it seemed impossible, a bad dream, disconnected from our safe and pampered lives, something that happened on TV or the movie screen, not with us in battle. We wondered where this Vietnam was anyway and why we were at war with the Vietnamese people. This too, the seeming senselessness of the Vietnam War, against a people who had done us no harm, defined us. It made us question our government and, by default, our parents and society itself. Couldn't everyone see the stupidity of war?

Conformity defined us—and then it didn't. Our parents, older cousins, and siblings had seemed content with the upwardly mobile version of the perfect family: mom baking after-school cookies in her all-electric kitchen; dad at work in his own business, which some of us were expected to join, or in offices downtown, or factories where the dulling hammer of repetition was itself dulled by the promise of a decent paycheck. But as we delayed adulthood with college and travel, the idea of settling down to the nine-to-five or the apron and wooden spoon began to feel like a version of hell.

As children born into a time of growth and plenty, we were defined by food, not just the abundance of it but its convenience, its symbolism of all things modern: TV dinners and canned vegetables, sugar-coated cereals, soft drinks and Kool-Aid, casseroles and box cake, white bread, yellow mustard, and, of course, bologna. When we discovered real food, crunchy brown rice and whole wheat bread, spinach from the ground rather than a can, vegetables harvested moments before eating, it was a revelation. Vegetables were good! Bread didn't have to stick to the roof of your mouth. Bologna was creepy.

Slogans and pejorative "instruction" had defined us, too. Don't be a wimp, a queer, a fairy, a slut, a commie, an egghead. Big boys don't cry. Girls don't do that. Act like a lady. Be a man. Lucky Strike: it's light up time! Rest assured; be insured. They'll know you've arrived when you drive up in an Edsel. You can't have too much. Rejecting all that, we made our own slogans: Hell no, we won't go. Make love, not war. Everybody must get stoned.

We were defined by myths—the myths of our religions and our race, the idea that Americans were good and pure, that we were all equal. Education,

Mississippi, books upon books, the very education and opportunities our parents gave us, stripped away these illusions. The Trail of Tears, slave ships, voter suppression, Japanese internment camps, atomic bombs—how could one continue to believe we were always the good guys with that history?

Most of all, however, we were defined by privilege. We had Erector Sets and bikes and dolls and clothes our parents never dreamed of possessing as children. We were perhaps the first generation to spend much of our childhood outside playing, not working, free to roam neighborhoods, woods, and backstreet alleys, free from "stranger danger" although there was unspoken danger in those homes in which the cardinal rule was what happened at home stayed at home. For most of us, it was white privilege that defined us although we hadn't yet identified it as that, there in our segregated schools, neighborhoods, and suburbs. When the reality of black lives came to us, we tried to make a difference, but we did so from a place that we could always retreat back to, a privilege those we tried to help did not possess. That, too, defined us.

And so, some of us said no. No to conformity, to suburbia and the "straight" life, no to haircuts and ties and button-down collars, no to permanents and rollers and bras, no to nine-to-five and church on Sunday, no to segregation and bigotry. But, most of all, being human after all and spoiled and self-protective, we said no to war. First we raged against it: demonstrating and getting arrested, burning draft cards and, then, for some, taking more drastic measures, making bombs to stop the dropping of bombs. When all that failed, many simply chose to walk away from the whole mess—moving to places alien to our parents: to communes in Vermont; ashrams in California, pueblos in New Mexico, lofts in Greenwich Village.

This is one story about that time, the story of Vermont, a state most dramatically affected by the counterculture, by the ragged, leaderless, and divided assemblage of scruffy young people who came by the thousands to Vermont's hill and valley towns to try something else, not protest so much as rehabilitation—of self, of a dream, of a future. If there was a commonality among us it was love of the land. Vermont's emerald hills and sweet valleys were better than Oz; the place felt womb-like, nurturing, simultaneously old and pristine. Beyond that, there was the promise of cheap housing in remote locations, a place that provided, as Bob Dylan put it, shelter from the storm. I count myself among the thousands.

My Vermont story began in 1967 when my first husband and I left graduate school at the University of Dayton to move to Vermont, which seemed saner than the Boston where I had grown up or the New Jersey of Steve's childhood. I, too, had been a war demonstrator. The Vietnam War had transformed me from the daughter my parents knew to the girl calling them from a police station, a girl who said goodbye to her high school sweetheart one Easter Sunday to learn of his death less than a month later, the first of many close deaths from war. I was very close to my parents as a child, especially my father. It was he who informed me of Philip's death and accompanied me to the funeral parlor where there was no casket, just the large photo of him in uniform. Dad cried with me then, but we argued about the war on the way home, the first of many arguments to come.

I had a single memory of Vermont, from a childhood ride across the Connecticut River while on summer vacation in New Hampshire. My father was showing off his amazing sense of direction, a favorite pastime that took us to unexpected places, only this time he had taken a dirt road that dead-ended in a muddy dooryard where a straw-hatted farmer awaited, leveling a shotgun at our new, fancy Pontiac. My rearview movie, as dad sped us away, remains vivid in memory: acre after acre of rolling green pastures, a falling-down barn with a cedar-shake roof, iconic heifers grazing under a perfectly blue sky, and that farmer grinning at me as he grew tinier and tinier, his arm raised in defiance of the coming of us, the outsiders.

Steve taught at Otter Valley Union High School in Brandon for a year or two before abandoning any idea of normalcy. We lived in town that first year, then moved to a farm in Goshen with the first of our five children. Goshen, to this day, is a community without much of a center. There's a town hall in the church basement—the church itself rarely used—a town garage, and a town office. No stores, no meetinghouse, but miles and miles of dirt roads that lead to deep, old woods. I had convinced myself that I had to live in the town and had been searching for a house to rent when I saw an older man standing in the front yard of an iconic white farmhouse, gazing at it in reverie. The man was Peter Romilly, a New York educator who had bought the farm in his youth and, after his wife's early death, visited rarely. He was returning to New York the very next day but, as I introduced myself and launched into my dream of living on a farm surrounded by woods, my infant son on my hip and probably wearing a long, flowered dress, he offered that two-hundred-year-old farmhouse, an immense barn, and seventy-five acres nestled beneath Hogback Mountain for $75 a month—no credit check, no nothing. He hadn't even met my husband.

For the next decade, I grew vegetables, flowers, and herbs and for a while ran the area food co-op out of that house. We were soon surrounded by like-minded friends, all exiles from elsewhere who rented or bought homes and camps even further into the woods. My hippie name was Boston because of my ridiculous accent. In my circle of close friends, everyone had their own homes but we lived in one another's, sharing communal meals, communal vw bugs and busses, our individual families part of a larger family connected by politics, pot, a single electric mixer, a rototiller, books and music, the things we learned together. The harder it was to do something or the more rudimentary our tools, the better: I had a loom, sewed my children's clothing, raised goats named Moonbeam, Rainbow, and Waterfall, made yogurt and cheese from goats' milk, gardened with spade fork and hoe while Steve, with his graduate degree in chemistry, tried his hand at working on the roads, building chimneys, and chopping wood. One day early on, the road commissioner and Steve's boss, Hawley Hathaway, quipped in his strong Vermont accent, "Your husband mustn't love you much." When I asked what he meant, he said one word: "Elm." He was right; the elm and poplars Steve had cut for our two Ashley woodstoves didn't burn for shit. But we were learning.

As with so many other transplants to Vermont, the locals were suspicious of our motivations or sanity. Why would well-educated young people give up the comforts of the city or the suburbs for a poorly insulated farmhouse in the middle of the Green Mountain National Forest? We knew we were the subjects of gossip, some of it derisive, or worse. But within a few years, I was elected a justice of the peace for the town of Goshen, was recording oral histories of old-timers, and had organized a community club. The locals didn't know that I and the other hippies living at the end of the North Goshen Road had formed the North Goshen Secessionist Society, where we followed news of the war and harbored ideas of seceding from the union.

Of course, it wasn't always rainbows and roses. After the interview at Otter Valley, Steve and I had stopped in downtown Brandon, parking our rusty old vw bus in front of the Brandon Cash Market. Despina Louras, the diminutive storeowner, had posted signs by the magazine rack that read, "This is not a library." That should have been fair warning.

"Is that your thing out there?" she demanded as I gathered a few items. When I realized she was talking about our van, I conceded it was. She was so small she had to stand on a wooden box to look over the register, but she was formidable. "Move it," she commanded. "That's my parking place for my customers and you are not one of my customers."

I looked at the candy bars and soda in my hands.

"Put them back," was all she said.

It wasn't long, however, before Desi welcomed me for late-night milk when the only grocery store in town, Humiston's Market, had closed, one time calling on my party line at dawn to report that my oldest son was in the store "in his cowboy pajamas," buying candy for a party he planned to have at daycare later that day. He'd ridden his bike down the mountain with a few dollars poached from my cookie jar only to be stumped in his bold enterprise by Desi who, I'm sure, loved dispensing that story for the next day or two.

* * *

A succession of hippies lived in two houses located outside of town on Short Swamp Road owned by the writer Willis Barnstone. This little enclave attracted much unwanted attention. Barrie Bailey, who lived there with her first husband, Jim Nelson, tells frightening stories of young local men repeatedly driving by their home, screaming to put some clothes on the kids by day or pointing rifles at their home by night, even sneaking up to look in their windows. On that occasion, Jim snuck behind the voyeur and nearly gave the guy a heart attack.

I must confess that in those early days I was a little anxious about walking past LaDuke's bar and restaurant, Brandon's most popular hangout, known for its amazing perch over the Neshobe River waterfalls, and also for having to replace its huge front window after occasional brawls. I was far from sure how the locals, mostly men, felt about me with my waist-length hair and painted clothing and Steve with his corkscrew curls and motorcycle boots.

One day, one of the newcomers to our group, a longhaired, skinny guy named Mike Lewis, stopped by to invite us to LaDuke's for a drink. First of all, most of the hippies I knew weren't into booze or bars, and, second, I wasn't interested in testing my popularity at LaDuke's on a Saturday night. Mike quipped he'd never seen a bar he wasn't welcome in and off he went. The next day he showed up with the story. He had been sitting at the bar next to three colorful regulars: Hugh Moffett, a journalist famous for interviewing Dr. Albert Schweitzer in Africa and Soviet leader Nikita Khrushchev for *Life* magazine before moving to Brandon and becoming a state legislator; John-John the Indian, as everyone called John Dedam, a Canadian Micmac artist; and Ray Downes, a plumber who'd saved Steve's and my butts every time our gravity-fed water pipes froze up. Mike hadn't even sipped his beer before Ray began teasing him about his hair. "Hey, hippie, what kind of job you got that lets you grow your hair like a lady," Ray asked, putting special emphasis on the word lady.

Ray Downes was more of a local celebrity than either John-John or Hugh Moffett. Considered the strongest man in Vermont, he had rescued us our first Christmas Eve, working outside in three feet of snow to free up the water line before coming inside with a bottle of something. Steve was a weenie when it came to booze and spent the next hour in the bathroom, then bed, while Ray and I wrapped presents and shared his bottle. I heard about the deer he'd wounded then tracked for a day through the woods, put out of its misery and carried home, a two-hundred-pound buck carried for miles on his back. And the story of the black bear he kept out back of his house and the bobcats he kept in his cellar. If someone doubted that he had a bear, he'd go home, get the bear onto the back of his truck, and drive it to town to show he was no liar. He was one hell of a storyteller and everyone in Brandon swore those stories were true.

Mike didn't know any of this. If he had, this might be a different story. Mike was a wannabe poet but at the time he was working at the Brandon Training School, the state residential facility for people with developmental disabilities. The school attracted conscientious objectors who could complete their alternative service there, and it also had a tight lesbian and gay community. Mike was not gay and took umbrage with Ray's remark that he looked like a lady. As Ray ragged on, Mike responded that he could grow his hair any way he wanted because he was a poet. The two really got into it then and soon a scuffle ensued with Mike hauling off and knocking Ray to the floor.

At that point in his story, Mike conceded he was fairly alarmed, surrounded as he was by Brandon locals, many of them twice his size and already in their cups. Alarmed, that is, until Ray reached his hand up from the bar floor, cracked a grin and announced, "Buy the lad a drink. We always needed a poet around here." Unbeknownst to me, Mike had had polio as a child. As a result, despite his scrawny appearance, he had great upper-body strength. The next night, a bunch of us returned with him to LaDuke's, which, we discovered, served the best hamburgers, French fries, and homemade raspberry pie in Vermont, food we rarely ate at home and secretly longed for. In no time whatsoever, we got to know all the locals and became regulars ourselves, and the nighttime drive-bys on Short Swamp Road ended.

That made life a little easier for Barrie and Jim Nelson. Jim was the quintessential hippie, flowing hair and beard, overalls and no shirt his favorite warm-weather costume, creating lightshows in the living room to Holy Modal Rounders music, dispensing pot and LSD while Barrie, who had no interest in drugs, nursed the babies, grew the family's food, and learned the uses of wild plants. After their divorce and her marriage to Wally Bailey, Barrie and her family became stalwart residents of Salisbury where she taught for twenty-five years in Vermont's Migrant Children Education Program and volunteered with Salisbury's Conservation Commission.

Her story, like mine, is representative of so many young people who came to Vermont in the 1960s and '70s. While many were familiar with the excesses of the times, from sex to drugs, once the kids started coming, life got real. Like Jim, my first husband was not very good at keeping a job. By the mid-1970s, as the economy changed, we found living on next to nothing less glamorous . . . or possible.

* * *

Life is an ever-changing venture, and, as the women's movement gained momentum in the 1970s and the economy also changed dramatically, many of our marriages were challenged. My girlfriends and I, like our counterparts throughout Vermont and the nation itself, began to get itchy to use our own educations and follow our passions outside the home. It wasn't that we wanted to return to the suburbs or the city; we began searching for ways to stay in Vermont and have careers. The term *supermom*—invented for women who were raising children and running a home while also having a career—became attractive. We could do it all, couldn't we?

In 1975, a group of women activists and nationally renowned writers such as Rita Mae Brown and Dorothy Allison, Vermont novelist and poet Grace Paley, and fellow poet Ruth Stone organized Sagaris University, an institute for serious political study of feminist issues at Johnson State College in northeastern Vermont. Sagaris had been preceded by a convocation on women's issues at Middlebury College. Burlington bookseller Kathy Roberts remembers collecting Gloria Steinem, the founder of *Ms.* magazine and a speaker at the event, at the airport in her vw bus. "These women's gatherings were life-changing," Roberts, who worked for decades as a school and city librarian, recalled. For some women in attendance, these meetings were the first time they had spoken openly about their reservations about their marriages or the restrictions of motherhood, and such subjects as orgasms, stalled careers, and abortion. How did the word get out to women across Vermont about these events? Word of mouth, I imagine. One weekend, some of us traveled to one such event held at Johnson State College; there we listened to lectures on women's potential, danced topless, and vowed to not get lost as so many of our mothers had in the never-ending chores of house-keeping.

Sagaris, along with a plethora of women's and men's support groups that sprang up in the early and mid-70s along with the founding of women's health centers in Burlington, Rutland, Brattleboro, and Montpelier, were vehicles that launched a second wave of exploration into gender roles and sexual freedom. Couples tried open marriages; people came out as gay and lesbian; women began to demand more autonomy, and counterculture fathers became more involved in raising their children. Some of the dropouts returned to school and careers. Many marriages ended, mine among them. And, truth be told, many of the fathers drifted away . . . to other states and other families. Of course, not all of the marriages dissolved; nor did all fathers move away. Nonetheless, despite attempts to "share" child rearing after divorce, many children of the counterculture were raised in single-family homes, most often led by mothers negotiating careers and motherhood simultaneously. New marriages followed and new families as a generation began the redefining once again of what it meant to be a family.

* * *

As many of us discovered, making our way back into "normal" life after a decade or more on the commune or other counterculture experiment was not quite simple. After the marriage and farm-life ended, I applied for a job at the *Rutland Herald,* carrying the little book of poetry I'd published under my arm; the editor was justifiably unimpressed, but I eventually got the job, writing my first articles on those old-timers whose stories I'd collected on my old reel-to-reel recorder. And in the next years, as I developed a career as a journalist, I came to understand that Vermont was of interest to people far and wide. Outsiders regarded us, whether it was the hippies who were transforming a state into a more liberal place or the natives who supported or resisted the changes we brought, with a kind of curiosity that suggested we were a sort of foreign country, American to the core, of course, but fundamentally independent, quirky, unpredictable, even incomprehensible in our allegiance to old ways, to making do or doing without, to choosing values over money, to blending new ways of doing with the old.

What I didn't realize until I started reporting on people and issues far from Vermont in my middle years was how lucky I'd been to have spent my hippie years in the Green Mountains and to have begun my journalistic career in Vermont, how remarkably trusting and open Vermonters had been with me at every step, not as closed down emotionally or suspicious of motivation as I found people to be in more urban areas. While Vermonters' reputation for reticence has its basis in fact, that characterization masks a general curiosity and generosity of nature that members of the counterculture generation were the beneficiaries of.

An example: My second son, Erik, was born during one of Vermont's more famous snowstorms, in the early morning hours of February 9, 1969. Having already given birth once by natural childbirth, I was comfortable with a home birth when the town plow broke down a quarter mile from my house and it became apparent I might not make it to the hospital in time.

Hold on, my neighbors said, turning out with shovels and even a mule-driven plow to open up the road so we hippies could get to the hospital in time for Erik's birth. Years later, I came to see that it wasn't just that we needed those natives to teach us which wood burned best or how to protect our delicate tomato plants in a mountain town where frost might come in any month, to dig us out so we could deliver a baby at the hospital, whether we wanted to or not. They needed us, too, as many of their own children were less than interested in learning the crafts, tasks, and occupations of the country. Indeed, just as the counterculture kids were arriving, Vermont youths were departing in droves, off for the lives and jobs we'd rejected.

In those first years in Vermont, I spent many afternoons with a neighbor named Doris Reed, traipsing the roadsides, learning the use of colt's foot, wild ginger, and chokecherries, hunting morels and wild asparagus, and finding rare Vermont wildflowers, the calypso orchid and the lady slipper, passions her children did not share. When I stopped by her neighbor's house to buy raw milk, Guy Goodrich and his wife, Dorothy, welcomed my interest in their bantam hens as long as I wasn't interrupting Dorothy's TV soap operas. From them and others, I learned how to can vegetables, make anadama bread, elderberry wine, and crock pickles. There were even a few who asked about marijuana. For, as curious as I was about their way of life, it turned out they were also interested in what they assumed was mine.

* * *

The journalist David Talbot tells the story of the counterculture transformation of San Francisco in his book *Season of the Witch*. While he celebrates the city's reputation as the epicenter of the cultural revolution, Talbot also catalogues the dark side of that time, from the Zodiac and Zebra killers to Charles Manson, who did his recruiting in San Francisco's Haight-Ashbury, and Jim Jones, who convinced his congregation to move to Guyana where they were forced to drink poison-laced Kool-Aid. Meanwhile, cops beat up hippies giving away free food and health care and Dan White, angered by the changes in his city, savagely murdered Mayor George Moscone and city supervisor Harvey Milk, San Francisco's first openly gay politician.

As I read Talbot's book and thought of those same years in Vermont, I realized how fortunate Vermont had been to avoid the worst of the era's over-indulgences. Over the past three years, I've talked with hundreds of people who were part of the hippie invasion of Vermont, locals who embraced the counterculture movement in their youth, sociologists, politicians, educators, and ordinary people who lived through those times, including some who lament the changes that we brought to the Green Mountain State.

There are, of course, scores of Vermont residents, both native and transplant, who do not welcome gay marriage or environmental regulation or any of the myriad other changes that are associated with the counterculture. Yet even they will concede that the very character of Vermont, a place that has always honored independence and the right to be different, a place whose residents have always been grounded by weather and the land, remains strong. Simply put, the right to be different is what attracted the counterculture kids to Vermont in the first place. Somehow, I think, we've found a courteous balance between old values and new. Indeed, I like to claim, although many will deny it because I was not born there, to be a Vermonter, one who came seeking a place to call home after the disappointments, heartaches, and excesses of the 1960s and found it among the rolling green pastures my father raced away from.

* * *

Our generation came with a soundtrack, anthems for all the elements of the movement from love and war, to resistance and rebellion, environmental concern to getting it on. It's only right that I share some of what I listened to as I've written this book. You'll find a soundtrack of suggested songs, recorded from 1967 to 1980 and organized by chapter, in the appendix.

A list of people who shared their stories with me can also be found at the back of the book. Following that is a list of sources, keyed by chapter, and some recommended readings.

The Hippie Invasion

The April 1972 *Playboy* magazine featured an article by Richard Pollak entitled "Taking Over Vermont." Among cartoons and articles about sex orgies and wife-swapping and the usual array of pin-ups wearing a tiny bit of "hippie" clothing, Pollak's story about a very un-*Playboy* place called Vermont warned of the impending invasion of "unwashed troublemakers" about to descend in marauding hordes on the quiet little state. Here's the opening paragraph: "Suppose the nation's alienated young decided to stage a takeover of Vermont. Not by staging a weekend rock festival at Rutland and then hanging around the Green Mountains like freaked-out trolls. Not by lacing the water supply with assorted chemical brain scramblers. Not even by trashing the 14-kt.-gold-leaf dome off the Statehouse in Montpelier. Suppose they decided to do it within the system, the hard-hat-approved American way— by ballot!"

Well, power to the people, how right Pollak was because that is exactly what happened.

The seeds for a takeover were well planted by the time Pollak's article appeared. Between 1965 and 1975, up to 100,000 young people with counterculture ideas had traveled north to the Green Mountains. Most were temporary visitors but, by 1972, thousands of hippies and people who identified with counterculture values were living on Vermont communes and collectives, in group houses and teepees, school buses, sugar shacks, and farmhouses across the state. They were smoking dope, making music and babies, growing food, and organizing statewide networks to provide one another with free health care, auto repair, and legal advice. They were buying brown rice by the fifty-pound sack and learning where the wild asparagus grew. They had established their own newspapers. Commune members from north and south had met on a farm hillside, harvested crops together, then made plans for how to transform Vermont. And then, you know what? They did it. Well, sort of. In a place like Vermont, a stubborn and ancient place with a unique history of independence, the transformation went both ways. Because of their sheer numbers, there's no question that the hippie invaders changed Vermont into a more radical place, one recognized by the outside world as socially quirky and politically liberal. The state's longtime residents and the realities of Vermont's environment and economic challenges changed the newcomers as well, imprinting them with traditional values that over time balanced the more radical elements within the counterculture. It has made for a most unusual story.

Contrary to Pollak's story, the majority of the newcomers had no intention of taking over the state through the political process. By the time they arrived, many had given up on the electoral process altogether. Many did, however, envision being part of a cultural revolution or rebirth, one that would imbue the small state's celebrated agrarian practices with their more progressive values and self-congratulatory standards. Many thought of Vermont as a refuge, believing that a national apocalypse was at hand, one brought on by any number of villains: the man, the masters of war, the titans of industry, big brother. The list was long. As racial and political divides tore communities across the country apart, the newcomers viewed Vermont as a place where they might work together to create alternative ways of defining families, doing business, teaching children, and making decisions. In time, they hoped their ideas would spread to the wider community. In that, indeed, they did see their roles as revolutionary. However, the apocalypse they envisioned didn't happen the way they feared or hoped. And, as it turned out, Pollak's proposition turned out to be right: a generation of hippies and free thinkers did transform the small state using the tried and true American way, by the ballot, electing more progressive politicians per capita in the intervening decades than any state and enacting legislation that routinely resulted in Vermont ranking among the most liberal states in the union.

The subtler and more meaningful impact of the counterculture generation on old Vermont, however, happened because the Green Mountains had long harbored radical elements and independent attitudes, attributes that contributed to the counterculture's ability to blend into the Vermont landscape. The most important of these qualities was the residents' undying respect for minding one's own business or, as eighth-generation Vermonter and longtime legislator Andy Christiansen expressed it, the right to do what you wish as long as your actions didn't hurt others or interfere with their property.

Christiansen had grown up on a multigenerational farm in East Montpelier and hung out with the freaks and dreamers at Goddard College and Bread and Puppet Theater, a kid with one foot in the counterculture and the other in old Vermont. While the hippies were grooving on summer meadows and wearing daisies in their hair, they needed Christiansen, and his parents, and their neighbors, strangers all at first, to keep them from freezing to death, burning their homes down, eating something really bad for them or failing in any number of ventures.

* * *

The state's motto, Freedom and Unity, provided a framework for balancing two valued but oppositional aspirations, ones that the counterculture could embrace. To live in Vermont, you had to accept the responsibilities of personal freedom and the demands of unity, of being part of a community. Today, in every town and village, you will meet people who fled the cities and suburbia for Vermont, part of a nationwide flight back to the land in reaction to the Vietnam War and the Nixon era coupled with a fascination with country living espoused in 1960s-era songs celebrating the redemptive value of nature as epitomized by Joni Mitchell's "Woodstock." Over the decades, as they infiltrated every aspect of Vermont as teachers and merchants, bakers and bankers, artists and social workers, mechanics and carpenters, fiddlers and poets, ice-cream makers and farmers, nurses and—yes—politicians, the hippies joined their neighbors on volunteer fire departments and rescue squads, bought old houses and rehabilitated them, built new businesses and raised their families much the same as the native people who became their neighbors, coworkers, and friends. Simultaneously, however, they brought dramatic changes that celebrated the old ways of doing things while reinventing them. For example, they embraced natural childbirth and midwifery, practices that had been the rule rather than the exception in Vermont well into the twentieth century, while also promulgating the idea of free health care, holistic medicine, and alternative treatments such as acupuncture and medical marijuana. In desiring healthy food, they took to the land, using rudimentary tools and techniques for farming while creating new job opportunities that have buoyed Vermont's agricultural and economic health from organic farms and farmers' markets to Vermont-made products sold widely. In the business world, they created jobs in the same old way, with ideas begun in garages and home offices, small shops and studios. Simultaneously, they introduced groundbreaking ideas, resulting in Vermont leading the way nationally in the fields of socially responsible business practices and employee-ownership of corporations.

* * *

Many of the people identified by statisticians, journalists, and others as hippies or members of the counterculture might not have used those words, then or now. Any number of terms applied—counterrevolutionary, back-to-the-lander, communard, transplant, radical, flatlander, seeker, acid head, Jesus freak or just freak, nonconformist, flower child, dropout, peacenik, free spirit, baby boomer—or none of the above. After all, nonconformists resist labels. As do Vermonters. There are differences, however, that should be noted. The word *counterculture* applies to the movement as a whole, as in its dictionary meaning of pursuing a way of life and behavioral attitudes that stand in opposition to the social norm. The term *hippie*, too, has general application, although many people who were called or perceived to be hippies disliked the word because it insinuated lack of hygiene. It comes from the word *hip*, more often associated with beatniks, to suggest a person who was in the know or aware. The term *activist* applies to those who were motivated politically, who believed their actions could make a difference and that it was immoral not to fight wrongs, whether political, social, racial, or economic. Freaks were more interested in physical pleasure than in the nuances or demands that changing a society or political circumstances would require. And back-to-the-landers were committed to a simpler way of life and were generally hardworking and focused, even when the work was beyond their physical capabilities or their long-term stamina.

Not all the newcomers felt radically alienated or revolutionary; as with any group, there were broad variations in both temperament and motivation. Most had been influenced by the notions and philosophies of the day, from the idea that "War is not healthy for children and other living things" to "You are what you eat." Many simply wanted a more peaceful and rural way of life. Senator Dick McCormack, a Democrat from Bethel who came to Vermont in 1968 from New York City with a guitar and little else, said "free spirit" would have best described him. He believed his generation was turned off to suburban and city life because American citizens had lost their connection to decision making. In Vermont, the newcomers discovered that the political system they were eager to replace with a more participatory system of

Senator Dick McCormack of Bethel as a young troubadour.
Photo by Jack Rowell

government was already in existence in the form of the annual town meeting at which residents elected town officials, approved or turned down budgets, and decided whether to allocate tax money to local causes, whether to show appreciation for veterans, support fire survivors, or fund a silly parade celebrating a weed like burdock or a vegetable like the Gilfeather turnip. For the young people who had felt disenfranchised from the political system, Vermont's long-standing tradition of local democracy allowed them to voice the convictions of the commune and the food co-op in the public arena; given their numbers, it's no surprise that dozens of Vermont towns have since passed resolutions against war, nuclear proliferation, and GMOs, supported the impeaching of President George W. Bush and efforts to provide universal health care. While few of their parents had taken their causes before their local governmental boards, the newcomers discovered they could petition their local select board or city council and, depending on the merit of their argument, get a fair hearing—not always, of course, especially in the early years of their intrusion into town affairs. They were newcomers, after all, and thus had no cachet. But with Vermonters, perseverance furthered their efforts—unless, of course, you acted like a jerk, whined, made a big deal about nothing, or otherwise acted superior or pushy. If so, you could probably wait forever for your cause to be considered.

As McCormack put it, "Vermont remains the most democratic state in the union and, at times, the most ornery; it's always been a radical place, a place where ideas and values mattered more than money or prestige. That hasn't changed much, or as much as in other places, with the coming of the hippies. It's evolved over time but the basics remain: one person, one vote. And, because of our small size, it's true that one person can make a big difference."

Pollak had come by the idea for the *Playboy* article from a treatise written by two Yale Law School graduates, James Blumstein and James Phelan. Since the world was in a mess and it would be impossible to overthrow the federal government or a large state, they promulgated the creation of "a truly experimental society in which new solutions to today's problems could be tried, an experimental state which would serve as a new frontier and encourage imagination, local innovation and, by its example, spur change in society as a whole."

Two national conditions supported their proposition. First, America was young. The median age in the United States in 1970 was twenty-eight because of the high birth rate after World War II, the so-called baby boom. By comparison, in 2016 the median age was thirty-eight. In 1971, for the first time in America's history, eighteen-year-olds were granted the right to vote. Thus, young people carried more political and cultural clout than they had previously. As the nation's third-least populous state, with 444,732 residents in 1970, and its proximity to the more populated states of the Northeast, Vermont was the logical place for such an experiment, preferable to the two less populated but more remote states, Wyoming and Alaska.

* * *

Forces other than a hippie invasion were already at work that unintentionally led to the reshaping of Vermont. Perhaps the most important had resulted from a 1962 U.S. Supreme Court ruling on apportionment. Until then, each Vermont town had sent one representative to the Vermont house, meaning a tiny town had the same power as a large city. The court found that system violated the idea of representative government; as a result, representational districts had to be created based on population. This decision obviously gave more power to large cities such as Rutland and Burlington over rural areas.

And, as places like Burlington and Brattleboro became populated with more and more liberal young people, their influence on the state increased dramatically, while the power of residents in smaller, more rural, and often more conservative towns decreased accordingly. As with all change, not everyone was happy with the ruling and its result. Emory Hebard, a representative from the small town of Glover, was heartsick. "Vermont has ceased to be Vermont," he told his fellow legislators.

Simultaneously, while most Vermonters in the 1960s and '70s identified as Republicans, the state's Republican Party experienced a division with a growing number of forward-thinking members challenging the status quo. Meanwhile, Democrats were flexing their political power statewide for the first time, following the revitalizing election of Massachusetts-born Phil Hoff as governor in 1962. To understand the full force of Hoff's election, consider that he was the first Democrat elected to that office since 1854. Add to these changes the construction of two interstate highways into and through Vermont, making the state more accessible to metropolitan areas to the south. No wonder there was trepidation when the *Playboy* article came out, filled with words like *take-over, freaked-out trolls,* and *chemical brain scramblers,* and the suggestion that 50,000 hippies were on their way, adding to the hippies already living in Vermont. Edward Corcoran, the public safety commissioner, responded to public suggestions that Vermonters form a modern unit of the Green Mountain Boys to repel the invaders by cautioning that overreaction could be more treacherous than the projected influx. It's easy to understand why native Vermonters felt that movements beyond their control were about to wreck a place they loved and wanted to protect. And, as it always is with human reaction to change, while the seeds of transformation and reinvigoration were planted, so too were seeds of resentment and frustration, ones that nearly three decades later led to the Take Back Vermont movement in which some residents sought to reverse the social changes they were uncomfortable with, changes they came to associate more with the coming of the young out-of-staters with their new and progressive ideas than with the fact that nowhere does time stand still.

It would be unfair to characterize the Take Back Vermont movement as one supported by only longtime or native Vermonters; its support came from old-timers and newcomers alike. As Steve Terry, the former managing editor of the *Rutland Herald* and legislative assistant to Senator Aiken, pointed out, conservative blowbacks in Vermont are in step with national trends in which the country has become more conservative since 9/11. Beyond that, he pointed out that the Take Back Vermont movement had its roots in even deeper resentments.

"Throughout time, there has been a strain in Vermont politics based on a fear of change and a desire to keep the Vermont stock pure," Terry, a Vermont native who subsequently became a Green Mountain Power executive, observed. He described how a 1930s-era plan to build a high-altitude roadway called the Green Mountain Parkway along the length of Vermont's mountain ridges showed that residents treasured their unspoiled wilderness more than tourist or federal grant money, while the debate also brought anti-Semitic feelings into the light as Vermonters openly expressed the fear that among other unwanted visitors, Jews from New York would have easy access to Vermont. The proposal was defeated 43,176 to 31,101 on Town Meeting Day 1936.

The parkway proposal came as Vermonters were concerned about rising poverty, increased illiteracy, and deteriorating health among the state's residents, as seen by the fact that the state had earned the second highest rate of "defect" among Americans taking the U.S. Army's draft-board physical exam. This led to another movement in the state, one that was national in origin, to consider sterilization as a way of weeding out these "defects." The eugenics movement, in which "undesirables" were sterilized to "improve" the "pure Vermont strain," led to sterilization, institutionalization, and/or a prohibition against marriage for people with developmental or mental disabilities, people of Abenaki and French-Canadian heritage, repeat criminal offenders, and the poor. Vermont was not alone in the eugenics movement, being the twenty-ninth state to pass a sterilization law for its purposes. But, in this context, one can see that the arrival of counterculture youth with their long hair and sloppy appearance could raise concerns about protecting the "real" or "pure" Vermont.

Of course, that fear of "invasion" from outside and the desire to control the Vermont stock became moot with the building of the two interstate highways. "With that, there were no more walls around Vermont," Terry observed. In came the hippies and lots of other people, and the debate over whether that has been a good or a bad thing will probably go on forever.

* * *

That instinct for self-protection was evident in the wake of Pollak's article. Seeing a controversy, Vermont newspapers soon whipped up the frenzy. Former UPI bureau chief Rod Clarke wrote in a recollection of the times,

"Bold, black newspaper headlines warned of the impending 'HIPPIE INVA-SION,' sending more than one old farmer scurrying for his shotgun." Governor Deane Davis, who served during the heart of the migration, from 1969 to 1973, received so many letters expressing apprehension that he reluctantly issued a press release to allay the fears. "It has become apparent that speculation about the so-called 'Hippie influx' this summer is causing mounting concern around the state," he wrote. "Like most people, the bulk of the young transients go about their business in a self-sufficient, peaceful manner, although their habits and appearance may not be to our taste."

On the other hand, it could be argued that by the mid-1960s what Vermont needed most was people, specifically young people, to stop the brain and energy drain of young Vermonters leaving the state for jobs elsewhere. For while the rest of the nation had experienced a dramatic population growth, especially following World War II, Vermont's population had grown by less than 9 percent between 1930 and 1960. Between 1950 and 1960 alone, 15,000 Vermonters between the ages of twenty and forty-four left the state. With an increasingly aging population, how would Vermont raise enough revenue to pay for education, road maintenance, and other services? The so-called invasion changed everything. By 1970, approximately 35,800 hippies were estimated to be living in Vermont, representing roughly 33 percent of the total population of 107,527 Vermonters between the ages of eighteen and thirty-four. The 1980 census showed that Vermont's population grew even more dramatically over the decade, from 444,732 to 511,456, making it the largest increase since the Revolutionary War; 57 percent of that growth were people from out of state.

* * *

Of course, Vermont was far from the only place to attract counterculture youths in large numbers; hippie enclaves flourished in San Francisco, Taos, Seattle, Portland, and elsewhere. But while these cities maintain strong influences from the era, they are not states. Nor did they elect a Socialist to represent them first in the U.S. Congress then the Senate. If one looks back to Blumstein and Phelan's theory, that the experiment in revolution begun in a small state could "spur change in society as a whole," one need look no further than Senator Bernie Sanders's 2016 and 2020 presidential bids. His national popularity brought ideas that Vermonters had been hearing for decades, ideas about shared wealth and shared responsibility, caring for veterans and workers rather than Wall Street, ideas forged decades previously in college classrooms and activist meetings dating back to the 1960s, propelled into the national spotlight.

Perhaps more than anything else, Sanders's record in Vermont—coming as a radical activist and successfully running for city and national office since 1981, losing just two campaigns in the intervening years—provides evidence of the counterculture's influence on Vermont. While the national pundits raised fears about his identification as a Democratic Socialist, that label hadn't hindered Vermont voters from electing him once he'd shown his success as Burlington mayor.

Sanders's story has often been told, how as a teenager he and his older brother took the subway from their humble Brooklyn apartment into Manhattan and stumbled upon a promotional campaign advertising cheap land in Vermont. They were captivated by the photos of beautiful panoramas and iconic farmhouses, the appeal of land and space after living in a cramped two-bedroom apartment. A decade later, Sanders and his first wife bought a chunk of that childhood fascination in the town of Middlesex, eighty-five acres off of Shady Rill Lane for $2,500, and his life in Vermont, a most dramatic one by any estimation, began.

But what about so many others of his generation? What was it about Vermont that attracted so many?

For many it was the very essence of Vermont and the lure of living in relative peace and quiet surrounded by nature. Stephen Sherrill discovered his affinity for Vermont in 1957 when he was eight years old and flew with two of his three siblings from Boston to Burlington. While nearly everyone else on the DC-3 was tossing their cookies, Sherrill was glommed on to the window, his aerial view of Vermont in full-on summer a panorama of greens, nestled villages, and ribbonlike rivers whose trajectories kept his mind off the roller-coaster flight. At home in the Boston suburb of Sherborn, the humidity had been so brutal that sleeping had been difficult, but in Vermont "it was so lush and the air so cool and crisp," he said. "From that moment, I was drawn to Vermont. That was my habitat, about the forty-fourth parallel; I discovered that's where I'm comfortable."

Sherrill was so charmed with Vermont and with living as remotely as possible, deep in the woods if possible, that he dropped out of Middlebury College in his senior year, despite the risk of being drafted to fight in Vietnam when he lost his student deferment. Middlebury had brought him to Vermont but, as he discovered, "the college was too pretentious for me. I was more comfortable in the hinterland."

He had been "peripherally involved in antiwar stuff and knew where I stood. Under no circumstances did I want to serve, but I steered clear of public involvement in demonstrations. I was more inclined to go for a hike or camping trip or swim in Goshen Dam." He also needed time in nature to mourn the death of his mother with whom he had been close. One day, while riding his bike down a dirt road in Goshen he noticed a barely discernible two-wheel path into the woods. When he followed it to a clearing with a simple camp set amid a bowl of trees, he was enchanted. Goshen was just the place Sherrill was looking for with its small population and dirt roads. The camp belonged to Arnold Magoon, the local game warden. With his wire-rimmed glasses and youthful face, Sherrill didn't look the type to survive a winter in the hinterland, but Magoon eventually agreed to rent to him and, just a few months later, surprised Sherrill by offering to sell the camp and five of its six acres. After some negotiation contingent upon getting that sixth acre, Sherrill bought the camp for $3,000 down, taking over the $30 monthly mortgage payments. Altogether, his little piece of paradise cost $5,500. The bankbook has remained among his treasures.

Armed with his copies of the *Whole Earth Catalog* and *Mother Earth News*, the bibles of the back-to-the-land movement, he set about learning how to live far off the grid. "I had an affinity for the climate and the culture, learning from the geniuses of the rural life," people like an older local couple, Doris and Heine Reed, "so symbolic of the acceptance of the hippies by some of the long-timers," he said. To avoid the draft, he paid $1,800 to an attorney in Bellows Falls who sent him to a psychologist who helped secure a deferment based on his mother's recent death. He further protected himself by securing a job at Brandon Training School. In 1971, he married Elsie Elliott, a young woman who had grown up in East Warren and brought her own deeply endowed skills in rural living to the union. Justice of the Peace Heine Reed officiated, thus giving the couple the town's unspoken blessing.

Until 1979, the couple and their two sons lived in the camp, which had no electricity, a hand pump for water, gaslights, gas fridge, and hand-pumped flush toilet. They heated and cooked with wood. The Home Comfort cookstove had been a wedding gift from a BTS coworker. Sherrill restored it back to wood burning from kerosene. That Home Comfort, positioned on one side of a double-flue fieldstone chimney with a Vermont Castings Defiant stove on the other side, took center stage in the handsome log cabin Sherrill built two years after he was hired to work for the Vermont Department of Highways. In 2007, nearly thirty years later, he retired as the regional traffic investigator for the Vermont Agency of Transportation. Like many who came to Vermont to drop out of society, over the years Sherrill took on leadership roles in his adopted town, serving as justice of the peace, road foreman, and member of town school and select boards.

Reflecting back on how a suburban kid with counterculture ideas came to be an integral part of a rural town, he recalled the elders who influenced his life, natives who taught him carpentry and stone masonry, how to manage his property, and live in harmony with the seasons, local men like Harold Mitchell, Hugh, and Hayden Hooker. "They were pure and good as gold, never had a cross word to say about anyone and were so very nurturing to a young guy with a different background and a longing to learn," he said. "They were my teachers."

* * *

Affordability was essential to the movement. Poet David Budbill initially moved to Vermont for cheap or, in his case, free housing. Born in Cleveland, Budbill grew up in a family that valued the plight of the underdog. A graduate of Union Seminary, in 1967, at the height of the civil rights movement, he and his wife, the artist Lois Eby, took jobs as teachers at Lincoln University, an all-black college in Pennsylvania. They didn't like the label *hippie* but they embraced many ideas that fell under the general rubric of the counterculture, especially the value of each and every human life and abhorrence of racism and war.

The couple wanted to balance work in the world with time for their creative endeavors. After two years at Lincoln University, they planned to take a year off to concentrate on their writing and art but worried about making ends meet. Budbill had attended the Bread Loaf Writers Conference in 1964. He disliked Bread Loaf, considering it an elitist institution with a male-dominated hierarchy, but he had developed a deep affection for Vermont and began to dream about returning to write. Even then, he was aware of Vermont's strong literary tradition and wanted to experience it, to see what would happen if he could put himself in a place where he could be free to write without economic pressures or the distractions of urban life. The only thing missing was diversity.

"I had fallen in love with the mountains because I'm a flatlander. I said to my wife, 'Jeezum, let's go to Vermont.' Well, I didn't say Jeezum yet," he said, laughing at his use of the most famous Vermontism, "Jeezum," as in Jeezum Crow, the fictitious state bird. As luck would have it, a friend of a friend of a friend owned an old schoolhouse in South Albany, a town of 528 residents in Vermont's Northeast Kingdom that had been losing population since 1870. The friend many times removed was willing to let them live there for nothing. This is a perfect example of the blind trust prevalent at the time, a level of faith in individuals of presumed commonality that seems Pollyannaish from today's perspective. People hitchhiked and picked up hitchhikers without much fear. People moved in with virtual strangers without forethought. And people rented to friends of friends without worrying about being ripped off. While this trust was common among members of the counterculture, it was not uncommon among Vermonters, who until fairly recently were apt to leave their doors unlocked. Equally difficult to explain was the ability to connect and communicate among friends and associates without the use of cell phones or the Internet. Payphones and letters were the means by which transactions occurred, especially in Vermont where it was not uncommon in rural areas not to have phone service.

Budbill and Eby had saved $5,000 for their year's reprieve; they planned to return to their college jobs after their sabbatical. They never left Vermont, eventually buying a reasonably priced parcel of land and building a home in the nearby town of Wolcott. Wolcott, too, was seriously depressed. By 1970, the town named for one of the signers of the Declaration of Independence had lost nearly half its 1860 population, when it boasted a high of 1,161 residents. Budbill and Eby loved the Kingdom, that isolated and relatively unchanged corner of Vermont that presented him with his material, an ever-fascinating panoply of characters whose stories he felt had long been ignored —not the stuff of *Vermont Life* magazine, but the real life stories of the rural poor and disenfranchised, proud farmers and loggers. Economic inequality, rural poverty, loss of job opportunities, and lack of support for the arts became Budbill's new causes, promulgated in plays, poetry, letters, blog posts, and diatribes aimed at the Vermont Arts Council and the state legislative body. Eby, who had been the first professor to introduce African and African American literature into the curriculum at Lincoln, found herself inspired by the starkness and beauty of Vermont, assimilating these emotional qualities into her art.

"People talk about how easily we integrated into Vermont, but it's only half true," Budbill said. "We inserted ourselves into the state. We imposed ourselves. We judged and dissected, congratulated ourselves for finding this place. We changed it, there's no doubt. But the bigger change has been on us. You live here long enough and you learn to be practical, to be prepared when you set out for all kinds of weather. You learn the value of simplicity. You learn you can do without that new thing. Most of your neighbors are poor or just getting by; they're comfortable enough but never rich. You learn to be comfortable with what you have, too. Not striving all the time, not competing. Being. These are Buddhist values. Vermonters have them intrinsically, or some do. Or did. That's changing now. But my generation learned these values from the long-timers," he said. These values in turn resonated with the couple's interest in Buddhism and Asian art, music and literature, interests the two had brought with them.

"Sure, rich people are putting up big houses along Lake Champlain and elsewhere. But they don't live here," Budbill said. "They just pay taxes and visit once in a while. The rest of us, we get to live here, which has been a perpetual joy." A curious statistic supports Budbill's theory about the Zen-ness of Vermont: while fewer Vermonters per capita routinely attend church services than in any other state, more Vermonters per capita identify themselves as Buddhists than residents of any other state in the union.

* * *

Another commonality explains the choice of Vermont among the hippies. Like Sherrill, a remarkable number of the transplants recalled a memorable Vermont experience in their childhood, whether visiting relatives, vacationing with family, or attending summer camp. Today, they speak of these experiences with a kind of reverence, making Vermont seem like a fairyland, an Eden, a place of adventure where you could swim in the cleanest of water, shoot a rifle, ride on snow, or watch some old codger tell your grandmother where to go. The last comes from Dick McCormack, a folksinger, teacher, radio broadcaster, and longtime Vermont senator.

McCormack's family goes back several generations in Bethel but his grandfather couldn't wait to get out of Vermont. As soon as possible, he moved to New York, where he worked as a teacher. "We were summer people. We would take turns at the Bethel house, a wonderful time with hiking and berrying and just being outside. One day, a man came to scythe the hay. My mother and grandmother, all of us, we're out on the veranda with nothing to do. I'm wearing my seersucker and we're all up there watching him work. He's looking at us, these little fat kids and these ladies in their wide-brimmed hats and you know he's thinking, 'They're using me for their entertainment.'

"All of a sudden, he yells out, 'Move your arses, you old goddam bitches,' and other swears and insults. 'Salty, isn't he? Rustic,' Mother says. 'Let's go inside, shall we?'

"I loved it. I loved that freedom he had to say exactly what he was thinking with no regard for how we might react. That's independence, the kind money can't buy. I used to cry when we went home to Long Island. I loved New York but I never felt like a New Yorker. I felt like an exiled Vermonter. To me, moving to Vermont was something I decided to do when I was four years old."

For others, it was the dramatic changes occurring in the places where they had grown up. For just as Vermont was undergoing change, so too were the cities and suburbs to the south, all within driving distance of Vermont. As other young people married and had families, the suburbs outside Boston, Hartford, New York, Trenton, and beyond expanded farther and farther, and those precious meadows and woods where 1950s kids once played filled up with prefab, look-alike developments. Meanwhile, racial strife was tearing inner cities apart throughout America. Garrison Nelson, a University of Vermont professor and state historian, suggested that racial discord contributed to the urban exodus to Vermont, one of the whitest states in the union. "Suddenly, the cities weren't safe. It wasn't overt racism," Nelson said, "but rather an escape to, not from, to something that felt safe and nonthreatening."

For Larry Plesant, it was the sameness of the new suburbs being built to serve the growing population of Long Island, then as now primarily white, that sent him north to Vermont. He calls his generation "eco-tourists," running off to places like Vermont to escape the ever-increasing development of developments, the traffic on roads like the Long Island Expressway, the building of ugly plazas, and the destruction of traditional downtowns. In an unpublished novel based on his experiences as a teenager who dropped out of high school and suburban life to live at the Quarry Hill commune in Rochester, he wrote, "One day, in my cozy little bedroom on the South Shore of Suffolk County, I woke to the sound of bulldozers. It never went away. They were widening Sunrise Highway three blocks away. The noise and dust were tremendous. When at last the circus of men and machines moved on, car and truck traffic increased until its roar nearly matched the construction racket. Behind us, in the seemingly endless woods, a housing development was chopping its way across the island."

During a two-week bicycle tour of Vermont and New Hampshire as a young teenager, Plesant heard about the fun, free drugs, and freer sex available at the Quarry Hill commune. He rode his bicycle to Rochester, found the rumors to be true, and as soon as possible, moved in. Later, he and his wife, Sandy Lincoln, built a solar-powered log cabin just a few miles from Quarry Hill. They named their cabin Further Farm after author Tom Wolfe's electric Kool-Aid acid bus. Plesant subsequently founded Vermont Soap, a successful purveyor of skin-care products, while Lincoln became a central figure in downtown Rochester, where her Seasoned Books & Bakery, housed in a pretty Victorian painted lemon and lime, served as the town's comfort zone in the wake of Tropical Storm Irene.

* * *

While Plesant was looking for asylum from suburban sprawl, others sought solace from an antiwar movement that seemed ineffectual, especially after the deaths of Rev. Martin Luther King Jr. and Bobby Kennedy, the savaging of demonstrators at the Democratic National Convention in Chicago in 1968, and the shooting of unarmed students at Kent State University on May 4, 1970. The transplants included two of the Chicago Seven defendants who had been charged by the federal government with conspiracy, inciting to riot, and other crimes stemming from antiwar protests that disrupted the convention. David Dellinger, the oldest of the protesters, had been imprisoned as a conscientious objector during World War II and later joined freedom marches in the South. After the trial, he moved to the far-north town of Peacham with his wife, Elizabeth Peterson. There, the couple continued to speak out against war, racism, and economic inequality, their home a beacon for others from the peace movement, old radicals and new who traveled to meet the aging veterans of the war against the war.

Another Chicago Seven defendant, John Froines, moved to Vermont while awaiting trial on the Chicago charges. He'd been hired to teach chemistry at Goddard College and subsequently headed Vermont's Occupational Health Division where he established what's considered the first and most extensive health and safety-enforcement program for workers of its time. Froines was one of only two of the defendants to be acquitted. He went on to a fifty-year career in academia and public service, first as deputy director of the National Institutes for Occupational Safety and Health during the Carter administration, and subsequently at the University of California Los Angeles where, as an activist scientist, he translated science into policies that protected the health of migrant farmworkers, blue-collar employees, and low-income families residing near freeways. He was a lifelong champion of sane water policies. "Vermont was my refuge after Chicago and a place where I learned how to work within the system for the greater good," he said. "I really found myself there. I always say, everything came out of Chicago and then Vermont."

* * *

Anthropologist Dan Chodorkoff of Plainfield came to Vermont in 1967 as a student at Goddard College, a fairly wild place in those days when a large proportion of the students were simply squatters—attending classes, eating in the dining hall, and sleeping in friends' rooms without the burden of paying tuition or room and board. In 1971, then elevated to a faculty position, Chodorkoff and anarchist Murray Bookchin created the Institute for Social Ecology, an international organization still working on global environmental, political, and social issues. Their names and books are fairly forgotten in America, while both are known worldwide in scholarly, community-planning, and anarchist circles.

"The Vermont I moved to is not the same place as the one we live in today," Chodorkoff acknowledged, reflecting that 1960s Vermont was still somewhat isolated, its residents sometimes wary of outsiders. While living on a commune in Woodbury, Chodorkoff came to see two sides of the Vermont character he believed were still present. One man, Harry Thompson of Cabot, "was very open and welcoming, a little odd, and always interesting. He was a legendary figure in our part of Vermont. He had a barn full of old equipment and tools. Goddard students would go there all the time. He was the patron saint of the hippies," Chodorkoff said. "If you needed tools, old doors, plumbing, almost anything, really, he and his brother, Dude Thompson, would help you out. They were generous with their time and knowledge. I often wonder what many of us would have done without him and others like him who taught us so much about rural living."

When the ruddy-faced, full-bearded Thompson died in 2012 at age ninety-eight, his obituary read, "He was renowned for his kindness and ability to find anything a person might need among his treasures, from a kitchen sink to a gold locket and sometimes even a little baby Chihuahua to warm a lonely heart. Harry's door was always open for a cup of instant coffee, homemade jam and, if you were lucky, a piece of fresh pie with lots of sugar and a perfect crust."

On the other hand, Chodorkoff met Vermonters whose hostility to the newcomers was downright scary. He told the story of a young couple who were part of a makeshift settlement along an old railroad bed outside of Plainfield. One night, "a group of local guys—we think one was from a prominent family and the other a state trooper, but we could never prove it —burned their cabin down." Perhaps the couple was singled out as they were interracial, while the other hippies, all white, were left alone. Overall, "the mythology was that Vermont was a place of tolerance and self-reliance and local democracy," he said. "That was what brought us here. But there was an underbelly to that as well."

Thus, it was important that Governor Davis emphasized the terms self-sufficient and peaceful in his effort to defuse potential rancor toward the "invasion." Vermonters were not immune to the general dislike of hippies prevalent in the country and the sense among "straight" people that the country was coming apart. It can't be emphasized enough how disturbing the cultural changes were to the general populace in the late 1960s and early 1970s as they read and watched reports of unruly demonstrations, stoned and naked teens cavorting at Woodstock, and members of radical groups like the Weathermen blowing up police stations. Davis needed to remind Vermonters that most of the newcomers fleeing north were peace loving. Of course, there were radical activists among them, individuals who felt that the war in Vietnam and racial conditions in America warranted more than slogans and folk songs. Communes in southern Vermont, in particular, provided refuge for some members of the political underground. The Weather Underground or the Weathermen were a radical faction of the Students for a Democratic Society; their name taken from the Bob Dylan line, "You don't need a weatherman to know which way the wind blows." Between 1969 and 1977, the Weather Underground was implicated in twenty-seven bombings at Selective Service, National Guard, and police offices, the U.S. Capitol building and the Pentagon, and for aiding prisoners like LSD promoter Timothy Leary escape from prison. No one was killed by the group in these actions, although three members died in an accidental explosion of a Greenwich Village townhouse where they were making bombs. Today, the people who took part in these more radical movements would likely be viewed as terrorists.

The truth is that most of the newcomers were clueless about the depth of anger among some members of the movements they felt connected to, and they had no plans for violent revolution. Nonviolent revolution they would embrace, or secession—a perennially popular subject with native and transplanted Vermonters alike. And not all of the interlopers stayed, of course, and thank goodness, in part because it's not easy to live in Vermont, and some of the more clueless or lazy or dangerous ones might not have survived.

* * *

As the baby boomers reached retirement age, some became interested in chronicling the history of their movement. Becky Armstrong, who lived for more than thirty years at the Quarry Hill commune, gathered together the histories of thirty-five people who had lived there along with thoughts on the commune from a few Rochester residents. The interviews were the basis of her master's thesis from Dartmouth College, a place she would have disdained in her twenties as "a tool of the capitalist system but, nevertheless, a good place to take a shower or crash for the night—as I did while hitching north from Woodstock in 1969." Armstrong wrote that her birth on January 8, 1944, placed her in "the perfect moment to fully live through the 1960s, observing and acting in many of the core-dramas of the vital, joyous, painful and transcendental era. I was 10 years old when the first American troops went to Vietnam and the upheavals over racism and civil rights began. Ten years later I was in Washington to protest the war. I lived the archetypically hip life (we called ourselves Freaks) in the Sixties, hitching across the country with no shoes and only the little change I had panhandled in my pocket. At the peak of the psychedelic era in Haight-Ashbury, 1967, I lived there on the street, took every drug available, and participated in every sort of psychic and sexual connection possible in that most open and uninhibited of times." And then, she came to Quarry Hill, where she found a family and a profession as a teacher for the kids born into the commune, and a place to live until it no longer served its purpose.

Scholars also realized the importance of recording the history of this time while the stories could be collected. To that end, the Vermont Historical Society conducted a two-year study from 2014 to 2016 in which interviewers traveled the state, gathering first-person stories; the society also hosted regional meetings on the generation's impact on Vermont.

A few years previously, two Harvard researchers wanted to understand why Vermont had become increasingly progressive while neighboring New Hampshire, similar in many broad aspects that include geography, size, and location, had remained relatively conservative. Jason Kaufman and Matthew Kaliner's conclusion is that like-minded people attract like-minded people, and over time, and given enough similarly attuned people, they tend to change the social character of their adopted place to make it more suited to their preferences, which in turn attracts others who share these values. They wrote, "Absent a major inter-generational shift in Vermont but not elsewhere in the United States, it seems hard to explain Vermont's trajectory without reference to newcomers: people like Howard Dean, Bernie Sanders, Ben & Jerry—all archetypal Vermonters born and raised out-of-state."

Of course to lump Sanders, Governor Dean, Ben Cohen, and Jerry Greenfield together is ludicrous to those with even a slight knowledge of the four men, all quite different, and to suggest that any of them is typical of the sixties generation of newcomers to Vermont is misleading. Sanders may have been counterculture but he never liked the word *hippie* nor thought of himself as one. He was a radical. While left leaning, Dean was certainly not a hippie nor a member of the counterculture; he was too straight for that, and conservative by some Vermont standards. Indeed he sometimes appeared more liberal as presidential candidate than he had as governor. And while Cohen and Greenfield embraced all things counterculture, Greenfield described himself and Cohen, as well as their enterprise, Ben & Jerry's Homemade Ice Cream, as "the beneficiaries" of the hippie invasion, noting that they arrived in Vermont toward the end of the 1970s to find a ready audience for their product and their message.

The Made in Vermont label has always had distinction. As far back as the end of the nineteenth century, Kaliner and Kaufman discovered, Vermont promoted itself as the best of New England and a place set aside from the rest of the world. In 1890, for example, Vermont's Board of Agriculture encouraged farmers to sell "authentic" crops and homemade goods to tourists, going so far as to urge farmers not to mention modernization improvements on their farms when tourists visited.

Harsh realities accompany the privilege of living in Vermont but, as historian Nelson pointed out, necessity can break down barriers. "The co-operative nature that exists here doesn't necessarily exist in urban cultures. Borrowing—bartering—they've been part of the Vermont culture since time immemorial and naturally they were appealing to counterculture people who were urban kids who had grown up where there was much less trust. It worked both ways, however. Vermont is far and away the most accepting of the Northeast states. The reputation to the contrary is just plumb wrong.

"Of course that rural nature had a winnowing effect as well," Nelson said. "It could rid a community of the drifters, the ne'er-do-wells, those who couldn't take the winters, scraping off the windshield, and shoveling out, the whole mess of mud season. Those who stayed actually were not that different from native Vermonters, except in the ways they expressed their values and politics. Eventually the hippies even started dressing like the natives, pretty much giving up the tie-dye for work pants, corduroy, chamois shirts, flannel, and work boots, clothing that made sense and lasted."

Life on the Commune

The commune was the natural outgrowth of camp and dorms, sleepovers and all-nighters—but without the rules. Sexual exploration and ten-day marriages were the hallmarks of one Vermont commune, while recording the experiment in the wilderness in story, poetry, and art became the trademark of another. On some communes, animals were workers and partners in the fields and helped feed the community; hard work had to be in these communards' character. On another, sensitivity to Mother Nature and her creatures prevailed, and thus, no meat was consumed nor any animal products, even leather, permitted. Some communes and collectives were for anarchists plotting a takeover. Some were for pacifists, hiding out in old camps and houses off the beaten trail.

And while the commune provided a way to extend childhood into adulthood, to live cheaply with people with whom you might share history and ideology, it was also a place to discover what made you uncomfortable, to discover your own limits. Some communes were successful and others were deadly; some communards lost their virginity; some lost their minds. Some found their reason to be. They had names like Frog Run, Tree Frog, Total Loss Farm, Maple Hill, Mad Brook Farm, May Day, Milkweed Hill, Johnson Pasture, Mullein Hill, Rockbottom Farm, Green Mountain Red, Mount Philo, Quarry Hill, Wooden Shoe, Redbird, Earth People's Park, Entropy Acres, Free State of the Arc, Fisher Family, New Morning, Pie in the Sky, and many, many more.

Robert Houriet, whose book *Getting Back Together* introduced America to the commune movement and the founder of Frog Run commune in Vermont's Northeast Kingdom, noted that the more politically active communes grew out of the freedom houses of the South. Freedom houses were safe homes for volunteers working in the 1960s to register as many black voters as possible, particularly in Mississippi. Living together for common cause provided security in difficult times, something that activists connected to antiwar groups like Students for a Democratic Society or the Weather Underground soon discovered. In the early 1960s, activists were living in inner city "hip ghettos," as Houriet described places such as Greenwich Village and Hell's Kitchen where cool and offbeat people had long inhabited as much for the grit and drama as for cheap housing. As the grit and drama accelerated, some began to look to Vermont as a safe haven where they might create a new society.

"The movement was urban to rural," he explained. The idea of going back to the land was secondary, not primary. Safety and getting out of unstable cities and "getting someplace connected to others who had abandoned the cities" was quickly followed by the realization that one needed a reason to *be* in the country and a way to survive in an unfamiliar environment. Living in concert was thus appealing.

Scott and Helen Nearing's book, *Living the Good Life: How to Live Simply and Sanely in a Troubled World,* provided instruction and inspiration. The book described the Nearings' nineteen-year experiment in homesteading in Vermont after the couple purchased a large parcel of forestland for $2,200 and a small farm in Winhall for $2,500 in 1932 and set about creating a self-sufficient life. Over the next two decades, three intentional communities grew up around the Nearings in the Pikes Falls area of Vermont. These alternative communities attracted forty to fifty people who shared the Nearings' opposition to war, greed, and overconsumption. Some were followers of Gandhi; one invented time-saving devices from scrap material; others had served time for refusing to go to war. They arrived as Vermont's subsistence farmers were giving up the farms. And while there were potluck dinners and dances at the community center they created, there was also arduous, dangerous labor as they harvested wood and built their community.

The communal experiment eventually failed. As historian Greg Joly of Jamaica wrote, while the Nearings and their cohorts "espoused philosophies [that] seemingly were in agreement with one another, [they] yet proved to be the foundations of discordance." Despite similar views among the Pikes Falls settlers, the Nearings' strict work schedule and abstemious lifestyle led to rifts within the community, rifts that were compounded as town residents learned of their leftist leanings. Encroaching development around Stratton Mountain ski resort exacerbated the Nearings' discomfort, leading them to abandon their experiment in Vermont in 1952 to begin anew on a remote cape in Maine.

While these developments might have given fair warning to the young idealists who read their book, few of the back-to-the-landers explored the more complicated reasons for the Nearings' departure. Scott Nearing was said to disdain the hippie lifestyle and excess of all kinds. As Joly observed, the couple abhorred stimulants, including coffee and tea, and strongly disapproved of the drug culture.

* * *

Dozens of communes came and went in Vermont, leaving little record of their existence except in the memories of the young people who briefly fashioned their lives around them. The seeds of one of these, the Baloney Brothers commune—often simply called The Land—were planted among young activists at Lafayette College, the "non-jocks, misfits, the literary, disparate guys who weren't quite sure why they were attending the then all-male college," as Jeffrey Kahn, a business owner in Woodstock, recalled. The commune produced a major museum director, a celebrity doctor, famous lawyers, and at least one esteemed professor, most of whom left Vermont after spending their postgraduate years at the Sharon commune. When they gathered together for their first reunion in 2014, the two-dozen friends who traveled from as far away as Texas and London were happy to share their youthful exploits but uncomfortable being identified publicly as former hippie commune members. Kahn was the exception. Not only was he one of the few who remained in Vermont, he was also unabashed about that chapter in his life, having concluded that the freedom of his early days had provided lifelong lessons he benefitted from daily. "Why deny your past?" he asked. "It is your story, what made you who you are."

The group's first commune had been off campus, a place for antiwar activities and group trips with LSD, mescaline, and peyote, always starting their experience with meditation, then "heading into the woods or some expedition somewhere, always in nature," Kahn recalled. "A friend had a house in Vermont, a place that seemed exotic to us. When it came time to graduate and we weren't ready to enter the world we were supposed to," the friends found fifty acres for sale in Sharon. While the price was right, their fifty acres had little road frontage, went almost directly up a very steep hill, and was heavily wooded.

"We pooled our money, moved onto the land, and built a road that went

Jeffrey Kahn in the Baloney Brothers days. When he opened his store, Unicorn, in downtown Woodstock, the billionaire Laurance Rockefeller, his landlord, questioned his ability to make the monthly rent.
Courtesy of Jeffrey Kahn

up to an overgrown meadow that we cleared and planted right away. Within no time, there were tent sites and makeshift structures, thirty of them, on the hill, including a 1950s school bus that someone had purchased in Nova Scotia." But living together was not perfection, as they soon discovered. "People were smoking too much. We had stopped tripping. Urges to grow up or go in different directions were happening. I left November 30, 1975, at 2:00 a.m., after my girlfriend woke with her hair frozen to our tent site. I hauled everything down the hill and moved to Woodstock into a communal house there called Apple Acres."

Just a few years later, Kahn was owner of Unicorn, a gift shop in Woodstock's handsome downtown selling an unlikely mix of hippie, New Age, practical, and whimsical items. Kahn recalled the day Laurance Rockefeller, who owned considerable commercial property in Woodstock until his death in 2004, discovered his new tenant was a longhaired hippie. "Do you really think you're going to last here," the billionaire asked, surveying the store's offerings. "I hope you know your rent is due at the beginning of each month." Kahn bought the building from Rockefeller's estate.

Today a village trustee, Kahn has helped raise money to save Woodstock's movie theater and Pentacle Arts center and contributed to the creation of Woodstock's Jewish community center. In some ways, he said, the community center represented the blending that took place in Vermont as a result of the counterculture's influence on Vermont, considering it an embodiment of the religious values he grew up with softened and broadened by the principles of the counterculture, especially inclusiveness, openness, and shared decision making.

Other communes, particularly the intentional communities and collectives that grew out of social and political activism, had a more visible impact on Vermont. Fear that the world, and America in particular, was on the verge of an apocalypse strengthened the activists' zeal to work for change, whether it was the members of the Red Clover collective in Putney, who hoped to transform Vermont into a more progressive place so it could embrace refugees from urban areas to the south of Vermont, or the New Hamburger commune in Plainfield, whose founders were dedicated to making a small footprint on the planet and using natural resources to create beautiful homes and furnishings while offering respite to refugees from far away.

Ideology and shared political views of a different sort were the basis of Redbird, a radical lesbian collective formed toward the end of the commune movement as women across Vermont were flexing their feminist muscles. Euan Bear, who grew up in Maine and New Hampshire, learned about Redbird at a women's music festival in Boston. She was already politically active, having been arrested at protests with the Clamshell Alliance against the Seabrook nuclear power plant and raising money for a lesbian woman involved in a child-custody battle in Vermont. At the Hinesburg collective, women built their structures without power tools and ate no meat or sugar as much for the health of their bodies as to take care of Mother Earth. Out of this short-lived collective came long-lasting services for victims of rape and physical abuse that eventually evolved into the Burlington organization Women Helping Battered Women.

* * *

Interestingly, two opposite regions of Vermont saw the largest number of communes. At least eight were located within fifteen miles of Brattleboro on both sides of the Vermont-Massachusetts border while another dozen or so were established in Vermont's Northeast Kingdom. Easy access to Boston and New York contributed to the abundance in southern Vermont. Together, estimates suggest a full-time population of about three hundred among them, while several attracted many more transients over the course of the fair-weather months. These communes received considerable media attention, in part because the founders of Total Loss Farm commune in Guilford had created and written for the influential Liberation News Service

Room for many: laundry drying and a table for twenty at Johnson Pasture.
Photo by Roy Finestone; courtesy of Charles Light

during the early years of the Vietnam War. After moving to Vermont, they published several popular books about their experiences.

Howard Lieberman, a commune member who became a corporate head-hunter, explained the differences between the better-known communes in the Brattleboro area to a *New York Times* reporter: Total Loss Farm was for the "intellectuals and writers"; Red Clover was for "the educated, affluent kids" with radical ideation; and nearby Johnson Pasture was "the Ellis Island of the commune movement, drawing people with nowhere to go and nothing else to do." He was speaking at a reunion of several communes that had been located along the Vermont-Massachusetts border.

Journalist Sally Johnson was harsher, writing that Johnson Pasture was "a resettlement camp for thousands of youthful refugees, many of them runaways and draft resisters and evaders from middle-class society." Charles Light, a filmmaker and musician now living in Guilford and New York City, told Johnson that while the first communards at Johnson Pasture "had shared values and education . . . it quickly sank to the lowest common denominator —the criminal element. What happened at the J.P. was a colossal failure." He was referring to an incident during the summer of 1969 when someone upended a candle after a night of drinking. The old farmhouse went up like kindling; four people died, an event that broke the hearts of Michael and

Annie Carpenter, who had bought the land in 1968 and opened it to anyone who wanted to come "with the full belief that only good could come of doing so," as Michael expressed it.

The Carpenters had spent four years traveling the country, visiting communes and alternative communities before deciding to buy land of their own "to see what we could make it into. We had no expectations. I simply thought it would be interesting to find out what would happen if everyone contributed to our new community," he said. He soon realized that "'contributing' just meant being there in those days," as his invitation attracted hardworking people who wanted to be part of a self-sustaining communal enterprise as well as freeloaders simply looking for a place to catch the buzz. Others, like Michael "Rapunzel" Metelica, took advantage of the Carpenters' generosity to promote their own ideology. Metelica led a group called the Brotherhood of the Spirit whose followers worked in Metelica's many businesses located in nearby Turners Falls and Warwick, Massachusetts. Some were members of his rock band, Spirit in Flesh. One story goes that Brotherhood members dynamited the top of a mountain on Carpenter's property as part of their

The rules painted on a barn at Johnson Pasture.
Photo by Roy Finestone; courtesy of Charles Light

preparations for a forecasted flood. "They left, then came back, hoping I would give them the property. I didn't," recalled Carpenter. After the fire, he sold the property and moved with his wife to Ithaca, New York, where he worked as a carpenter.

The deaths have continued to haunt him. "Life is a learning process," he said. "You learn hard lessons, you learn easy lessons. Some you never forget."

While sheriffs who came to investigate Metelica's dynamiting expedition apparently did nothing, Peter Simon (of the Simon & Schuster publishing empire and singer Carly Simon's brother) tells the story of a standoff between commune dwellers and cops at his eighty-acre Tree Frog Farm in Guilford after residents complained about "all the nudity and psychedelic drugs." Simon *had* been attracted to the idea of just walking around naked in the privacy of nature, but a common theme emerged as he and a friend discovered they were paying all the bills and doing all the work.

"The normal boundaries that people put up are changed. Everything was shared. We shared food. We shared sex. We shared clothing," Simon, a successful photographer headquartered on Martha's Vineyard, observed. "Ultimately, it was the downfall because I started getting sick of it."

Elliot Blinder, whose photo graces the cover of this book, had been part of the Boston University gang involved in the Liberation News Service and Total Loss Farm. He moved to Tree Frog Farm when Total Loss became too crowded for him, only to have the same thing happen at Tree Frog. Blinder had dropped out of BU to "do something to stop the war," a commitment he carries on today. He left Tree Frog with the birth of his son Amos, named for the first man to farm Tree Frog land. Blinder and his first wife established their own farm, Hill House, across the border in Charlemont, Massachusetts, made maple syrup, raised vegetables, and sold hay, until 1976 when California dreaming took him away. He hoped to make a movie from his published book, *The Bloom Highway*, an account of his journey from a Long Island suburb to a hippie farm in northern New England. That didn't work out, but the years since have brought success as the founder of three art galleries in California.

"My Vermont commune experience was a life-changer. Living in a community of artists, writers, and photographers, *communing* with artists from the heart and the mind, that's where and when I really got to know the soul of the artist, which has been my life's work and pleasure," he said.

Blinder's companion in the photo on the book's cover, Jewell Greco—friends back then knew her as Jenny Buell—found her "first home" at Tree

Frog. Growing up with a father in the CIA, she lived in six countries including Cold War Poland, a place of few freedoms or comforts, before moving to the states at fifteen. Her mother died two years later, and she found herself at Tree Frog, where she built a retreat of twigs and recycled material. She found she loved growing things, a love that led her to Quebec where she homesteaded for seven years. Now living just across the Vermont border in Shutesbury, Massachusetts, she works as a plant-based spirit healer. "I was one of the younger ones at the commune," she said. "I thought I had died and gone to heaven. It was a lovefest—not a sex fest—a real festival of love. My own healing came out of that, which is why I became a healer."

Reflecting back on the impact that the communal movement had on the Guilford-Brattleboro area is best from the long view, Charles Light observed. "It's wrong to call the commune movement a failure" because so few remain and tragedy occurred at one or more. Tragedy occurs anywhere daily. From the long view, "the movement influenced the entire area in terms of art, politics, food, music, and community," he said. And for those communards still in one another's lives, and there are many, the bond goes deep. As Light expressed it: "Those relationships have lasted forty years. . . . We're all one another's family, something so lost in most of today's society."

* * *

While the Northeast Kingdom is readily accessible from the south by Interstate 91, then as now its attraction lay in the area's sparse population and relatively cheap land—and, for some, its proximity to Canada. Some of the area's best-known communes were Frog Run, Mullein Hill, and Earth People's Park. Operating under the radar in nearby East Charleston, Mad Brook Farm, founded by Peter Murray and others in 1968 as a collective for artists and dancers, still attracts creative people who share some aspects of communal living while enjoying the autonomy of their own homes. Murray, who died in 2007 at age sixty-five, was featured in a 1974 *National Geographic* photo essay and a subsequent documentary that chronicled his process of building maple rocking chairs held together with wooden pegs without the aid of nails, screws, or glue. Later, Murray lived fairly isolated in a one-room cabin on the property, painting the landscape outside his window and the corners of his sparse dwelling.

World-renowned improvisational dancers Steve Paxton and Lisa Nelson, along with other artists and artisans from Mad Brook, integrated into the local community, while others helped transform New York's culinary scene by marrying art with cooking at a pioneering SoHo restaurant called Food. There, artist Gordon Matta-Clark, who died in 1978 at age thirty-five, was one of several artists who celebrated the historical connection between food and art by turning meal preparation into both spectacle and political statement. A *New York Times* review of a 2007 retrospective of Matta-Clark's work at the Whitney Museum noted that the restaurant Food introduced "many of the vaguely countercultural ideas fostered" at Mad Brook Farm to New York City, ideas considered radical at the time, such as "fresh and seasonal foods, a geographically catholic menu, a kitchen fully open to the dining room, cooking as a kind of performance—[ideas] now so ingrained in restaurants in New York and other large cities that it is hard to remember a time when such a place would have seemed almost extraterrestrial."

Loraine Pingree Janowski was one of the founders of Mullein Hill, the commune celebrated in Kate Daloz's fascinating book, *We Are As Gods*. Janowski's experience illustrates the struggles many women living on communes faced, one that was exacerbated by motherhood and the isolation of the Northeast Kingdom. A Rutland native whose great grandfather, Samuel E. Pingree, was the fortieth governor of Vermont, Janowski grew up middle-class—her father was an optometrist in town—but she was strongly attracted to a bohemian lifestyle. After high school, she and her first husband sang folk songs at ski areas in the Rutland area and her first child was born. After the couple divorced, she moved with her daughter to Cambridge, Massachusetts, where she loved going to the coffeehouses and became involved in antiwar demonstrations until one of the demonstrators handed her a bag of marbles to toss at the feet of the mounted police. In that moment, she realized she missed Vermont. Moving to Plainfield, she attended Goddard and began dreaming of a way to have a communal family in Vermont, which led her and her friends to Mullein Hill.

There, "the women and children tended to stay home. We had no electricity, a hand pump, and ran a candle-making business, all very primitive. The men went off to sell candles, to take down barns we used to build our first house. I was the earth mother, at home, cooking and caring for the children," she said. When her second daughter was born, a young journalist named Bernie Sanders came to interview her for a story on home birth.

"At some point, a neighbor, Tony Chapin, a very cultured person interested in what we were doing, asked me, 'Why do you do all the cooking and cleaning and taking care of the kids and let the men sit around the fire and smoke pot?' That got me thinking" she said, and eventually, she went back to college, earned a degree in mediation, and took a job at Sterling College as a baker and chef.

She lived twenty years at Mullein Hill before the communal experience finally ended. Now she lives in an apartment in St. Johnsbury but still gardens. "It took me a while to see that I could be a mother and have my own life, but I have few regrets and the time on the land remains precious in my memory," she said. "I've been blessed."

* * *

While the north and south commanded the most communes and collectives, others were scattered around Vermont. Indeed, it's safe to say that they were present in every county. Detailed stories of six follow, selected for the variety of goals and experiences they offered.

TOTAL LOSS FARM

In 1967, a stone's throw from the White House, a group of young people were hoping to start a revolution, one fomented by information not aggression. Ray Mungo from Lowell, Massachusetts, and the former editor of the *Boston University News*, and Marshall Bloom, an Amherst College graduate who'd lost his position as director of the United States Student Press Association over Vietnam War coverage, had moved into a townhouse at 3 Thomas Circle where they founded a kind of Associated Press of the left. They optimistically called it the Liberation News Service. All the pressing issues of the day—the Vietnam War, civil rights, draft resistance, the nascent women's movement—consumed them.

Soon, other idealists and activists from the Northeast, journalists Allen Young and Marty Jezer, photographer David Fenton and poet Verandah Porche, joined the news service. Over the next two years, they worked tirelessly, writing, editing, and sending packets of articles twice weekly to underground newspapers across the country and abroad. By February 1968, roughly 150 underground newspapers and 90 college papers boasting as many as two million readers had subscriptions. But in the hours and days after Martin Luther King Jr. was assassinated on April 3, 1968, as D.C. erupted in riots, they experienced a feeling of powerlessness. Porche prowled the city, her press pass a shield of invisibility. She watched the National Guard set up machine gun nests aimed outward from the Capitol building. She watched young white men in army camouflage look away while looters, singing and crying, wheeled racks of suits from department stores or stacks of steaks from the grocery, or set fire to their own blocks. When Porche and her cohorts asked black friends and neighbors what they could do to help, the answer was guns. They declined, of course; they were peace activists after and despite all. Nonetheless, D.C. was a war zone. Thirteen people died and thousands were injured during three days of riots.

Meanwhile, differences over strategy had created hairline fractures on the Left that opened into bitter disputes; the peace movement was unraveling as some chose to protest the war more and more forcefully. Even the Liberation News Service was under attack, with Marxist-leaning members at the press's New York office attempting a coup. Porche began to long for personal peace, release from the relentless accounting of war deaths and racial strife, from the sense that she had nothing to offer that could make it all end.

On Easter morning, 1968, she woke Mungo and said, "Raymond, I want to go home."

She wasn't referring to Teaneck, New Jersey, where she had first entertained her family with her songs and poems, her instinctive facility with language, nor Boston where she and the other activists had met at Boston University. She was done with cities.

Mungo opened his eyes, said, "I know the place," and returned to sleep.

The place turned out to be a worn-out farm in Guilford; friends who owned a nearby camp had learned that the widow Rosie Franklin was anxious to be rid of it. "It was Memorial Day weekend when we went to look at the farmhouse. The house itself was ugly, the color of pee. The door was locked but we peeked in the windows, and thought, oh well. Then we looked up the hill and saw a pinkish haze, the peach orchard in bloom, and we climbed above it and looked down and saw it all there, below us, the house, the orchard, the hills across the way, and I just thought, I'm going to live here forever," Porche recalled. There was truth in that.

Soon other LNS staff members and their college chums, ten or twelve of them, joined in purchasing the farmhouse, barn, and chicken coop on ninety acres. They each contributed what they had, Jezer cashing in the Israel bonds he'd received as a bar mitzvah gift toward the down payment on the $26,000 farm. They named their commune Total Loss Farm after a category on an Internal Revenue Service income-tax form.

Reflecting on the days before the move, Porche said, "It was exciting and horrifying. I could wander through the city almost invisible. The National Guard wouldn't move in on a twenty-three-year-old white girl. Yet I was so aware of the broken lives of the people who were passing me. Each had one life and I felt as if my life, my privilege, was full of possibility while theirs were circumscribed by horror and oppression, and there was that shame, that same recurring feeling that I couldn't go on with my life as planned, living in D.C., working for the news service. I had nothing to offer. . . . This is reflecting on it forty-eight years later, of course."

And so, they bought the farm, and, since it was never a total loss, Porche preferred to call it Packer Corner Farm for the section of Guilford where it is located.

In the early days, publishers clamored for anything the tribe could write. There was Mungo's 1970 *Famous Long Ago: My Life and Hard Times with Liberation News Service*, then *Total Loss Farm: A Year in the Life*, filled with the raw honesty of youth from tales of drug-fueled road trips to the challenges of city kids learning how to live off the land. *Home Comfort: Stories and Scenes of Life on Total Loss Farm* followed, written by Porche, Mungo, Jezer, Peter Gould, and a dozen other residents, and edited by Richard Wizansky with illustrations by Alicia Bay Laurel and Gould. *Home Comfort* is a delightful if unpolished conglomeration of stories, poems, drawings, and recipes that provided entrée into their communal dining room, nicknamed the Café Depresso, where the hippies invented myths, wore the costumes of the day, and performed and read their ramblings to one another.

More books followed: Porche's poetry collection, *The Body's Symmetry*, already showing the poet's intense relationship with syntax and wordplay, her ability to express emotion without pathos or platitude; Peter Gould's *Burnt Toast*, a surrealist story that reads like a rite of passage located in the golden days of the counterculture; the late Marty Jezer's articles in WIN magazine and columns for the *Brattleboro Reformer*. In the intervening years, there have been many more books: books on American history, ballparks, stuttering, and love, several dozen as of this count.

Ellen Snyder recalled receiving Mungo's "occasional drop," his term for the missives he sent to college and movement friends, while she was finishing her degree at Radcliffe. "Dear nymphs and shepherds, come to Vermont," Mungo commanded. She came and went, then returned to stay in 1970 in time to work on *Home Comfort*. "I was unprepared for how green and calm Vermont would make me feel. It was both the beauty and the drama among us, among the immigrants, with LNS and the other people who were there," she said. She and Gould became a couple, had a son, Eli. The relationship didn't last but the friendship and connection to the farm did. Snyder lived

Total Loss Farm keeps growing: front row (*left to right*) Peter Simon, Dale Evans holding Oliver Kittoon, Barf Barf the dog, Elliot Blinder, Harry Saxman. Back row (*left to right*): Laurie Dodge (late partner of Richard Wizansky, disappeared 1972), Mark Fenwick, Richard Wizansky, Ray Mungo, Marty Jezer (died 2005), Connie Silver, John Kaplan, Ellen Snyder, Don McLean, Verandah Porche, Michael Gies. *Courtesy of Verandah Porche*

there more than fifteen years. Eli Gould became a successful architect and designer whose company, PreCraft, a custom design-and-build operation in Brattleboro employing a dozen craftspeople and project managers, weds environmental concerns with creative design.

And, while residents of other communes often stayed aloof from the local community, the folks at Packer Corner became fully integrated into the Guilford and Brattleboro area. Snyder worked as a nurse in area hospitals. Peter Gould runs a half dozen Shakespeare camps for kids throughout Vermont and has continued to write about the sixties. His latest book, a memoir, *Horse-Drawn Yogurt: Stories from Total Loss Farm*, richly describes the communards' appreciation of what they found in Vermont. One story in particular describes the group's work to save and repurpose some of the priceless wood from the old Boston & Maine freight depot in Bellows Falls that the fire department was about to burn down for practice. Gould's wife, Vermont

Rep. Molly Burke, a progressive with back-to-the-land roots of her own, founded Art in the Neighborhood, a program for economically disadvantaged children. Others were active on town committees—Wizansky on the Guilford library board; Porche as a cemetery commissioner. Perhaps more to the point, in the intervening decades, many of the communards have gone beyond telling their own stories to telling that of their neighbors. Porche has written poems and created narratives that celebrate the road commissioner, the farmer down the road, and the town of Guilford. And she has worked to bring poetry into Vermont schools, nursing homes, cancer treatment centers, and dozens of communities as a teacher and mentor. In 1998, the Vermont Arts Council awarded her its Citation of Merit for her contributions to the state's cultural life. In 2017, she was elected to the Guilford select board.

Wizansky, whose sensibilities were formed in earliest childhood growing up in Boston's West End, "a wonderful neighborhood of refugees, Italians, eastern Europeans, and Jews" met Porche and Mungo at BU. In college, he was fascinated by the Transcendentalists and, after taking LSD, felt he'd had a transcendental experience of his own. "They hadn't done LSD but the world had opened up to them so they could see and know that trees are material manifestations of a spiritual world," he said. He felt that magic in nature himself, simply being in Vermont, and moved up full-time in 1971. You can imagine what his parents thought; here he was with a masters degree in English literature, cleaning the chicken coop to fertilize the onions, milking the cow, and living with a bunch of dropouts from society. They were happy when he got a job teaching English at Greenfield Community College across the Massachusetts border.

"My father said to me, 'Why are you going backwards?' But my father had been a kosher butcher," Wizansky recalled. "He taught us how to butcher the cows and the pigs. He or Fenwick would do the cutting. He wrung their necks under the supervision of Luis Ygelesias of Cuba," the celebrated humanist, poet, and teacher who lived at the commune for several years. "It was a whole-day affair; you'd have the taste of blood in your mouth. You'd be filthy. But you knew where your food came from."

Wizansky, cofounder of BoldMoves, a support and fund-raising business for nonprofit organizations, and his husband, Dr. Todd Mandell, the former medical director of Vermont's Division of Alcohol and Drug Abuse Programs, built a handsome home just down the road from the commune's main building.

The Fenwick Wizansky referred to is Mark Fenwick, a wood sculptor who moved to the commune in 1968 as a renegade from high school. Porche described him as "the boy wonder, taciturn, strong, and gifted at learning. He carved up the pigs they raised for the freezer. He built a towering chimney from fieldstone, and a fireplace of scavenged bricks with a marble mantle. The chimney outlived the building it once warmed." Later, he built his own, ever-evolving "castle" just down the road from the main farmhouse.

From 1975 to 1981, the Monteverdi Players, founded by creative director John Carroll and made up of commune members and their local comrades, produced ingenious outdoor plays with elaborate sets built by Fenwick. Perhaps the most memorable was for Shakespeare's *The Tempest* in 1971. As Porche described, "Over the winter in a neighbor's heated barn Fenwick finished his craft. In September, when his white boat with the figurehead of a mythic bull and swan at the stern sailed through the man-made mist, the audience gasped at Fenwick's artistry. Few realized that he'd also built the island: homegrown planking over deck logs floating on lecithin drums."

Certainly, this life was more entertaining than the dreams their parents had nurtured for them. Well into the 1980s, the commune was home to a dozen or more residents at a time, founders, their children, and newcomers alike, along with refugees from other movements and, briefly, Patricia Elizabeth Swinton, known locally as Soshana, a fugitive from justice arrested in 1975 at the Good Life Health Store in Brattleboro where she worked. Swinton had been implicated in the Weather Underground's bombings of government buildings in 1969. She was acquitted of the charges five months after commune members paid her bail.

While Porche is the only fulltime resident of the farmhouse, others come and go. Along with Wizansky and Fenwick, other former communards, friends, and relatives have built or purchased homes nearby, populating the acres around Packer Corner. "We sort of made a shtetl," Porche said, using the word for a small Jewish town or village such as those once widespread in eastern Europe. Each year on May Day, those connected with the commune, many now in their late sixties and older and living far away, gather around a Maypole, share a potluck, and remember a time when solving the world's problems seemed possible.

When Mungo last visited from LA, he stayed in an old schoolhouse across from the farmhouse that serves as a communal B and B. "It's no accident that Vermont pioneered civil unions and so many other progressive ideas. Ethan Allen stopped in this very house, in this very room, Schoolhouse #10 at Packer Corner," he said. "Our coming here was just another chapter in the amazing story of Vermont's history of independence, whether newcomer or old stock. Our neighbor, Ronnie Squires, a fifth-generation Vermonter who owned the farm down the hill, the Franklin Farm, was gay and died of AIDS at forty-one. He got elected and reelected to the legislature. He was a great friend to us and a local hero. He taught us to be open about being gay, to be proud of who we were."

As historians and newspapers began chronicling the stories of the hippie invasion and their impact on Vermont, Porche rejected some of the "self-congratulatory" expressions she heard and read from the aging baby boomers. Like Mungo, she was more interested in noting what Vermont had provided her and those of her generation, the generosity of those who took the time to share what they knew with a bunch of clueless kids—from what to do if the chimney caught fire to putting an electric dipstick in the oil pan so the car would start in the morning. "In order to write or speak about the counter-culture and Vermont, you have to address the issue of class," she observed. "You have to ask uncomfortable questions of people. Who are your friends and who are you not friends with." Those who have had the greatest impact on Vermont, she suggested, were those hippies and activists and farmers who took the opportunity to know their neighbors and befriend them rather than isolate themselves with people who think just like they do.

Even at Packer Corner, this had sometimes been a challenge but one with unexpected rewards. "Up-the-road neighbors, one of the guys, Larry Chapin, told me how he had hayed this farm for a dollar a day with Forest Franklin. He came to our twentieth reunion; we welcomed him very warmly. We were knocking back vodka drinks when he took my hand. 'You people taught me to respect what I couldn't stand, meaning your lifestyle,' he said, meaning our privilege. I was initially so surprised by that but then I thought about it. We got to live here and play here and work here but we had other options. As I've thought about what he was really saying, I've felt more re-flective, grateful that Larry and I had a chance to explore the differences between being neighbors and friends. There were times when our neighbor-liness was a power struggle over land issues or something else, but I'm happy we ended up friends."

Reid Frazier was fascinated by the sociological implications of so many counterculture people integrating into the Brattleboro area. He interviewed people from both sides of the divide for his master's thesis from the University of Vermont, entitled "1960s Communes in Southern Vermont." In it, he deftly summarized what the hippies came for and what some of the old-timers were ready to hand over to them: "The sale of the farm was in itself symbolic of the transition witnessed by many small communities in Vermont. . . . The seller, a woman who married into a family with roots in the community dating to the 18th century, had tired of the hardscrabble existence of life without central heating or indoor toilets." Frazier wrote. "She opted for the amenities of modern middle class life in a heated apartment in a small New England city. By contrast, the young people who would form Total Loss Farm were making the opposite journey, from the suburbs of mid-century middle America back to the agrarian lifestyle that people like Rosie were happy to leave."

THE FREE VERMONT MOVEMENT: RED CLOVER COLLECTIVE AND EARTHWORKS COMMUNE

Roz Payne was smoking a First Class cigarette, a discount brand sold at the general store near her Richmond home, as she recalled her decades as a social and political activist. For Payne, even smoking was a political statement. She bought the brand for the irony, chuckling that someone who had fought class struggles all her life could finally "go first class" for cheap. More than a self-deprecating joke as a senior citizen still smoking cigarettes, the comment reflected her general attitude toward conformity. Raised in New Jersey, where Allen Ginsberg was occasionally her babysitter, and later in Hollywood, Payne had grown up on political activism. Her father once ran for the New Jersey Senate on the Socialist ticket, while her mother gained the ire of a Catholic priest for her union activism in Lowell, Massachusetts, leading the priest to label her a "red flame straight from hell."

After graduating from UCLA, Payne settled briefly into married life and teaching in New Jersey before divorcing "Mr. Muscle Beach Jr." and deciding in 1967 to move to New York City. During her apartment hunt, a departing tenant offered her several cameras he no longer wanted. She didn't take the apartment, but left with a camera. Back on the street just minutes later, camera in hand, a stranger noticed her and shouted rather urgently, "Hey, you! You're a photographer, right? There's a meeting tonight of all the political film people. You have to go. It's very important." The stranger was filmmaker Melvin Margolis. He was working to unify three groups who were separately covering the various political movements of the moment. The activist filmmaking collective Newsreel was born at that meeting. Over the next decade, Newsreel members produced dozens of films that captured the Vietnam War and antiwar activities; the struggles, trials, and convictions of civil-rights activists, especially the militant Black Panthers; and, also, the life of the Red Clover Collective in Putney where the filmmakers launched an effort to unify Vermont's counterculture youth in what became known as the Free Vermont movement. If it sounds complicated, it is. As John Douglas, on whose Putney farm Red Clover was located, put it, "Thank goodness we were young and foolish . . . and committed. We knew what we were doing was dangerous but we were convinced that we had no choice. As people used to say, if not us, who?"

Payne's first documentary recorded the 1968 student takeover of Columbia University, using the approach Newsreel photographers had adopted—up close and personal. She, Margolis, and others shot their footage inside university buildings with the demonstrators rather than safely outside with the press. The protests had erupted after King's murder, which closely followed the discovery of the university's tacit support for the war. Simultaneously, students had heard rumors that Columbia was considering a segregated gymnasium to be constructed in nearby Morningside Park. As the student occupation of university buildings continued, New York City police moved in and violently removed many student activists, all recorded by Newsreel.

Payne soon focused on the Black Panthers. "I was interested in the Panthers because I'm interested in people and, in particular, people who have gotten a raw deal, who are put down, beaten, made to feel inferior, but somehow have the courage to fight back, to say their lives matter," Payne explained at her home in rural Richmond, the rooms filled with documents, films, photographs, alternative newspapers, and posters, the history of the sixties and of Red Clover and the Free Vermont movement that had been launched there.

✳ ✳ ✳

"Red Clover was not a commune. We were a collective. We were fucking serious revolutionaries," Douglas proclaimed passionately. The name was significant, an intentional double-entendre that combined the Vermont state flower with the oldest symbol for socialism. Douglas grew up in Lake Forest, Illinois, in the wealthy family that had founded the Quaker Oats Company. He attended Harvard University, but didn't like its "conservative atmosphere," dropped out after a year and a half, and spent a year sculpting and painting on Martha's Vineyard before enrolling as an art student at Boston

University. Because he had interrupted his education, he was drafted in 1963. Two years later and out of the army, a friend invited him to visit Vermont. One day, the two stopped by a real-estate office run by Les Snow, whose name enchanted Douglas, as did the opportunity to purchase an old hill farm in Putney—150 acres complete with the largest standing barn in town, five outbuildings, and farmhouse for $18,000, paid for with money he'd inherited from his grandmother.

Douglas spent the summer fixing up the place, then headed to Mississippi to make a film with a friend from Harvard, Tom Griffin. Griffin had worked on registering black voters in Mississippi during the 1964 Freedom Summer and wanted to see what progress had been made, while Douglas wanted to see the black struggle for voting rights for himself. The two had an innate sense that this was a pivotal moment in the struggle and wanted to record it. Their film, *Strike City*, tells the story of black laborers who went on strike in 1966 to protest their living, work, and pay conditions. For Griffin and Douglas, as with many young people who were there, Mississippi was a life-changer, with the stark contrast between the comfort of their lives and that of poor blacks made evident. "Everything that followed grew out of the Mississippi taproot," David Harris, a leader of the anti-draft movement who had served fifteen months in prison himself as a draft resister, told Clara Bingham in *Witness to a Revolution*. "We learned how to organize by working with sncc [the Student Nonviolent Coordinating Committee] in Mississippi, and perhaps much more important was the spirit of Mississippi; there was a kind of inspiration in the heroism of the black people in Mississippi. . . . You come back from that, and you can't look at [America] the same way." It was precisely that experience that led Douglas and Griffin to connect the black struggle with what they saw as the imperialism of the Vietnam War: rich people using poor to fight their battles and protect their investments.

As luck would have it, the nascent filmmakers were back in Vermont editing *Strike City* when they learned that Bill Jersey and Norman Fruchter, two activist filmmakers associated with Newsreel, were showing their antiwar film in Bennington. Douglas and Griffin introduced themselves, showed the rough draft of *Strike City*, and soon were introduced to Tom Hayden, a president of Students for a Democratic Society and Chicago Seven defendant, and Robert Kramer, another sds organizer with deep activist roots. Kramer and Hayden were at the core of Newsreel and the antiwar movement. Soon Douglas, like Payne, had joined Newsreel and Kramer began suggesting they create a commune on Douglas's farm. In this way, these national movements were brought to Vermont and the activists as well.

Strike City won first place at the 1967 American Film Festival. Like other Newsreel films, it was gritty, unpolished, black-and-white, shot with 16-millimeter cameras. The idea was to capture "civil rights and civil wrongs" as they were happening. While Payne chronicled Panther trials and, in one instant, accompanied a Black Panther back to his apartment only to be greeted by FBI agents with guns drawn, Kramer, Douglas, and others traveled to North Vietnam to record a version of the war they thought was not being shown at home. Eventually, they were spending more time in Vermont than New York. "By the end of 1967, there were people living in a shed, a barn, a chicken coop, everywhere, and we began to figure out whose milk it was in the icebox and began to live communally, loosely, and, as time went by, we figured we could get out of New York and work together in Vermont more cheaply," Douglas recalled. While there was the initial illusion that Vermont offered a bit of protection from government surveillance, that fantasy dissolved when the FBI learned that Carl Oglesby, who had been connected to the Weather Underground, sometimes stayed at Red Clover.

In July 1968, Douglas was asked to join a delegation of American activists negotiating the release of three American prisoners from North Vietnam. David Dellinger's National Mobilization Committee to End the War in Vietnam was leading the negotiations rather than the International Committee of the Red Cross, the traditional go-between in matters affecting war prisoners. Initially, the North Vietnamese offered to return the prisoners in exchange for the opportunity for Ho Chi Minh to be filmed speaking directly to the American people. CBS had agreed to make the film, but wanted Walter Cronkite to conduct an interview. The North Vietnamese refused. Although still under indictment on the Chicago Seven allegations, Dellinger somehow arranged to travel to Hanoi to negotiate with the North Vietnamese, taking Douglas, Kramer, and Fruchter as filmmakers, Rennie Davis, also under indictment on the Chicago charges, several other SDS members, and the writer Grace Paley. As it turned out, Ho Chi Minh was too ill to be filmed, but Douglas and company were invited to stay in-country and record what eventually became the *People's War*. The film portrayed the North Vietnamese fighting Americans while attempting to raise their standard of living after centuries of colonial rule. Dellinger was successful in gaining the release of the prisoners, the third such release he negotiated. Nonetheless, his willingness to negotiate with America's enemy put him and those connected to him in jeopardy of treason charges. The U.S. government confiscated Douglas's film upon his return to the states. The film was eventually released but it was clear that he would remain a target of government surveillance.

In a subsequent film, *Milestones*, Grace Paley discussed her reaction to spending time with the North Vietnamese people: "They were like us. I liked them. At that time, I had a lot of troubles in my life. I stopped thinking about them. That's what we brought back from Vietnam, the realization that we are all the same." These activities predated her move to her husband's family's property in Thetford and her later honor as Vermont State Poet.

Douglas's subsequent film, *To Our Common Victory*, presented a critical look at U.S. policies in Vietnam and included a rare interview with Madam Binh, the Vietnamese leader who negotiated on behalf of the Viet Cong at the Paris Peace Conference.

All this while, Payne was filming Panther and other radical groups' activities around the country, including *Mayday*, which records a May 1, 1969, rally in San Francisco organized to demand the release of Huey Newton, the Panthers' cofounder charged in the murder of an Oakland police officer, and *Off the Pig*, featuring Panther training and recruitment practices. She traveled in 1970 to Cuba to record the Vinceremos Brigade, in which young people from around the world, including Americans and North Vietnamese, defied the American blockade to help Cubans cut sugar cane. In Vermont, she recorded Black Panthers rallying on the campus of UVM. These films have been collected in a twelve-hour compilation, *What We Want, What We Believe*, considered the most complete record of Black Panther activities.

* * *

As the 1970s dawned, members of Red Clover met members of the Earthworks commune, located in Franklin and not far from the Canadian border. Despite living on opposite ends of Vermont, they began exploring ways of working together for common cause. Looking to the future, they envisioned that Vermont could be a place of refuge for the disenfranchised, a place where a new society might evolve after the war had been ended. Two couples, Barbara and Jim Nolfi and Mary Pat and Bruce Taub, had traveled with their children from Sebastopol, California, to Franklin in 1969 to establish the Earthworks commune. The Nolfis had met at Berkeley where Barbara finished her undergraduate degree and Jim earned his doctorate in zoology. In establishing Earthworks, their goal was to question societal restrictions on everything from the economy and gender roles to the structure of the nuclear family. As Barbara expressed it, they rejected social traditions whose purpose was "not to enlighten but to constrain." Other young people, including several of Jim's coworkers from UVM, where he'd been hired as a professor, quickly joined their enterprise. They planted crops, farmed with horses and rudimentary equipment, constructed outbuildings, and began to dream of a small community on their land. But the next year, a fire leveled Earthworks' communal house and barn and destroyed a year's worth of firewood, obviously a major setback. With the optimism of youth, they set to rebuilding the structures while attempting to raise food for the winter. Friends from other communes helped, especially residents of the Mount Philo commune established in an old inn in Charlotte. Mount Philo had hired a teacher for their kids and invited the Earthworks children to live with them while the main building at Earthworks was rebuilt. Despite these difficulties, that summer, Earthworks and Red Clover organized a statewide gathering of communards, the first of several.

"We envisioned a collaborative effort, north to south, east to west," Barbara explained. "We traveled to the Dreamers [commune] in Montgomery, to Johnson Pasture and Total Loss Farm in the south, talking wherever we went about how to unite for common goals. We wanted our food to be good quality, healthy, and inexpensive. Health care, transportation, and newspapers—communication between us—were essential issues. Publications like *Free Vermont*, the *Vermont Freeman*, *Vermont Railroad*, and the *Vanguard Press* all came out of our efforts as ways to keep us together and informed, to spread our ideas throughout Vermont."

Robert Houriet, the chronicler of the national commune movement, became a friend and joined the effort. As he recalled, "The communes moved into a loose-knit federation and began to meet twice a year on solstices. The first gathering was held the solstice of 1970 and was hosted by Earthworks in Franklin, a commune which fell roughly in the middle of the spectrum from hippie to radical. The morning of the first day they harvested by hand a field of oats. Then they hunkered in small circles on a meadow high above the complex of farm buildings. Each group sketched a part of the new society: a cooperative system for buying food, primarily grains such as brown rice; a separate children's' collective; a medical clinic which would ride circuit between communes to assist at homebirths and treat all the chromic illnesses and infections; a traveling caravan of people's music and theater: a people's bank endowed with $5,000 from Red Clover; a shortwave hookup

A young Barbara Nolfi.
Courtesy of Dylan Nolfi

for communication and defense alert; a car pool of '62 Fords for standardized exchange of parts and mechanics' knowledge.

"From the first gatherings, two sometimes opposing approaches were advanced: Red Clover's urban, take-up-a-gun was moderated by the rural communes' cooler advice to adopt the dress and customs of the natives and be good farmers. These differences were contained in a unifying feeling that we were all on the edge of a growing movement that would transform all of us, personally and collectively, into a new people, new families, new tribes, a member of the Woodstock Nations not in a few months, certainly no longer than a few years. The gathering closed in a huge circle of clasped hands around the meadow and a singing of 'Amazing Grace.'"

To support these goals, members of the various communes toured colleges and farms, other communes, and collectives, spreading the word about the services they had created and the opportunities they envisioned for working together. Wherever he went, Douglas also brought a political message, connecting the dots between the war in Vietnam, racial discrimination in the United States, and poverty in Vermont. Douglas had devised a way to make a copy of a film each time he showed it and would leave the copy with whatever group he was visiting so they could share it with others. For him and other activists, apathy in the face of these problems was not only deadening but dangerous. One needed to fight the system on all fronts, from monetary and political to intellectual, social, and spiritual. To that end and in response to what some viewed as harassment by law officials, a few Red Clover members acquired guns and learned self-defense. Others were interested in simply organizing for a more sustainable life. After all, the movement needed food, a health system, car repair, and a way to educate its children.

In Putney, the residents of Red Clover began to make these ideas a reality. They opened the Liberation Garage, a free automobile repair shop, along with the Common Ground restaurant, a worker-owned-and-operated endeavor considered the first all-vegetarian restaurant in New England. As if life weren't complicated enough, about this time, Douglas's first child was born. Not long after, in the fall of 1970, the FBI raided the collective looking for Bernadine Dohrn and other Weather Underground fugitives. Douglas recalled the agents arriving in the middle of the night, lining everyone up and searching the house. Although there were no fugitives to be found, news of the raid spread quickly to the wider community.

As it turned out, forces within and without led to the dissolution of both Earthworks and Red Clover. "At Earthworks, people had wanted to break what they saw as restrictive and conformist ideas and that included marriage, but the reality of open relationships was not an easy one to navigate. The mores were open marriage but it was more what the men were into, to be honest," Barbara Nolfi conceded. "New alliances outside of marriage began and some of them lasted, but the bottom line is I went there married to Jim Nolfi with Dylan [her son], and at the end of the first summer Jim left." As someone who had little experience in rural life and as a new mother, she felt overwhelmed. In 1971, she left the commune but not the movement. Barbara moved to several locations around Chittenden County and continued her activism as part of a large group of women and men who in the coming years would establish the area's first food co-op, first free health clinic, and first women's health-care center. Eventually, other members of the commune moved on as well, some making their own contributions to Vermont in areas of the environment, land use, and farming.

That same year in Putney, problems between townies and Red Clover came to a head after collective members "liberated" vacant land belonging to nearby Windham College. They plowed and planted the vacant field, dubbed it the Free Farm with the intention to freely share both the produce and their ideology. They believed the farm would demonstrate to the wider community the benefits of cooperative action without the need for constant striving after more and more money. All summer, the land served as a gathering place for potluck dinners and political gatherings; food was given away with no questions or commitments required. Bikers showed up, local kids. There was music and frivolity and hard work. When fall approached, however, college officials said it was time to go. Hell, no, the Free Farmers said; that's not what liberation means. The standoff reached a climax on parents' weekend. Demonstrators had planned to meet at the land to protest the loss of their garden plot but were greeted by sheriffs and state-police officers. Like any dedicated liberators, they didn't give up, but marched off to the parents' barbecue at the college, made a big ruckus, gave speeches, helped themselves to hotdogs, and generally embarrassed the college before the parents. Police stood by in riot gear, but college officials never asked them to intercede. Indeed, media reports of the time suggested the college president was somewhat sympathetic to the Free Farm's argument that they were making good use of vacant land.

Townspeople were less forgiving. One night, a group of townspeople ripped up the vegetables and drove vehicles through the garden, spoiling the food. A fistfight ensued and the Free Farmers were told to leave or else, which they did, but the next night, local vigilantes by the carload drove by the farm and shots were fired into the air. Douglas began to realize it couldn't go on. He explained the dissolution this way: "There had been a lot of feeling that I was abandoning the collective. A lot of people were having babies, so it was heading in other directions. The kids collective, Red Paint, had moved into the main house at Mount Philo in '71. About then, also, the FBI met me at the bus station in Brattleboro and 'offered' me a ride home. We were well aware that black Panthers were being gunned down and the feeling was, maybe we were next. And then, the townspeople turned against us after the Free Farm episode. It was time to move on. People spread out, some moved toward Burlington."

Douglas eventually sold the property to people who had been living there and wanted to continue the farm. Another collective was briefly formed in Westford, with Mary Pat and Barbara Nolfi and their kids, Douglas, his son Leif, and others sharing the home. With the end of the Vietnam War in 1975 and new realities as Douglas found himself "a single dad a lot of the time, although I'm close to both moms," other demands took over. Sometimes he lived in Greenwich Village, sometimes in Vermont. Eventually, he became quite adept in computer graphics, from which he has made a living, while also continuing to make experimental films, the most recent of which was his contribution to the 2015 six-part documentary *Freedom and Unity*, a collaboration of more than four dozen Vermont filmmakers who tell the Vermont story thematically, not chronologically.

All the while Payne continued to record the stories of the Panthers, eventually interviewing the FBI agents who had investigated them. She created what's generally considered the most extensive archive on the Black Panther movement. Like Barbara Nolfi, she contributed to the creation of the Onion River Food Co-op, the Burlington Women's Health Center, and the People's Free Clinic, all radical enterprises that came out of the counterculture. In 1981, she worked as a legal investigator and law clerk for progressive Burlington attorney Sandy Baird and subsequently completed the Vermont Law Clerk Program. Her interests remained eclectic: she taught history, focusing on civil rights, the sixties, and women's rights at Burlington College, an alternative college Jim Nolfi helped create. She became an expert mycologist and spread her knowledge of mushrooms through classes and mushroom-hunting field trips in northern Vermont. In 1989, first as a joke, she ran for Richmond constable—and won. She soon came to hate receiving phone calls at all hours of the day and night from "people who wanted you to solve all their problem. But I got a badge and could get into things for free," Payne said, again enjoying the irony in her words.

Jim Nolfi taught briefly at UVM but was fired for counseling students on the draft. No worries; he went on to teach at Goddard College, where he worked with Dan Chodorkoff and Murray Bookchin at the Institute for Social Ecology. His work in determining how much land would be needed to feed the Vermont populace and what would be needed as the population grew remain important guides for farmers and planners. He also helped organize the Vermont Institute of Community Involvement, which eventually led to the creation of the recently closed Burlington College. In all these efforts, he was trying to break down barriers that kept people like Vietnam War veterans and single parents from gaining useful education while also working to sustain the organic food movement.

After working for decades with other like-minded people, Barbara Nolfi saw her dream of a new form of communal living come to fruition with the creation of the Burlington Co-Housing East Village, a multigenerational, cooperative living center located near UVM. There, in the tidy apartment she shares with her husband, Don Schramm, she enjoyed many of the benefits of communal living such as the opportunity for common meals, a full calendar of workshops, films, and cultural presentations; access to a rooftop terrace, community living room, playroom, laundry room, and garden—all in a setting that allowed residents the privacy of their own living space.

One of her lasting disappointments has been that some people in the Franklin area retained negative impressions of Earthworks, a sentiment shared by cofounder Bruce Taub. Taub became a lawyer and moved to Cape Cod, but he never forgot his time in Vermont. In 1993, he wrote a letter to the Franklin town librarian, responding to what he considered a "derisive" and "limited" mention of Earthworks in Franklin's official town history. Earthworks, he wrote "was founded in an effort to 'return to the land,' to master the skills that would promote agrarian self-sufficiency, and to help create a society that would provide an alternative to the despair and destruction we were experiencing in our culture, our country, and our environment. We were upset about the state of world affairs and had set about in a manner we acknowledged to be experimental to improve them.

"We were particularly opposed to our government's military violence, to the competitive behaviors we felt were inherent in capitalism, and to the selfish, male-dominated non-cooperative values we then believed were wrongly engendered by the nuclear family. The Vietnam holocaust was to us a source of daily pain. So too was the perceived destruction of our natural environment and the permanent annihilation of other living species. We hoped we could make things better. We intended to be social reformers."

With those words, Taub summarized the aspiration of the counterculture and commune movements, especially those of the radical activists who had formed Free Vermont. In writing, he expressed the hope that these goals would not be lost to history but also emphasized the knowledge that, for all its idealism, the goal of the activists was only partly achieved.

QUARRY HILL

Ten-day marriages, shared parenting, Socratic discourse, polyamory—for decades, these elements characterized the interpersonal drama at the Quarry Hill Creative Center in Rochester. Established by Irving Fiske and his wife, Barbara, as a writers' and artists' retreat in 1946, by the late 1960s Quarry Hill had evolved into one of Vermont's larger communes, with Irving at its center. Quarry Hill was a world apart, almost free of rules, where hundreds of hippie kids over the years experienced what some described as an idyllic family life in which sexual exploration and freedom trumped the rules that had been deeply engrained in their psyches by their parents, educators, and religious leaders, a place where children would be raised with a degree of autonomy their parents had not experienced as children. Others felt in retrospect as if they had been caught in Irving's social experiment, at times manipulated or influenced, their emotional and sexual behaviors part of an "old man's power fantasy," as a former resident put it. Regardless of which view one accepts, Quarry Hill has endured, and, while a split in the community caused some longtime residents to leave in the late 1990s and early 2000s, it remains Vermont's oldest alternative living community, with roughly forty residents in 2017.

Irving Fiske was thirty-eight and his wife Barbara twenty-eight when they bought the property as a retreat from their busy, bohemian lives in New York. Irving enjoyed an audience. In New York, he would give public talks on Tantric yoga, the yoga of sex, and other avant-garde ideas such as the notion that traditional schooling was deadly, that children should never be spanked or physically or emotionally harmed; that monogamy was unhealthy and encouraged possessiveness, which in turn led to aggression and restriction; and that people should live as fully as possible, enjoying their avocations and one another rather than labor in boring, repetitive or demeaning jobs. The talks often ended with an invitation to join the Fiskes in Vermont, where these conversations would continue, everyone gathered round Irving.

By 1965, as stories of the wizard in the woods and his free-love commune spread, more and more young people arrived. Old school buses and trailers became shelters. Tents filled upper meadows. Plywood shelters and large homes were built while people divided up the farmhouse attic, lined with mattresses, into bedrooms. Barbara Fiske said this of the hippies' arrival: "They danced nude in the neighbor's pond and in the streets of Rochester, one girl at least, just generally raising hell. Irv was struggling to make mortgage payments. Some of the people could contribute, and that struck him as being a very fortuitous thing."

Decades after his death in 1990 at eighty-two, Irving's legacy continued to engender complex emotions. Some remembered him as a brilliant intellectual who could converse with anyone, a mentor who used questioning as a teaching tool. Others believed he'd helped them free their minds of sexual hang-ups and admired his espousal of personal freedom, especially for children. For these people, Irving was a generous soul who allowed them to live on his land for next to nothing or half of whatever they had. Others, however, viewed him as a libertine who manipulated those who trusted him for his own entertainment, sexual fantasies, and economic support, leaving behind a chaotic community whose members would soon end up in a legal battle over compensation for their contributions to Quarry Hill's long existence and other issues. Among the more controversial stories were that he arranged pairings or urged someone to stop sleeping with a particular person, and that he had sex with young women who visited or lived at Quarry Hill.

Becky Armstrong conducted oral histories of dozens of former and current residents for a thesis she wrote toward her master's degree at Dartmouth College. "Quarry Hill, 1966–1976: An Oral History of a Time and Place" describes how "We would gather in the Farmhouse, especially after dark, and Irving would suggest, playfully, that this person or that person was particularly sexy, or he would propose that someone give a certain percentage of their lover to him or to someone else, or that the whole universe might be transformed if two particular people got together. The sexual energy would begin sparking through the room. Some people were very uncomfortable with this and would depart the room or the whole place the next day.

"The women would get together for sex with the man who had attracted the interest of one or both. Eventually the women were having sex in groups of six or seven, still with one man. There were only a few men who could be counted on to behave properly for such an event. Irving suggested that men could not be illuminated without the intercession and aid of a woman, a bodhisattva. He would say that women were all goddesses and should be treated exactly like the Empress of the Universe," Armstrong wrote.

While there's general agreement that Irving arranged his schedule to allow for his own social and sexual encounters, Allen Sherman, often referred to as Irving's "lieutenant," insisted that Irving used these encounters as ways to promulgate his various ideas or, in the parlance of the day, "to expand one's consciousness." Sherman dismissed claims that Irving had sex with minors. Irving employed and taught a technique called "running," similar to a practice used in Dianetics or Scientology for self-improvement. Ladybelle Fiske McFarlin, Barbara and Irving's oldest child who still lives at Quarry Hill with her husband, Brion McFarlin, explained that her father had known L. Ron Hubbard, the father of Scientology, slightly until they had a falling-out. The concept of "running" is based on the power of repetition in a quiet, soothing voice as a person is falling asleep or otherwise relaxed, she said, adding that Irving had purposefully made his voice "mellifluous. He'd gotten rid of his Brooklyn accent . . . by listening to records of his voice and then by imitating his favorite actor, Ronald Colman." One former Quarry

Irving Fiske.
Courtesy of Isabella Fiske
McFarlin/Quarry Hill Archives

Hill resident recalled Irving reciting to her, "When you see me, you will be filled with overwhelming sexual desire." Residents practiced running on one another.

One woman told Armstrong, "Running was reconditioning to think you were wonderful, to feel good about ourselves, to be confident about our sexuality and in all ways. I was run, and I ran people, six or eight different people." But another woman called running "evil. It was a way that Irving and the men close to him manipulated women. It was a kind of mind control. For 20 years after, I had nightmares that I'm at Quarry Hill and can't leave."

Irving remains an enigma to former resident John Rosenblum, who once regarded Irving as a father figure. "When I think back to who he was, I wonder whether those moments in which I derived my opinions of him were him acting a role or the real person," he said.

For Spring Cerise, who grew up at Quarry Hill and now lives in Oakland, it was painful to watch her mother go to Irving's cabin "to be run."

"There were no illusions. They had their sex schedule. They made no effort to explain to us what they were doing. They were just participating in this polyamorous running thing with Irving. She would spend the night there," she said. "I'd beg her to stay home. I knew she was going to be with another man. It brought up overwhelming anger for me. I felt threatened by it." As for Irving, she said, "I never understood what anyone found charismatic about him. I understood everyone revered him but to me he was an old man with this really bad temper. He would come out of his little cabin, screaming and stomping. I'd think, this guy is crazy, a loose cannon."

One way or the other, they stayed and stayed, some for twenty or more years until what came to be known as the "big divorce."

A Cornell graduate, Irving grew up comfortably on Long Island but eschewed the family's bourgeois life and the dictate that he must become a doctor. He studied what he liked, culling from science and the humanities. After Cornell, he held forth at the Waldorf Café in the East Village on metaphysics, sex, politics, and happiness. Barbara Fiske had come to New York from Arizona as an aspiring artist who found herself drawing cartoon characters named Girl Commando and the Blond Bombshell. It wasn't until her last years that she received recognition as a pioneering woman cartoon artist. Her editor at Harvey Comic Books introduced her to Irving. She had been enchanted as an only child by *The Woodcutter of Olympus*, a 1904 novel by Mary Ellen Waller of Bethel, about a fictitious Vermont woodcutter who lost the use of his legs only to discover he had the talent of Michelangelo as a wood sculptor. "It made her yearn to come to green Vermont and go into the hills and pick raspberries," Ladybelle said.

On April 10, 1946, with $1,000 from their mothers, the couple placed a down payment on the Lawrence Spencer Farm, 180 acres of woods, meadows, pond and brook, an old swayback-roof farmhouse, falling-down barn, and outbuildings. The farm was located on a hill northeast of Rochester, not far from the fictionalized woodcutter's home. The village, located on the edge of the Green Mountain National Forest, with dark valleys and rich farmland nestled along the White River, then had a population of about 1,130 people, roughly the same as in 2017.

Soon, the Fiskes built other cabins for friends and relatives. The couple initially agreed on no children, but as Barbara neared thirty she began to want a baby. Their friend, the abstract artist Joachim Probst, took Barbara's side. "You two will be the mother and father of a new race," Probst was said to proclaim theatrically, a prophecy Irving could not ignore. That was the story Ladybelle always heard, and that her parents put their hands together, made love in the hay and she was born nine months later; she was followed by a brother, William.

"My mother discovered babies don't just lie there in a drawer. They make art difficult. And so they started looking for people to take care of us by putting ads in the New England Dairy Farmers newsletter and the like for an artistic young woman to watch the children in return for art lessons," Ladybelle said. "We had an outhouse until 1990, computers before a septic system or good running water. It was even more primitive in the 1950s." Irving quickly came to believe that "children are ambassadors from another dimension and ought to be treated with the utmost welcome and courtesy."

The family's early years were spent between New York, often staying with intellectual friends and artists, and Vermont, where the children ran naked, free as the wild creatures living on the land. Irving called schools "Dark Satanic Mills That Grind Men's Souls to Dust," quoting William Blake. Once Ladybelle reached school age, "We traveled constantly in a handmade travel trailer pulled by an old Chevrolet up and down the Eastern seaboard to escape truant officers, from Vermont to Florida where we had a little cabin in the Ocala National Forest. We learned by Socratic discourse, visiting historic battlegrounds and by constant reading. I engulfed books, reading by age three." Barbara remained quiet in the background until she struck out on her own, opening a gallery with a friend named Gwen, but soon Irving took over Gallery Gwen for his talks, and later became sexually involved with Gwen, a situation that pained Barbara so greatly that she had a nervous breakdown. As she told Armstrong, "From the time we met, [Irving] tried to reveal to me that I had either a bisexual nature or a lesbian nature. . . . That was his direction, having and arranging relationships with many women at the same time and women with each other. . . . I was crazy about him. From my point of view, we were in a state of bliss but it really irked Irv. Irving liked to fool around with human relationships, to experiment to find out what turned people on. Irving was interested in women who were not orgasmic. I didn't fit the scenario at all and never had. The idea of a monogamous domestic relationship practically killed Irving. When he couldn't get anything else going, he felt like he was dying and said so. He wanted to eliminate jealousy between women. . . . It was the Oneida idea that jealousy could be prevented if everybody's partner was sleeping with another person."

"My going under in a shambles [after Irving became involved with Gwen] was a terrible thing for Irving," she said. "He cried and cried. Then he had to pull himself together and go on another basis. Being Irving, he saw the advantages of it almost right away. He met and was able to facilitate his relationship with many, many girls." In 1976, she divorced Irving and moved to Randolph, later marrying Dr. Donald Calhoun, a Quaker writer and sociology professor

A young Ladybelle Fiske.
Courtesy of Isabella Fiske McFarlin/Quarry Hill Archives

who had been her mentor at Vermont College. After Irving's death the couple returned to Quarry Hill where they lived into their nineties.

Armstrong was among the first hippies to discover Quarry Hill. She spent a few weeks there in 1966. By 1968, when she was twenty-four, she felt her "life had been an irresponsible glory of drug explorations, which touched on madness" and returned to Quarry Hill to stay for thirty years. "It was Irving who attracted me most to Quarry Hill. He challenged me to make Socratic self-exploration a way of life and espoused Tantric sexual practices as holding the potential for personal illumination. Quarry Hill had no religion, no political dogma, apart from William Blake's view that 'Everything that Lives is Holy.' There were no rules beyond a prohibition of violence—especially against children. Spanking and scolding were prohibited—and the 'NO DISHES IN THE SINK!' sign posted by Irving in the Farmhouse kitchen."

Of the seventy to eighty-five people living at Quarry Hill in 1999, two-thirds arrived between 1969 and 1976, the dates Armstrong used in choosing her interview subjects. Quarry Hill was not political, nor did residents integrate themselves into the town. At the commune, women had elevated status. Indeed, at least in the early years, mothers had what passed for permanent housing while men went from house to house or room to room or mattress to mattress, depending on which woman they were with at any time. Mothers could apply for welfare support and food stamps, which were shared with the community. Others found ways to qualify for public assistance or food stamps. Some lived on student aid. Some begged money from parents. The general idea was, if you got money from any source, you would give half to Irving, who would parse it out for bills or treats, such as hot fudge sundaes at Lyon's Pharmacy. As Armstrong wrote, "We didn't question that our minimal resources should constantly be stretched to include more and more people. . . . Our philosophy allowed us to work outside the community for wages only in dire emergency." There was rarely enough food. Sherman recalled being so hungry he once shared a dog treat with a dog. He remembered the milkweed casserole someone created and something called "bulgur boom boom," made from bulgur wheat, broccoli, and cans of cream of mushroom soup. He swore these were good.

Parenting, too, was shared. A kids' list was posted for people without kids to sign so mothers would have time to themselves.

Judy Geller was among the first to take Irving up on the invitation to visit Vermont. She was nineteen years old, from Jersey City and living in Greenwich Village. It was 1965, the beginning of the hippie era. Timothy Leary was passing out LSD-laced sugar cubes and giving lectures at Cooper Union. Geller wanted a break from the craziness and thought Quarry Hill might offer respite. Ladybelle was fifteen, William twelve. Geller loved the idea of the place and the freedoms it promised, but she wasn't ready to settle down. By the time she returned nine years later, accompanied by her daughter, "the community was really thriving and growing and houses were being built; there was a sense of community. The kids' list was one of the elements that made the place so special to me as a single mother. It was the best thing about the community. I raised my daughter as a single mom at Quarry Hill." As it turned out, her daughter got a dad. "She picked one man to be her dad and he, being the wonderful person he is, he took it on. Now he's grandpa to her daughter and he and I are very good friends, so we're like a family."

The he she referred to was Rosenblum, a private business consultant and writer in Calais who lived at Quarry Hill from 1976 to 2001.

* * *

In summer, the commune members were more like the grasshopper than the ant. They grew food but put little by for winter. One good-weather task could not be avoided—moving the outhouse to a new location. Tommy Toilet, one of Irving's inventions described in hilarious detail by Armstrong, was a barrel half-filled with motor oil positioned beneath a toilet seat in an outhouse. The idea was that when the barrel got full, a trench would be dug and the barrel tipped so the shit and oil would flow into the trench, and the whole mess could be set on fire. In reality, the barrel only half-emptied and got stuck in the trench. Someone or some ones had to climb in, tip it to empty, and set it upright again—none of which sounded like a happy day on the commune.

In winter, Irving would travel to his little two-room cabin in Ocala, bringing some of the residents with him. For those left behind, keeping warm often meant burning green wood and thawing the hose that brought water into the main house by hauling it in overnight, only to have it freeze again. Cars might be buried in snow and, later, mud.

In Ocala, Irving and his merry troupe basked in the warm days, swam in a lake in the park, and enlisted new members for their family. One fourteen-year-old, recruited at a bar in Daytona Beach where she was working under a false ID, recalled meeting a young guy from Quarry Hill who invited her to visit the camp to meet "the Socrates of the Forest." From his description of the setup, she couldn't understand how her new friend could be so young and "have" so many kids. Soon enough, she was among them, learning a new definition of family.

In either location, poverty or not having enough food was often less challenging than coping with jealousy when a person someone had fallen for wanted to sleep with someone else, or if Irving suggested that idea. He came up with the idea of a "ten-day-marriage" as a way to deal with jealousy or to discourage a resident's desire for monogamy. He thought the arrangement would lead a young person to quickly tire of being monogamous. In his world, wanting to be married was an intentional or unintentional desire to limit one's partner's freedom, a leftover from childhood brainwashing. Ten-day marriages were community-wide spectacles with Irving officiating; photographs of several are prominent on Quarry Hill's Facebook page.

As time went on, however, residents matured and more children were born. The reality of parenthood, the need for privacy, and a desire for stability led some people to want to claim and create their own family units, if only to reduce the drama in their lives. Simultaneously, and for similar reasons, people began to improve certain houses for themselves, build new ones or add to existing structures. As Armstrong wrote, "By 1975, primary relationships started to be defined by parental relationships and small groups joined together in one building" as a kind of extended family. One resident lived in an eight-by-twelve-foot trailer designed by Irving and built out of Masonite. Twenty-five people carried it to a meadow. Another little room was added with a loft. Five people lived in that house. Mothers took in single people for help with the children. Eventually, the kids' list was abandoned. Rather than gather together for a communal meal at the farmhouse, people began cooking and eating together in smaller groups. As time passed, also, people became tired of being cold and uncomfortable and wanted more comfort for their children. This led them to improve their homes, which in turn led to people becoming more proprietary.

Ladybelle and William were often of two minds about the growing number of structures on the commune. While they generally enjoyed having a lot of friends their age around, it bothered them to see a structure go up on a favorite meadow or under a treasured tree. "William was always distressed by Irving's propensity of saying yes to everything. [William] wanted people to understand that if they build houses, the houses were ours. It was fine if everyone wanted to live with us but we want[ed] to hang on to our land," she told Armstrong. William died in 2008.

Some residents also worked to organize the commune's North Hollow School and apply for state approval. Geller was instrumental in these efforts. Relationships with the town improved; several parents from off the commune sent their children to the school and to art classes. Simultaneously, a number of Quarry Hill residents returned to college and earned degrees in part thanks to low-residency and satellite college campuses that became more available throughout Vermont. Several businesses were formed on the commune. Art Spiegelman, the Pulitzer Prize–winning author of the graphic novel about the holocaust, *Maus*, and his wife, Françoise Mouly, helped create Top-Drawer Rubber Stamp Company in 1978. Top-Drawer made pictorial rubber stamps featuring art by R. Crumb, Spiegelman, Barbara Fiske, and others. William Fiske, who had master's degrees in computer science and history, became adept in software programming. In the 1980s, he developed innovative programs for blood-bank management and founded two software firms, Bioheuristics and William Fiske Associates, both of which employed residents. As the economy changed and it became more difficult to live on less while desiring more, some residents took jobs away from the community as well.

Who knows how the commune would have evolved if Irving had lived longer, because what its residents might have called order seemed to fall apart with his death in Ocala in the winter of 1990 at age eighty-two. It had been one thing to adhere to his suggestions and theories, but another to follow Ladybelle and William. Almost immediately, or so it seemed to Ladybelle, residents wanted more say in decision making about investments in the community and the school. As one former resident explained, "We wanted to create a strong community where decisions were made fairly and funds we paid to maintain the community would be used in a transparent and fair manner." For years, the communards had lived on little while a few more wealthy residents contributed generously. Libby Hall was among the benefactors. A member of one of America's best-known families, the Halls of Hallmark fame, she lived at Quarry Hill for more than twenty years, contributing to the North Hollow School, the commune's water system, and other necessities. Initially Libby and her son Adam Sherman lived in a one-room, low-ceiling shack with no running water but in the late 1970s moved into the former summer home of a Grand Union executive. Adam named the property, located directly east of Quarry Hill, Magi-La for "magic land." One former resident described Magi-La as "a beautiful property with a large house, expansive meadows, ponds, and forest. We considered Magi-La part of Quarry Hill, and even buried a couple of people there." Cerise told how, when her father and Hall married, Hall embraced her as a daughter, and she spent her high school years living at Magi-La. Cerise may have feared Irving's temper tantrums, but said, "My stepmother had an incredibly involved relationship with Irving. I never hear her say a bad thing about him."

When Hall left Quarry Hill, she took financial support with her, part of what Ladybelle called "the big divorce." Feeling that their demands for autonomy were not being addressed and insecure about the future, some long-term residents took legal advice to clarify their rights to houses they'd improved. The upshot was a settlement between Ladybelle and some residents in which they received "lengthy leases on the land under and around their houses, the right to use a certain area of common land at Quarry Hill and the community building for gatherings and parties," Ladybelle said, adding that was something she always thought was a good idea. Quarry Hill's obligations and protections as a family-owned rental corporation, Lyman Hall, Inc., were further defined. Whether due to the conflict or not, many long-term residents, including Armstrong, Geller, Rosenblum, and Allen Sherman moved away. For most, the emotions are still raw and the versions of the story are many.

The divide can best be seen, however, in observations made by two men who were long close to Irving. While Rosenblum had long admired Irving, "I came to realize that there was a side to him I didn't see when I was there with him. Irving used 'psychodramas' to exert his control over others. He was always playing a Machiavellian game where there was something tangible he was trying to get for himself, sex with one of the women, domination over a man, and also to keep the pot stirred so that people had multiple relationships, which made it easier for him to get girls into his bed. I'm not saying Irving didn't believe he was creating a new and creative society. That was one side of him. The other was that he was an insecure megalomaniac who would completely freak out if he couldn't control everyone around him. Luckily for Irving, he was a brilliant Machiavellian tactician and could usually get anything he wanted."

Sherman continues to see the situation entirely differently. He was with Irving every day and insisted that "Irving didn't mess with people's lives in a direct way. Truly, he believed we had been damaged by our parents and society. He received constant feedback that what he was doing was what people desired. People would have problems and come to Irving for help and he would help them resolve the problem. Now that he's gone and many of us have moved away from Quarry Hill, it makes me sad that people blame him for decisions they made when he invested so much in trying to free us."

For Ladybelle, the years of dissent at Quarry Hill were particularly difficult, especially after her brother's death, the loss of Hall's support and friendship, and her husband's bout with cancer. On June 17, 2000, Hall's lawyer sent a letter to Quarry Hill, stating that she would not be returning, at least for the foreseeable future. The letter forbade access to Magi-La. The property has been sold. Adding salt to the wound, in 2010, Adam Sherman,

Hall's son by Allen Sherman, wrote and produced a "based on a true life" movie, *Happiness Runs*. The online movie database IMDb.com described the film thus: "A young man named Victor realizes the shortcomings of the Utopian ideals on the hippie commune where he was raised. Victor's mother is funding the commune where the guru Insley hypnotizes and seduces women with a technique he calls 'running.' Insley manipulates the minds of these women so that they give him their bodies and all their worldly possessions." The mother in *Happiness Runs* is played by Andie MacDowell, while Insley is played by Rutger Hauer.

"I concentrate on the beautiful days, the wonderful memories, the smart and compassionate children we raised here," Ladybelle said. "This *was* a magical place. It still is. While I feel a sense of betrayal that we let so many live here, have their babies here, live for next to nothing, enjoy the freedoms of the place, and hear it turned into something it never was, we have remained a strong community. The fact is that both before and after the divorce and the settlement, we have done all we can to help people here and even elsewhere, and have taken in many people who had nowhere else to go. And we still are doing this."

Geller, who taught in a private school in Berkeley after leaving Quarry Hill, was of two minds about the value of the Vermont experience. "On one level, what we wanted was to have a voice in how the community was run, to be partners in the venture. So many good things were happening, but it was like we were up against a brick wall with the family. It imploded. [Ladybelle] calls it the big divorce, like being married to eighty people and then getting divorced. Perhaps its time had just come to an end for some of us. It's better now; we're healing. My daughter and Ladybelle's daughter are good friends, but there's no way of not seeing that the end was a very difficult time for many of us."

There was nostalgia in her voice as she added, "It's a diaspora; our tribe was flung in different directions. There was something very satisfying about it for a long time; that's why we stayed so long. That family that we were always had people to help with the children. And, of course, the land itself is beautiful. There are times when I really miss it, miss it so much it hurts."

FROG RUN

Robert Houriet's book *Getting Back Together* made him an expert on the commune movement. Published in 1971, it featured stories of fifty of the roughly two hundred communes he estimated were operating in America by the late 1960s. Based on three years of research during which Houriet traveled more than 10,000 miles visiting communes from Vermont to Washington State, it attracted much media attention, including an appearance on the *Today* show in which three issues dominated the conversation: drugs, sex, and religion.

Wearing a herringbone-tweed jacket, cotton shirt, and tie and sporting a scruffy Lincoln-style beard, Houriet told host Hugh Downs that drugs were used on some communes, not all, that extramarital sex occurred but rarely of the orgiastic nature portrayed by the media, and that he thought most communards were more religious than the general population in that they were seeking spiritual understanding rather than material or physical comfort.

Houriet had become interested in the counterculture and progressive politics while a student in the mid-1960s at NYU and Columbia University, from which he earned a master's degree in journalism before becoming a reporter for the *Camden Courier Post* in New Jersey. Aware that antiwar tensions were increasing, he decided to cover the 1968 Democratic National Convention. There, he witnessed police and Illinois National Guardsmen manhandle dissenters opposed to the war as Vice President Hubert Humphrey, a supporter of the Vietnam War, was selected the party's candidate for president over the peace candidate, U.S. senator Eugene McCarthy of Minnesota. Unrest had been anticipated given the assassinations of King that April and Robert Kennedy in June, just two months before the convention. Dismay and anger over these deaths was confounded by the fact that, while roughly 80 percent of Democratic primary voters had chosen antiwar candidates leading up to the convention, the delegates had defeated the peace plank and chosen Humphrey. An estimated 10,000 activists faced 23,000 police and national guardsmen inside and outside the convention hall, leading to the disastrous confrontation.

Houriet had gone to the convention hoping to remain objective but was radicalized by the brutality he witnessed. He returned home convinced that the country faced several internal wars over race and foreign policy. With an eye for a good story, he was also curious about the commune movement, and shortly after the convention visited his first commune, located in western Pennsylvania. That trip led to his 1969 story in the *New York Times Magazine*, "Life and Death of a Commune Called Oz," a fairly dispassionate story about the Oz Commune, which had been run out of town by residents of Meadville, Pennsylvania.

The reaction to the *New York Times* article was swift and positive: nine literary agents offered to represent Houriet if he would write a book about the commune movement. He had already quit his newspaper job and moved with his wife, Mary Mathias, to a small parcel of land they had purchased two years previously in the Northeast Kingdom town of Derby. Houriet and Mathias had met in New York City as graduate students at NYU and bought the property in response to growing tensions in the city and America. Their initial reason for choosing that particular property had not been political. Houriet loved to fish for walleye pike; he had read that the small, deep lakes of the Kingdom were famous for walleye. Their first winter, living in a camp on Little Salem Lake with a three-year-old daughter and newborn son, without electricity, telephone, or running water, they discovered their lake had more salmon and lake trout than pike. With no money coming in, "We had lake trout or salmon every night," Mathias recalled, "each meal more delicious than the previous."

Beginning that first year, "We had that experience of how the land influenced us more than we influenced it, and the local people, who were so much smarter than we were, influenced us as well," Mathias recalled. "The first person we met was a fifteen-year-old named Albert who just showed up and sat there on his bike. I asked, 'How are you doing?' and he said in his strong, almost indecipherable accent, 'Just came to see who you folks were.' I invited him in. He declined, then asked, 'Want some help with that woodpile? You built it wrong.'

"He tore the woodpile apart and built one that wouldn't fall down. Next thing he told us was, 'Well, you know, the way you got your chimney, you're gonna' have trouble when the wind is coming from West Charleston.' He was right. He and Robert got up on the roof, made the chimney higher and it worked just fine. He knew all the stuff we didn't know. One time, I was distressed because I didn't have an oven. Next day, he shows up with a tin box. 'Here's your oven,' he said and set it on top of the woodstove. You could bake anything in it. He adopted us."

Houriet spent the next two years traveling for his commune book, gathering ideas for how to make a commune work while Mathias managed with two children, help coming from friends who, even though their place wasn't formally a commune, adopted the commune spirit of doing what needed to be done. Upon Houriet's return, family and friends moved into a chicken coop Houriet described as an "elongated [40-by-12-foot] shack down the road on the edge of our property. We rented it for $10 a month from the man who had raised eight kids under its low, sloping roof and, most recently, chickens. It came with an uncluttered view of hills, a hayfield, and a brook providing constant background music. Inside the door, over the peeling wallpaper, Mary stapled a saying of Bertrand Russell: 'It is preoccupation with possessions more than anything else that prevents man from living freely and nobly.'"

Houriet's journey across America had been spiritual as well as physical, and it had convinced him that he would spend the rest of his life in Vermont. "The Yaqui master of Castaneda's *Don Juan* teaches that every man has his appropriate spiritual and geographical spot in the world, a destined location where he should stand to attain his highest being. Mine was Vermont. I had not been seduced by Oregon's mountain forests or New Mexico's colossal spaces. Feet reinstated on Green Mountain soil, walking along the golden dappled roads under the green arches of maples, I knew that this was my place: This was where I once belonged and was to begin again." he wrote.

A year after the book was published and the interviews over, on July 18, 1972, along with three other couples and two single people, Mathias and Houriet bought the land upon which their commune, subsequently called Frog Run, was established. It was Mathias's mother who found the property, which they'd initially rejected because it was located right on Route 105 in East Charleston. The mother was not particularly thrilled with the couple's decision to live in the wilderness and had moved close by to help with the children, but she had a good eye for what they needed. "It had great fields for hay, sandy and yet fertile soil, wild black raspberries and asparagus, a farmhouse and barn. Frankly, we couldn't afford to go on looking. So many people had come to join our commune; they were all camping in tents on the Derby property. We needed to put in a garden and build the sugarhouse. The property had beautiful sugar woods," Mathias said. The name Frog Run came from a neighbor who stopped by to watch Houriet make late-season maple syrup in the new sugar shack he built. The old-timer quipped that the last run of sap was called a frog run because by then the frogs were coming out of their winter torpor. It might have been an insult but Houriet was not offended.

The couple had placed ads in *Communities* magazine and other forums looking for people to join them. "We built the sugarhouse in the fall, a pole building of cedar, rafters made from cedar poles with one side cut flat with an adze. We did everything by hand. We weren't going to use power tools, just adzes, saws, and axes. The house had an old Sam Daniels wood furnace that had been converted to oil. We unconverted it, got a Defiant from Vermont

Robert Houriet in the sugar shack at Frog Run.
Photo by Lucy Horton

Castings and knocked down walls to make room for the people who showed up, all young and penniless. They weren't going to build homes on our land, invest in the farm. They were going to work with us, people who wanted to live in a group, people who just dropped out of college or high school or work and wanted a taste of the commune experience," Mathias explained.

All went fairly well until 1973, when fractures in the relationship ended the couple's marriage. Houriet moved from the commune. As Mathias pointed out, none of the early relationships among Frog Run communards lasted.

Houriet, who has lived on several nearby farms, helped found and run the Northeast Kingdom Food Co-op and Northeast Organic Farming Association, two successful efforts to provide wide distribution and production of locally grown organic food. "I came to see that if we were to have self-sufficient communities, we had to form a larger cooperative movement. We had to pool our resources and work efforts, grow for one another, sell to one another, create networks to teach one another and grow our movement," he said. Houriet worked with NOFA from 1973 well into the 1980s. He became a pioneer in growing crops considered outside Vermont's growing zones, in part to prepare for climate change. More recently, he also worked to raise concerns about the impact of dairy farms and effluent from cow manure on the environment, especially the quite large dairy farms in Addison County that he saw as contributing to algae growth and other pollution problems in Lake Champlain.

From 1973 until 1981 Mathias lived at Frog Run with a changing group of communards, many of whom stayed close by after leaving the commune. These include Lucy Horton, author of *Country Commune Cooking*, a popular cookbook of the era, who now lives in Pennsylvania; Michael Poster, an accomplished photographer living in Putney; and Chris Carrington, who became the Northeast Kingdom health inspector. Like the transplants at Packer Corner, Frog Run residents blended into the community in other ways. Frog Run Band, later called the New Leaf Band, with Horton as lead singer, was popular with locals. There were several commercial ventures, including Antelope Highway, which made leather products. A friend, Maryann Thomas from Boston, started a sewing company called Native Moon with members of the commune. They sewed patchwork pillows and hand-embroidered

Winter Night at Frog Run commune.
Photo by Lucy Horton

Mary Mathias and calf at Frog Run.
Photo by Lucy Horton

shirts they sold on the streets of Boston and Cambridge. "Anything to feed the animals . . . and ourselves," as Mathias expressed it.

Carrington grew up in Florida, graduated from Florida State University and lived on a commune in southern France that she described as "very primitive; we were living in stone huts." There she learned about America's commune movement and visited several after reading Houriet's book. About a minute after arriving at Frog Run in February of 1974, she had "found home." By then, about fifteen people lived on the farm. "There was that strong feeling in our generation about our parents and materialism. Their values were all about what money could buy. I wanted to get as far away from that as I could. I discovered that doing with what you had, that being with good people and doing good hard work were Vermont values, and I embraced those values," Carrington said. "At first, the locals were askance, but over the years we developed good relationships. They needed help from us; we needed help from them. We helped the locals out with our horses and they taught us about farming. We were doing it eighteenth-century style, Jersey milk cows, pigs, a huge truck garden, bringing produce down to Boston to Erewhon [Trading Company, the natural food pioneer], or Faneuil Market, all organic. We were hardworking. I think they saw that. We interacted with the other communes in the area, Mad Brook in East Charleston, Mullein Hill in Glover, Earth People's Park, although not so much with the latter. We formed tight bonds with one another and have remained close."

After leaving Frog Run, Carrington lived in a huge old Victorian in Derby Line until she retired as health inspector in 2004, bought a twenty-one-foot camper and became itinerant. "I came to Vermont with nothing but a backpack so it was nothing to sell everything, and get back on the road," she said. She has spent every summer since in the Kingdom, however, parking her trailer on a friend's property. "In this way, Vermont is always home," she said.

Decades in the Kingdom offered Mathias daily lessons in generosity rather than opposition. Once, a highway worker driving a roadside mower cut the hose they were watering their big garden with, stopped to apologize then returned days later with a new and better one. After a bit of a mess with their first team of workhorses, Herbie Ovitt, a horse dealer from Island Pond, taught Martha Lasley, a seventeen-year-old from Princeton, New Jersey, how to farm with horses, harness a horse, and buy old harnesses and restore and keep them in good order. When Lasley moved to Troy, Pennsylvania, she founded an international coaching organization called Leadership that Works. She learned about leadership, she said, from the Vermonters who shared what they knew. "One generation teaches another," she said. "That's what I learned in Vermont."

Mathias's mother, who'd been "completely appalled" by the move to the wilderness, spent her last years on the farm. "She kept saying things like, 'Oh this is such a nice place, the people are so nice.' Finally one day, we were milking the cows, she was sitting on a bale of hay and she said, 'Oh it smells so nice here. You know my father always wanted to have a farm, but my mother wouldn't let him,'" Mathias recalled. "She saw her parents differently then and maybe my life, too. I like to think that anyhow."

In 1985, Mathias became friends with the women who had written *Our Bodies, Ourselves*, the iconic book about women's health and sexuality written by and for women, and the members of the Boston Women's Health Book Collective who had written it. As it turned out, she fell in love with Mary Ide, a contributor to the book. After selling the farm, Mathias worked for several years for the battered women's agency in Newport before joining Ide in Boston. There Ide managed the archives for radio station WGBH, and

Mathias worked for fifteen years in a refugee trauma program run by Harvard. As retirement age approached, Mathias and Ide began dreaming of returning to Vermont, but neither wanted to live remotely again. In 2002, they bought a small house in Brattleboro, embracing the strong women's network in the area, the natural outgrowth of the counterculture's impact on the region. "The country isn't what we envisioned it would be. We're still divided. Nonetheless, we know our generation has accomplished much," Mathias observed. "There's always pushback to new ideas, to change. We're in a time of pushback when it's sometimes difficult to see all that has been accomplished because so much that was good that came out of the movement feels under attack, and there's a lot of turmoil in the world. Change is scary, and some people respond by emulating a past that is a fantasy. The fifties might have seemed safe if you were white and male and growing up in a suburb, but it was exactly that stultifying sameness of the suburbs that we rejected, not to mention the lack of opportunities for women outside the home.

"Vermont remains a little place of sanity. The state, of course, has become much more liberal because of the counterculture. The Kingdom has changed less. That isn't why we chose not to live there. We need an easier life now. But, in terms of the whole experience, I wouldn't change a thing and cannot express how lucky I am to have found my way back to Vermont."

EARTH PEOPLE'S PARK

Note: Vermont journalist Rod Clarke wrote this piece about Earth People's Park shortly before his death on January 26, 2016. It describes life on Vermont's most notorious commune, busted in 1990 by state and federal drug-enforcement officials. On October 5, 1994, with Woodstock emcee Wavy Gravy the only signatory on the land deed present, the property became Black Turn Brook State Forest. Here, with permission, is Clarke's story, originally published in *Northland Journal*:

We are caught in the devil's bargain;
And we've got to get ourselves back to the garden.
JONI MITCHELL, "WOODSTOCK"

They came by the hundreds, looking for the garden. But what they found was 592 acres of tangled, bug-infested, logged out swampland, a wall of local hostility, and a climate so harsh and unforgiving that it brought tears to the eyes of the weak when the bitter winds of winter howled down across the Canadian border. Some took one look, hitched up their back-packs, and headed out without ever unrolling their sleeping bags. Others stayed, much to the dismay of the hard-working, French-Canadian locals who had viewed the invasion of their land by hordes of long-haired hippie freaks with fear and loathing.

It was called Earth People's Park (EPP), and to this day, the very name conjures up a host of images, most of them wildly off the mark. I should know. For a year, my family called EPP home. In 1971, I was a staff reporter for United Press International's Montpelier bureau, covering virtually everything that happened in the state: crime, politics, state government, the Legislature. The hot issue that year was the threatened hippie invasion. *Playboy* magazine started it off with an article explaining how easy it would be for counterculture (remember THAT word?) radicals from across the country to take over poor, old, naive, bumpkin Vermont.

A lot of people found that prospect terrifying. The Vermont media (which was much more conservative in those days) picked up the banner, warning that as many as half a million long-haired freaks might flock to the Green Mountains that summer. Bold, black newspaper headlines warned of the impending HIPPIE INVASION, sending more than one old farmer scurrying for his shotgun. Governor Deane Davis hastily called a news conference to explain that he hadn't really invited them. The Vermont League of Cities and Towns sponsored a workshop to brief local officials on how to deal with the so-called influx.

The focal point for all this hyperbole was a handful of dreamers with visions of a new utopia dancing in their brains who had begun trying to eke out an existence on a hardscrabble parcel of land tucked along the Canadian border in the Northeast Kingdom community of Norton.

Earth People's Park was an outgrowth of the fabled Woodstock Music and Arts Festival in neighboring New York State, and the celebrated People's Park rebellion in Berkeley, CA.

The concept was simple: The best way to keep the Woodstock Nation alive was to buy a piece of land somewhere and open it up to all the people. Led by the Hog Farm commune, which helped organize Woodstock, bands of disciples streamed across the nation, panhandling on street corners and passing the hat at rock concerts and college campuses. When enough cash had been raised, legend has it, the new nonprofit corporation bought the Norton property sight unseen out of a real estate catalogue. Why? Because it was big. And it was cheap.

The first settlers began arriving without much fanfare in the late summer and fall of 1970. A few actually stayed through the winter. But by spring 1971, word was out on the alternative grapevine that there was free land in Vermont.

On the first weekend of May, a colleague who wrote for the *Burlington Free Press* and I decided it was time to see for ourselves what all the fuss was about. I had an old, small school bus that had been converted to a camper, and we packed it up and headed to Norton. My friend and I spent the weekend at the park. We toured the land and met the people and lived the life. And a spark was lit inside me.

By this time, my wife Loretta and I had had five kids, and were living in Barre while I worked at UPI. My hair was down over my shoulders and my beard hit the middle of my chest. I was going through something of a philosophical and political upheaval as well, and EPP appealed to the latent anarchist that was growing inside my gut. Every weekend, we loaded the kids into the bus and headed to Norton.

In September, the park was hosting an ecology workshop, a euphemism for a fundraising party to make the $8,000 annual mortgage payment. My suggestion to UPI that we cover it was rebuffed by an editor in Boston, who pointed out that I'd just done a major EPP piece. "It's like the second load of moon rocks," he said. I went anyway, on my own time. It was a heck of a party. On hand was Hog Farm guru Hugh Romney, better known as Wavy Gravy, who made the stage announcements at Woodstock and later had a Ben & Jerry's flavor named after him. The problem was, I forgot to come back to work on Monday. And Tuesday. UPI fired me. With no job and a gnawing sense of unrest growling in my gut, I took what seemed then to be the most logical step. We became fulltime Earth People. It was a decision we've never regretted.

It may be easier to say what Earth People's Park wasn't than describe what it was. It wasn't a commune. To be sure, some people lived communally, sharing food, living quarters, resources. Others lived more solitary lives, guarding both their property and their privacy with pit-bull tenacity. There were the young and the not-so-young, male and female, black and white; the fugitive and the seeker, the idealist and the cynic, the lawless and the godly. Some hoped that by freeing themselves from their urban ways and material possessions, they might carve a new way of life and a new way of living from the land. There were druggies and drunks, hoping that a fresh start in a new place might help them break the chains of their addictions. Some made it. Others didn't, and have since paid the ultimate price for their habits. There were runaways hiding from their parents, and Jesus freaks who freely gave away all their worldly possessions.

There were peaceniks and pacifists, Buddhists and bikers. They came 3,000 miles from California and a long stone's throw from Island Pond, just down roller coaster Route 114. There was a young man who walked around buck-naked all the time, and a middle-aged engineer from Canada who built a sophisticated homestead and knew a little bit about everything. There were permanent settlers who built sturdy log homes and A-frames from scavenged lumber and dreamed of someday having a community school. And there were the transients who came during the summer because they'd heard it was a great place for parties, dope, booze, and free sex. (It wasn't.) They freeloaded off the residents and caused problems for the locals, then fled as soon as the frost began making threatening gestures toward the pumpkin.

The land. That's what we called it. Just "the land." It was the thing that brought us there and it was the tie that bound us together. The land, after all, was pretty much the only thing we had in common. The underlying tenet of Earth People's Park was deceptively simple: "Free land for free people." Only those living there could make rules. You arrived, staked out a piece of land, built or camped on it, and it was yours as long as you stayed. No deed. No lease. No payment. And no one had locks on their doors. The land would be open and free to all people. We took that very seriously.

A kind of basic, primitive anarchy reigned at EPP. There was no electricity, no running water, no plumbing, no telephones, no television. In the wintertime, the rough and rocky path that served as a road was closed by snow, and a trip to the Norton store meant a three-mile trek. Few of the full-time residents had cars. Those that did had to park them at the entrance to the land and hope they'd start when needed.

I was working harder at the park than I'd ever worked in my life, putting in 18-hour days trying to establish some sort of a homestead. We were older and more settled than most residents, and blessed with a few more creature comforts. Our trailer was heated with oil, not wood, we had a small generator, a chain saw, an indoor chemical toilet, a shotgun, a tiny black-and-white battery-powered television set, a propane gas cook stove, an old four-wheel drive jeep, a hundred-dollar snowmobile, even a gas refrigerator.

During the summers, the park filled with transients who partied all night and generally upset the backwoods tranquility. But they were gone by fall, and only the most serious, diehard homesteaders stuck around after the snow began flying. Those winters were magical, joyful, vintage times. Playing charades by oil lamp and sipping hot apple cider with the family up the road, the air so cold and brittle it would shatter like a pane of glass, and a full moon casting a blue-white radiance on a foot of fresh snow. No visitors could visit, no phone could ring.

But then summer returned, and the craziness began anew. By the fall of '72, it was time to move on. Because I was older and perceived as some-what more responsible, I found myself in a leadership role I wasn't ready to assume. I didn't want to be mayor of Earth People's Park; I just wanted to work my land. I didn't like having to account for the antics of the sum-mer transients. I didn't particularly like to be awakened in the middle of the night to go out in the woods and talk some freak down from a bad trip. And it bothered me when someone from the village would ask, "How do you people live like that?"

I had developed friendships with many Norton residents, I loaded their hay and poured their concrete and my kids went to school with their kids. I liked these folks, and was weary of the insurmountable barrier that I feared would loom between us as long as we lived at the park.

Within a few years, I was back in Montpelier and was rehired by UPI, eventually becoming bureau chief. Life went on pretty much as it had be-fore. I even wrote the stories about Earth People's Park as it fell on hard times. Many of the permanent settlers—those who gave the place soul and hope—had departed, leaving it mostly to the transients and the burn-outs. The reputation worsened, a guy was stabbed to death, and police raids escalated as troopers found large plots of marijuana.

Eventually, the federal government seized the land, then made a deal that turned it over to the state with the proviso that no one could live on it. Despite its apparent failings, EPP served a very real and a very valuable purpose. It gave people a little space when they needed it, and it bought them time when time was running out. It was a respite and a stopover, a way-station on a journey, not the end of the journey.

And, in a sense, its destiny has been fulfilled. It is still "free land for free people."

Far out.

If ever there was a college ready-made for the counterculture and a collection of young people ready-made for a particular institution, it was Vermont's Goddard College in Plainfield, located just 8.5 miles east of the state capital, Montpelier. Goddard describes itself as a "one-of-a-kind institution of higher education with a history of creativity and chaos, invention and experimentation, of growth, decline and reemergence." Locals called it "Little Moscow on the Hill" long before the hippies showed up; with their arrival, the school's influence in terms of bringing new ideas and people into Plainfield and surrounding towns only increased.

Imagine an accredited college where hundreds of young people, only some of whom were actually enrolled and paying tuition, could take a course in eco-anarchist theory or the politics of food, or just take acid all day and make something—a poem, a sculpture, a theory, a song—and somehow find a way to get credit for the experience. No grades. No curriculum. No dormitories in the way that most people envisioned what a dorm should operate like. Ginny Callan, the founder of Horn of the Moon Café in Montpelier, recalled that students "in the political dorm had shooting practice on Saturday mornings, preparing for the revolution."

Goddard had long attracted its share of brilliant and anti-authoritarian professors. In the 1960s and '70s, these included the Chicago Seven defendant John Froines, anarchist philosopher and writer Murray Bookchin, cultural anthropologist Dan Chodorkoff, and Peter and Elka Schumann, whose Bread & Puppet Theater brought dozens, perhaps hundreds of counterculture people to Vermont to work or volunteer on their protests against capitalism, corporatism, and imperialism. Dennis Murphy, a noted musicologist and instrument maker known for his efforts to bring the Javanese gamelan to the

Goddard College students near Northwood dormitory, 1971.
Photo by Keith Thompson; courtesy of Goddard College Archives

United States, taught music and music theory at Goddard where he created a gamelan ensemble. Students hammered gamelan instruments out of steel or made them from hubcaps, metal cans, and even an antique milk strainer.

The student body, too, was a mix of quirky and independent, the college chosen for its small size and location, along with the freedoms it offered, both intellectually and culturally. In 1960, Susan Green was listening to a friend read the Goddard College brochure when she heard two magic words: 90 students. "That's when I perked up," the Vermont journalist and book author said. Her freshman class brought enrollment to 150. Green grew up in Queens and on Long Island, best friends with Suze Rotolo, Bob Dylan's girl-friend who appears on the cover of his *Freewheelin'* album. Green once offered to bring Dylan to Goddard, but the school declined paying the $75 fee. Over the decades, Green has written about the impact of Goddard students and Goddard itself on the region. "Goddard drew the first batch of beatniks and bohemians into Vermont," she said. "Many liked it and they moved out into the country," followed by successive students. The college boasts many well-known alumni, such as actors William Macy and Piers Anthony, Phish band members Trey Anastasio and Jon Fishman, poets Ellen Bryant Voigt,

Jane Shore, and Mark Doty, novelist Mary Karr, filmmaker Jay Craven, and playwright David Mamet.

Phish's storied history with Goddard began the day band members were so whacked out on acid that they couldn't perform, but they returned for a successful performance, enhanced only by weed, so much so that one of the band members wandered into one of the theme dorms, the one inhabited by the militant feminist separatists. Nonetheless, two band members transferred from UVM to Goddard, embracing the idea of self-directed study, which in their case amounted to taking over the music building where they created "a new kind of psychedelic, one for individuals raised in suburban captivity and set loose in the New Earth," as Jesse Jarnow expressed it. That New Earth, apparently, was Vermont with Goddard as its epicenter. Band member Fishman titled his senior study "A Self-Teaching Guide to Drumming Written in Retrospect." By the time Phish was performing at and attending Goddard in the late 1980s, the counterculture movement was over but not so much at Goddard, a situation that may have contributed to its declining enrollment. In 2002, after fifty-four years, the college ended its traditional residential degree program to become a low-residency college while maintaining its open and egalitarian philosophy.

In her recollection about Goddard written that year, Green downplayed the drugs and stressed the contributions to Vermont from students and professors who stayed, people like Susan Meacham, one of the founders of the Onion River Co-op, which evolved into Burlington's City Market and one of the most successful food co-ops in the nation. "Her legacy is just one quiet example of how Goddard helped a poor rural state move into the second half of the 20th century," wrote Green, who ran Burlington City's Arts Council when Bernie Sanders was mayor and has been a reporter at both the *Burlington Free Press* and *Seven Days*, among many other publications.

Jane Shore of East Calais told Green how a mean girl at summer camp thought to insult her by declaring that Shore should go to Goddard. "That's the place for someone like you!" the girl said. Turned out it was. Shore's poetry bloomed there. One day during a reading by Allen Ginsberg, Shore heard him proclaim Plainfield "the spiritual center of the universe."

West Palm Beach's Norton Art Museum president Hope Alswang, who attended Goddard between 1967 and '71 and later ran the Shelburne Museum, was "expecting a school where people just sang lefty Pete Seeger songs. I was taken aback by the marvelous self-indulgence and decadence. People were smoking dope, naked and crazy."

Macy was among those who took advantage of the craziness. "I reveled in the atmosphere," he told Green. "The inmates had taken over the asylum."

The pleasures of Vermont remained with him and, in the 1980s, he bought several units of the old Toy Town Motel that had been moved from their original setting on Route 2 in Montpelier to a more remote location that Macy carefully did not disclose when he wrote about his cabin in the woods for the *New York Times*.

"The days I spent working on that cabin gave me some of the purest pleasure I have ever experienced," he wrote. "The cabin has outside plumbing and a woodstove for heat. I built one of the best swimming ponds in the Western Hemisphere there. There has been skinny-dipping."

"One summer I had a two-month gap in my schedule, and I decided to build myself a wood shop," Macy wrote. "I bought a book called *How to Build a Building*. At the end of the very last day of my vacation, it was almost too dark to see as I drove the last nail into the last piece of roofing on the peak of my new shop. That beauty is still standing, and some lovely pieces of furniture have come out of it."

❋ ❋ ❋

Lee Webb's experience at Goddard and with the Vermont legislature illustrates how the presence of even one activist in a small state can have great impact. A Brookline, Massachusetts, native, Webb was active in antiwar, antinuclear, and disarmament efforts at Boston University before becoming a national leader in Students for a Democratic Society and the National Conferences of Churches. In Washington, he tried to create opportunities for these organizations to engage decision makers in broad dialogue. Frustrated, he welcomed an invitation to teach economics and public policy at Goddard in 1968. Not long after arriving, he organized a rally against the Vietnam War on the statehouse steps, attended by several hundred protesters. He expected the police to clear them away when a stranger approached from the statehouse to ask if he needed a megaphone. The stranger was Vermont sergeant-at-arms Reide B. Payne of Rutland. Within minutes Webb was inside the statehouse asking the legislature to take a position on the war. In response, the state legislators held hearings on the issue that lasted several days. While the legislators voted to support the war, 77 to 52, Webb felt he had successfully raised important issues. The fact that 52 had voted against the war impressed him, so much so that he began working with the Vermont Public Interest Group to influence state policy. While still at Goddard, he got himself appointed to the Governor's Commission on Electric Energy where he helped pass legislation that created a capital gains tax on land speculation and the first-in-the-nation lifeline electric-rate bill. His next effort was a successful campaign to institute a sliding-scale payment program for dental care for children. Webb had learned that it wasn't just poor kids who had bad teeth due to the high cost of dental care in Vermont, but rather that it was not unusual for Vermont kids to receive false teeth as a graduation present as a way to help them go forward in life. Vermont's Tooth Fairy Bill, the result of his efforts, passed 140 to 1.

Reflecting back on the idea promulgated in Pollak's *Playboy* article, that progressive efforts started in a small state could engender wider action, consider that these efforts received local and national press, leading progressives from other states to contact Webb for advice. This led him back to Washington where he and others established the Institute for Policy Studies, a progressive action group that worked with people around the country on housing, health, environment, and utility issues. It's estimated that these efforts led to the passage of dozens of state bills and the election of many candidates interested in progressive issues, from land use and open meetings to rent control and police reform. Webb, a senior policy fellow at the Margaret Chase Smith Policy Center at the University of Maine, told Pierre Clavel that he learned the way to bring about change in Vermont was to choose issues that offered "the widest scope of benefits for the people . . . to make it an economic issue, not a social issue or a class issue," but one in which "70, 80 or even 90 percent of the people in the state or the city are going to benefit."

* * *

The degree of freedom students enjoyed at Goddard might not have been exactly what Tim Pitkin had in mind when he founded Goddard College in 1938. Pitkin was more a freedom *and* responsibility kind of educator and philosopher. A Marshfield native, he had graduated from Goddard Seminary, the college's predecessor, in 1923 before going off to UVM and subsequently earning a PhD from Columbia University and teaching around New England. In 1935, he was asked to help transform Goddard into a "college for living" and increase its enrollment. Pitkin had been impressed with John Dewey's progressive concepts about education and the ideas promulgated at the Highlander Folk School in rural Tennessee where people like Rosa Parks were later coached in social activism. From the beginning, Goddard was not to be an ivory tower, but rather a place where real life entwined with academia, a place where thought and action were wedded, a place where students were expected to perform good works in the wider world.

Under Pitkin the grading system, written exams, and required courses, as well as fraternities, diplomas, and athletics were done away with. Students were expected to help maintain the campus and design and implement projects that benefited their community. Andy Christiansen's story illustrates the ways in which Goddard, its professors, and students did just that, in the process integrating into the community despite the college's reputation for anarchism. Christiansen remembers Goddard students coming to his grammar school as volunteers, introducing students to pen pals from around the world and to gamelan music, organizing Halloween parties, and helping them with homework. The former state legislator may have been the youngest Goddard student, allowed to attend astronomy courses while still in junior high along with a friend whose father taught there. Christiansen's family goes back in Vermont "almost to the time of the Abenaki" and was "very education-minded" and musical. A pianist and trumpet player, he attended Adamant Music School, founded in 1943 by free-thinking musicians, writers, and artists. His grandmother, a speed-reader, librarian, and teacher proficient in Latin and Greek, had gone to Goddard Seminary; his mother, also a school-teacher, had returned to college there as an adult. She liked to tell stories at the dinner table about her fellow students, openly discussing their nudity or describing a gross guy who walked around campus barefoot with toenails that curled up into his feet. None of that kept his parents from letting Christiansen hang out there, playing pool and taking part in exciting conversations. When he graduated from Lawrence University's five-year program with degrees in neuropsychology and music theory and composition, he volunteered with Schumann's Bread & Puppet Theater and joined Larry Gordon's Word of Mouth Chorus and the Goddard brass quartet led by Murphy. Word of Mouth sang what's called shape-note music, a type of singing with a distinctive style introduced in the late 19th century for community or congregation singing. Shape-note music was popular in early New England, spreading throughout America and then to Europe. Gordon, an early member of the New Hamburger commune where he lived for fifteen years, sought to keep this original music alive, a notion Christiansen embraced along with playing in the local hobo band.

The hobo band's founder, Doug Franks, was "an itinerant painter who traveled the rails as a real-life hobo" and had played for the Ringling Brothers Circus until the Depression when he settled in Plainfield. "We met him when my mother hired him to paint the woodwork around our windows at home. He noticed that her little boy—*me*—had a trumpet, and convinced me to play in the band, which I did up into my first years in the legislature, but when he got old and eventually died, the other members drifted away."

How delightful it had been, he said, when that amateur band of locals, a vestige of an older time in Vermont, met new Vermont. He recalled the local reaction when Bread & Puppet joined the parade. There were the local kids from farm and town with hand-me-down instruments alongside Bread & Puppet's giant puppets, many manned by Goddard students and hangers-on and representing rather heretical notions, celebrating America's birthday together.

"Thanks in part to Goddard and also the New Hamburger commune, my second home, I had a solid foot in the counterculture and the old culture and couldn't understand why not take the best of both worlds. My values conflicted with both sides of that divide. I was politically radical and socially conservative. I didn't go much for the free love stuff, but I was liberal when it came to personal rights and decisions, which made for an interesting dynamic in the legislature," Christiansen said.

He noted that many of the politically radical types from Goddard went on to serve their Vermont towns, people like John Warshow, who attended Goddard in the mid-1970s, organizing Goddard students to attend protests at the Seabrook Nuclear Power Plant in New Hampshire. At Goddard, Warshow studied renewable energy and subsequently became an activist against the Vermont Yankee nuclear power plant while working to find alternative, nonpolluting forms of energy. A longtime selectman in Marshfield, his first business venture was an effort to redevelop a dam in Plainfield. That dam proved unsuitable for hydroelectricity, but he continued the effort and, with Matthew Rubin, he developed several power dams, including ones in East Montpelier, Middlesex, Winooski, and Springfield.

* * *

As Christiansen pointed out, progressive ideas have been part of the fabric of Vermont education since the state's earliest days—not surprising given that Vermont had been a national leader in fighting slavery. The state's original constitution as a commonwealth banned slavery in 1777. When Vermont was admitted to the union as the fourteenth state in 1791, its state constitution also contained the slavery ban, making it the first state in the nation to do so. Not stopping there, in 1854, the Vermont senate issued a report that questioned the right of *any* state to allow any group to enslave another human, which in turn led the Georgia General Assembly to pass a resolution authorizing the towing of Vermont out to sea! In 1860, Vermonters gave Republican Abraham Lincoln the largest margin of victory of any state in the nation, and the state takes somber pride in having lost more soldiers per capita during the Civil War than any other.

Progressive ideals came early to the University of Vermont. James Marsh, uvm's fifth president, was a leading Transcendentalist who embraced enlightened ideas. He not only transformed the university "from a struggling provincial college into the first American sanctuary of transcendental idealism," but he allowed part-time students to register so working men could attend. He introduced an elective system that revolutionized the way students pursued their vocations and avocations, giving them then radical freedom in the selection of course work.

Yet much of that progressive philosophy seemed to have diminished over the decades, so much so that, during the 1960s, while many uvm students took part in demonstrations against the Vietnam War and racism in the South, the university came under fire for its continuance of the annual "cakewalk," a popular activity during the university's winter festivities. Cakewalks were a dance competition that originated on southern plantations among African Americans; a cake was awarded as a prize. Even while uvm students demonstrated against discrimination at lunch counters in the South, the cakewalk, often spelled Kake Walk, continued to be a highlight of the university's social calendar until it was terminated in 1969 in the wake of continued criticism, much of it from outside the university.

Historian Nelson attributed the more recent liberalization of uvm and, by extension, Chittenden County, to Lattie F. Coor, a uvm president who made a big push for more out-of-state students beginning in the 1970s. Nelson opined that, even though uvm had been the first American college to guarantee in its charter that all activities and decisions would be free of religious discrimination or consideration, much of that early zeal for equality, especially in terms of race, was lost as Vermont remained among the whitest states in the nation. As uvm's out-of-state student population grew, native Vermonter college students came to understand and support racial equality and became increasingly liberal in their political leanings. Nelson postulated that the influx of more outside students also contributed to Bernie Sanders' surprise election as Burlington mayor in 1981. At the time, landlords seemed to raise off-campus rents year after year, leading to a renters' revolt led by

UVM students. When Sanders supported their fight for fair rent, "the renters became Bernie's base," Nelson said, fueling his defeat of six-time incumbent Gordon Paquette. And, as a percentage of UVM graduates remain in Vermont or return when they are ready to start families, Coor's decision, albeit as much a financial decision as anything else, has contributed to the influx of young out-of-staters, a trend destined to continue as, in 2016, UVM had the smallest percentage of in-state students in its history.

* * *

Middlebury College has its own egalitarian distinctions rooted in its earliest days: It accepted and graduated Alexander Twilight, a Vermont native born in Corinth, and the first person of color to earn a BA degree from an American college or university, in 1823. Twilight, a Congregational preacher, became the first African American in the country elected as a state legislator, representing the town of Brownington. Another Middlebury student, Marion Annette Anderson, known as Nettie, was also one of the first African American women to attend college; she was her class valedictorian in 1899. Anderson was a native Vermonter, born in Shoreham to a former slave who had moved to Vermont after the Civil War with his French Canadian and Indian wife.

Well into the late 1960s, however, as demonstrations against the Vietnam War and racism erupted on other Vermont campuses, Middlebury students remained comparatively conservative. That changed as more and more of their friends and relatives were drafted. Within no time, serious tensions erupted between the college and the town over the Vietnam War. Torie Osborn was one of the agitators in 1970. Osborn had transferred to Middlebury that fall, expecting it to be "an intellectual hotbed of leftist radicalism." Instead, she found a "preppie, unevolved place where Frisbees and skiing were more important than the war killing people our age." She dates her own activism to an incident she witnessed at age five when her father worked for the State Department. Osborn was born in Copenhagen and then lived in Spain. One afternoon while walking in Madrid, she came upon "a food riot led by women and children against Franco. I watched as the military opened fire at them. I was outraged that poor people were being fired upon by their own government."

"I was a sitting duck for the 1960s," she observed, having been raised in the liberal culture of Denmark then the militaristic atmosphere of Spain. Back home in the states as a teenager living in a suburb of Philadelphia, she was well aware of the differences between the haves and have-nots and longed to take part in the Freedom Summer efforts to register black voters, but she was too young. She soon became a "middle-class hippie," taking part in antiwar and civil rights rallies with white and black students, smoking pot, listening to the Beatles and folksingers at the Main Point folk-music club near Bryn Mawr.

Frisbee on the lawn was not what she had in mind. She considered leaving Middlebury until she met activist Steve Early and joined the growing political consciousness on campus. Osborn and Early brought different factions of the counterculture—feminist, antiwar, civil rights, and labor—together. Early had led several campus-wide actions against the Vietnam War, beginning with a student strike in the fall of 1969 during the National Peace Moratorium. A month later, he led two hundred students to Washington for the November 15, 1969, demonstration, the second moratorium against the war. The following spring, after the Kent State shootings, he helped lead the campus shutdown as many colleges around the country went on strike. He remembers only one dissenting student, Jim Douglas, who asked for a tuition refund when classes and finals were canceled. Douglas was the campus Republican club president who later served as Vermont secretary of state, state treasurer, and four-term governor.

Demonstrations and teach-ins continued throughout the next school year, culminating in student participation in the May Day 1971 action in D.C., where dozens of Middlebury students were arrested in the largest mass arrest in American history. While Osborn participated in these activities, she also founded the first feminist group at Middlebury, the Women's Union. She had been shocked her first week on campus when a coed had been denied birth control at the student health center. "I led a delegation of women from the freshman dorm into the dean's office complaining about the Catholic doc who ran our health services," Osborn recalled. Her efforts led to a policy change. Learning that male students had no curfew while women did, she also lobbied to remove the coeds' curfew. Given that abortion was illegal in the United States but not Canada at the time, she helped organize an "abortion underground," composed of students who secretly arranged and facilitated appointments with a physician in Montreal.

Osborn described Early as "never counterculture. [Other students] thought he was a narc. He dressed kind of collegiate." Early conceded he was fairly square. "I didn't even drink in college," he said. He had grown up in New York's Westchester County where he had little interest in politics. Ironically, he had joined the Reserve Officers Training Corps his first semes-

A young Steve Early.
Courtesy of Steve Early

ter and had even considered a military career, but "one semester's worth of
ROTC was definitely a radicalizing experience for me. Personally, and with
many others, I realized that a better way of dealing with [the war in Vietnam]
was to end the war, abolish the draft, and kick ROTC off campus, or at least
strip it of academic credit."

The demonstrations Early organized after the Kent State shootings led
Middlebury to cancel classes for a weeklong teach-in at which both students
and faculty discussed the issues. One early morning during the week, an
arsonist set fire to Recitation Hall, where ROTC offices had been located. A
campus history recalled the resulting tension between town and gown: "Due
to the number of colleges around the country that were striking and protesting the Vietnam War, people in the town began to worry that Middlebury
students were going to rebel in the same way. When the burning of Recitation Hall happened on May 7th, the feeling of goodwill between the town
and the college students was suddenly disrupted. . . . There were fears of
government intervention if the strike got out of control, and President Armstrong called an emergency meeting, but the faculty council decided to have
the strike anyway until May 11th. Dean Denis O'Brien added that even the
fire department was weary of the 'radical' college students. When they were
putting out the fire, they were sure they were going to be shot by the students.

In response, students formed The Community Involvement Group [whose] goal was to repair the relationship between the town and the students. Students and faculty volunteers conducted nighttime patrols to protect campus facilities, particularly the Alumni and Placement Building where ROTC offices were housed."

Early, then editor of the campus newspaper, had been awakened in his dorm room by news of the fire; destructive action was not his style. He'd met the Red Clover people, some of whom he dismissed as trust-fund activists whose coziness with Black Panthers and the Weathermen didn't impress him. "We prided ourselves on persuading people based on research and data. I found their politics out of touch and contra the approach some of us were trying. We were interested in broader working-class issues. Not to be too dismissive of their approach, but I think what we tried to do, including a big teach-in in the fall of '71 at Middlebury College with Lee Webb from Goddard, was to look at labor, welfare rights, utility company issues, and third-party strategies together. I felt that had more long-term potential than solidarity with the Black Panthers," Early said.

Looking back on his years in Vermont, he observed that there "was a porousness or an openness in Vermont. People who were successful in assimilating and getting involved in a broader range of issues could become successful in politics there. It led to the transformation of the state." He would know, having been active as a union lawyer and organizer, journalist, and political adviser since graduation in 1972, working first in Vermont then throughout the country. In 1976, he met Bernie Sanders after earning his law degree in Washington. He considered Sanders's support for labor issues essential to whatever strength labor unions still have in Vermont. Now living in Richmond, California, Early has written several books about labor and progressive politics.

It hasn't escaped him that there's some irony in the fact that he, Osborn, and Jim Douglas, the moderate Republican who followed Howard Dean as governor of Vermont, were classmates together. It was a time when people developed deep commitments on either side of the political divide. Recalling Douglas, Early said, "I think he felt the administration was dominated by peacenik liberals and that he felt beleaguered on campus, but he stayed around in Vermont and has remained committed to his ideals. While the state moved to the left, he had a successful political career on the right, ironically elected by some of the same people who vote for Bernie. But that, too, tells you something about Vermont."

Osborn has been much rougher on Douglas who, as governor, had vetoed Vermont's Marriage Equality Act, which legalized same-sex marriage. Douglas's veto was overruled. "In the excitement and swirl of new ideas and social change, I and my activist friends had one nemesis. He headed the small Young Republicans club on campus, and, whenever we had a rally or a speaker on women's issues or were fighting racism or about the war, there he was: one solitary, implacably conservative voice of opposition. His name was Jim Douglas," she wrote in response to Douglas's veto. "I must have argued with him a hundred times on a host of issues, in public forums, in the dining rooms, in the student coffee house, on the lawns of the sprawling idyllic campus. At the time, he seemed impossibly square ('straight,' we called it in those days . . .)—a decent guy but stubbornly out of touch with the zeitgeist. Today, 38 years later, he is once again out of touch. . . . When I heard his veto was overridden on Tuesday with a vote to spare, I whooped for joy. I have no idea if Jim even remembers his solitary wars against progress in the 1970s at college. He lost on Vietnam, on moving racial and gender justice forward too. This time he had the power to help make history."

Governor Douglas's take was, not surprisingly, a bit different. Yes, he said, he "was lucky enough to go to college when college campuses were hotbeds of activism." He felt that tension had honed his values and commitments; that Vermonters honored the right to dissent, even to dissent from the dissenters. "I came and dutifully joined the young Republicans, a good club, quite active on campus despite the backdrop of the political scene. I became president of my local and state club. I remember working simultaneously as news director of WRMC and trying to be a good journalist. There were demonstrations and vigils, and in spring of 1970 after Kent State, when the campus shut down for the end of the semester, yes, I felt they had gone too far. I didn't approve of burning draft cards. I felt the [student activists] had the right to have demonstrations. That was free speech. But it got out of bounds when they marched into the local high school and started depositing leaflets in classrooms. The activists were respectful for the most part, didn't harass me, but there were certainly points of disagreement.

"In the wider context, most of America isn't like a campus," he said. "We all felt the sadness and frustration of Ohio but, interestingly, the next fall at an alumni gathering where I was on a panel, I was introduced as 'Jim's sort of an unusual student, Jim's a Republican.' The alumni all stood up and cheered."

After Middlebury, Osborn joined the first group of activist lesbians living in Burlington. Recently, she wrote about that time, describing how she and "a colorful, merry, hippie-looking band of about 20 lesbians—no gay men—paraded down Burlington streets, pedestrians and shopkeepers gaping from the sidewalks" to demonstrate for equal rights. "I remember sometime in the mid '70s sitting under a tree with a gay male friend talking about what it would take to bring legal gay rights to the state. We agreed our advantage over other states was the small size, independent spirit and democratic town-hall traditions of our beloved Vermont. . . . We were just beginning to imagine how to translate our gay liberation counterculture into real-world policies, as part of a generational wave of young idealistic activists that turned Vermont very blue." That man was Bill Lippert, a psychotherapist who helped form Vermont's first men's support group as well as Outright Vermont, a service and support organization for lesbian, gay, bisexual, and transgender youth. As a longtime Vermont legislator, Lippert was instrumental in the passage of Vermont's civil union bill, the first state law to recognize same-sex civil unions, and in the vote to overthrow Douglas's veto of Vermont's Marriage Equality Act, which legalized same-sex marriage.

"I was profoundly changed by Vermont and those six years there," Osborn said. "I got to really grow in a free, libertarian, live-and-let-live spirit, which is a very good thing for young people who need to find their own way. I've watched my generation have an impact on the state and import that to the rest of the country. I grew my feminism there. Vermont consolidated my values." She also observed that, "Vermont is beyond left and right; it's free-spirited but has a sense of communal responsibility. I left at twenty-six because there was not the ethnic diversity I needed. Vermont couldn't give that to me, but what it gave me was important. I don't know who I would be if it hadn't been for Vermont." In the intervening years, Osborn served for eight years as executive director of the National Gay and Lesbian Task Force and subsequently as senior advisor to the mayor of Los Angeles, working specifically to reduce homelessness and poverty. Hers is yet another example of how activism honed in a small state can have impact far and wide.

＊ ＊ ＊

Students who attended Windham and Marlboro College, two of the nation's smallest, during the 1960s and '70s also found themselves caught up in the social, sexual, and political unrest of the times while simultaneously influenced by the activist communes located nearby. Marlboro and Windham were founded by Walter Hendricks, whose ideas about education, like

Pitkin's, were progressive for the times. Hendricks established Marlboro College in 1946 with the hope that students would be active at all levels of campus life from pounding nails to making decisions on how the college would operate. Marlboro always emphasized the arts, especially theater and music, and its town-meeting approach to decision making led to some interesting situations, such as a short-lived ban on cars on campus approved by students during one session. A geodesic dome built on the campus was taken over briefly by the vegetarians in the late 1960s. And, in 1980, during a two-day, campus-wide barn-raising effort, students and faculty together built a handsome post-and-beam structure to house a bookstore, coffeehouse, and game room. The college has long been associated with the Marlboro Music School, where for seven weeks each summer promising young musicians work alongside some of the world's most gifted musical artists.

Joey Klein, one of the founders of the Northeast Organic Farming Association and owner with his wife, Betsy Ziegler, of Littlewood Farm in Plainfield, joked that he ended up at Marlboro after being turned down by Goddard "if you can believe *that*." Goddard wouldn't accept him because he hadn't graduated from high school, having dropped out his senior year to attend the Friends World College. FWC was a kind of traveling college through which students studied in the South, and in Mexico, Scandinavia, and other countries. Not only did Marlboro not care about the high school diploma, but the college gave Klein a scholarship. He was precisely the kind of student they hoped to attract: students who were in the world. He studied soil and plant science, took part in antiwar demonstrations, "graduated into the burgeoning youth culture around there in 1970 and spent the next ten years moving between various households," including a short stint at Total Loss Farm. Everywhere he lived he worked the land. "You have no idea when you're young and you have these ideas and you're just trying them out, how your life will turn about. The soil, growing things, it got me right away . . . as did Vermont," he said. He had first visited the state at age fifteen while attending a Quaker camp in Greenfield, Massachusetts. From that moment, he believed, "It was the place that called to us. That's what you call good fortune."

Perry Kacik of Brookfield ended up at nearby Windham College by chance as well. Kacik, another Long Island transplant, had been on the swim team and was social chairman of his fraternity at the University of Massachusetts. But there was too much social life and not enough studying and he flunked out, twice. His parents gave him "one more chance," and in 1967 they paid $100 to someone who guaranteed he could get Kacik into college, which was a good thing because Kacik had already passed his draft physical; no way did he want to fight in Vietnam. He chose Windham because the college brochure featured a photo of young people skiing. Windham turned out to be "a lifesaver." He discovered he actually liked learning and that he was a good organizer, soon becoming vice president of the student government and successfully leading negotiations with Windham president Eugene Winslow to make dorms coed. Windham students were quite involved in the antiwar movement, holding teach-ins, rallies, and demonstrations, some of which didn't go over very well with local residents. He recalled the time he was leading students past the old Book Press factory on Route 5 in Brattleboro, carrying the American flag at the front of the demonstration. The workers came out en masse and threatened to kick the hippies' asses. Nothing came of the confrontation, but he felt the deep emotions on both sides of the political divide viscerally, perhaps for the first time. That was part of his education, too. On the other hand, during one teach-in, when Tom Hayden warned that a revolution was coming and urged the students to buy guns and bury them where they could get them in a hurry, Kacik decided something less dramatic might be more practical: demonstrate but don't agitate. "I learned that if your cause is just, logic and conviction are your best tools," he said, lessons that have come in handy during a lifetime of union organizing.

Kacik lived in Putney for thirty-five years, first as a teacher in Westminster, a job he got despite having been labeled an antiwar hippie. By then he was living with friends in a house with motorcycles parked outside and music blaring from inside, which didn't go over so well with the next-door neighbor, who happened to chair the local school board. Kacik was student teaching at Westminster Center School when the job opened up. No way was that school board head going to hire that "damn hippie" until John Porter, the principal at Westminster, threatened to quit if Kacik wasn't hired. He got the job, but that hadn't deterred his draft board. If Kacik wasn't already in love with Vermont and Vermonters, the next thing that happened convinced him the Green Mountains were the place for him. Porter and Assistant Superintendent John Barry drove with him to Long Island and talked his draft board out of drafting him. "They said they needed me. Who needed who?" Kacik asked rhetorically, recalling his relief when the school officials came out of the meeting that his draft board wouldn't even let him attend.

Kacik became a union representative and organizer for the Vermont Education Association, then executive director of vt-nea from 1997 to 2000, and then NEA's regional director for seventeen states until retiring and moving to Brookfield. The way to success, he discovered, was "not being crazy radicals but practical radicals." Kacik has remained involved in politics, serving on the Vermont Democratic Committee, and like others stressing the difference one person can make in a small state like Vermont.

While Marlboro College and its music school and festival continued over the decades, Windham did not. Its enrollment swelled during the Vietnam era when young men stayed in school to stay out of the war. At its peak from 1970 to 1972, it had around nine hundred students. After six years of dwindling enrollment, it closed abruptly in 1978. In 1985, it was reborn as another innovative educational institution, Landmark College, a school for individuals with learning disabilities.

Not everyone who studied at one of Vermont's innovative colleges found the experience rewarding, although some fell in love with the state during their early years and returned. Windham College introduced Bill Stetson, the grandson of Eugene Stetson, a corporate pioneer at Coca-Cola and J.P. Morgan, to Roz Payne, John Douglas, and other radical filmmakers living nearby at Red Clover. Today president of the Vermont Film Association, Stetson's interest in filmmaking and political activism were nurtured at Windham as he spent time with the activists who were recording an alternative version of America's history. Stetson had already been introduced to the excitement of political action as a campaign organizer for Roy Daley, an unsuccessful Democrat aspirant for Congress, the year before his family moved from Connecticut to Vermont's Woodstock. Windham's overseas academic programs had attracted him to attend, but after a heady year of study in Austria, he found Windham's party atmosphere and what he considered too little academic rigor disappointing. Off to Harvard, he went, his own form of radical behavior as everyone else in his family had gone to Yale.

At Windham, "I was really smacked by the issues, the war still going on, the importance of environmental issues," he said. At the same time, he found "it shocking, people taking their clothes off, acting strange. I thought, 'We're not in Kansas anymore.' I had grown up in an old-fashioned Republican family, even though I marched on Earth Day and worked on Daley's political campaign at eighteen along with Black Panthers. While I found it all interesting, I felt drugs got in the way of progress. We needed clear intellect so as not to be distracted if we were going to accomplish anything good as a generation. That's why I had to part ways with that school and get serious."

And serious he got. Stetson has worked on environmental issues from heading Laurance Rockefeller's Ottauquechee River Water Quality Program to serving on President Obama's National Commission on the Arts. He also transformed the traditional oil and gas company his father had purchased into a profitable, environment-conscious natural gas firm and then began focusing his efforts and investments into socially responsible companies. These have included Tom's of Maine, Amber Alert, and Beech Hill Farm, an organic blueberry farm in Rockport, Maine. He's been an environmental advisor to three Vermont governors—Dean, Douglas, and Peter Shumlin. His wife, Jane Watson Stetson, the granddaughter of IBM's founder, "started a support program for pediatric patients at Dartmouth, David's House. We had a child with leukemia who survived," Stetson explained. "Jane saw so many people in the hospital who couldn't live near to where their kids were being treated, and stepped in to make a difference. We grew up similarly. We were taught that when you were born with comfort, you should give back. These are Vermont values too, which is why we live here. They were hippie values, too, which explains why the counterculture had such an impact, at least initially. In Vermont in particular, people fell in love with the possibility of making a difference."

Food ... and Revolution

Ginny Callan became a vegetarian the day she watched her Barre neighbors chase two chickens down the road. Callan, who undoubtedly served many Vermont legislators their first tofu cutlet with mushroom sauce, hid one of the chickens in her living room overnight. The next day, she fessed up. "We've got your chicken," she told the neighbors. "You can keep it," they replied. "We cooked the other one, and it was scrawny and tough."

Callan "bought another to keep mine company. It started laying eggs, and I became a vegetarian at nineteen years old."

Callan grew up in a meat-and-potato home in Queens before coming to Goddard College in 1970 as one of the students taking part in Goddard's experiment in communal living at its Northwood campus. Two students were required to cook the evening meal, sometimes with not-so-welcome results, such as the night when dinner was oatmeal. A near insurrection ensued, even though there was brown sugar and raisins on the side.

By May Day 1977, when Callan opened Horn of the Moon Café on Langdon Street in downtown Montpelier, one of Vermont's first all-vegetarian restaurants, she could purchase whole-grain bread from local bakers, organic vegetables in bulk from several local farmers, and milk and yogurt from Jack and Anne Lazor at Butterworks Farm in Westfield, an indication of just how far the natural food movement had progressed in Vermont. The demand had grown, too. People lined up around the corner for her corn chowder and tabouleh salad. Soon, they were asking for recipes, and Horn of the Moon cookbooks found their way to other kitchens, even ones where meat and potatoes had long been the staple.

Much the way that Callan learned how to make delicious vegetarian offerings through sampling and inventing, adding flavor and depth with spices

Horn of the Moon celebrates its tenth anniversary. That's
Ginny Callan standing in the center wearing a sweater.
Courtesy of Ginny Callan

from far away, and finding more local, fresh, and increasingly organic ingredients, all the while feeding friends and senators, so too did the counterculture's food ethos evolve and become part of Vermont's culinary and business
landscape. Since those early days at Horn of the Moon, Callan has gone on
to other endeavors, including serving as executive director of the T. W. Wood
Gallery in Montpelier, while the people Callan relied upon for organic food
—farmers like the Lazors, Sally Coleman, and Richard Wiswall at Cate
Farm, or fourth-generation farmer Alan LePage of Barre—also prospered,
part of an ever-intertwining network that grew out of the back-to-the-land
movement and has sustained Vermont's farm-to-table industry throughout
the state and beyond.

Callan remembered her first purchase of brown rice, for a road trip to
Canada. On the way, she and her friends stayed at a commune in Woodstock, New York. When they hauled out their bag of brown rice, proud to
be outfitted with the proper hippie contribution to a communal meal, their
hosts groaned. "That was all they'd been eating. They wanted our instant-
cocoa mix," she said, laughing with the memory.

It's about as hard to explain how and why hippies suddenly began eating lentil loaf and serving their kids Tiger's Milk as it would be to explain why bartering came back into vogue during this era or how buying old clothes from the not-new shops became cool. Some of it was economics, of course. Rice was cheap, as were lentils and beans, second-hand jeans, and vintage shawls. But it was more than money. Just as Cool-Whip was being introduced to the nation, a generation was saying no thanks to artificial. They were willing to suffer for it, too. That Tiger's Milk was a concoction made from milk, of course, then more milk in the powdered form, blackstrap molasses, Brewer's yeast, and wheat germ. It was one of Adelle Davis's recipes in her book *Let's Have Healthy Children*, an early favorite of counterculture mothers. Hippie kids, not having been exposed to sugar-laden beverages, actually liked it. Some of it was groupthink, of course, while some of it was a genuine embracing of doing what their parents had always told them to do: the hippies were eating their vegetables, and their grains, and their adzuki beans. They were also saying no thanks to deodorant, hair perms, makeup, and all things that smarted of chemical alteration, except of course the more mind-expanding chemicals that came in a little blue tab or were soaked into a blotter. But that was food for the mind. When it came to the rest of the body, they wanted raw, whole, and natural, like the brown rice and granola that the Hog Farm members made in huge batches and passed out for free on Haight and Ashbury Streets in San Francisco and at the Woodstock music festival. And let's be honest: anybody can make brown rice. It just takes patience and enough liquid to keep the rice from sticking and burning.

* * *

Callan's restaurant was not the first vegetarian restaurant in Vermont; that honor goes to Common Ground, the workers' collective Free Vermont created in Brattleboro in 1971. It might have been the first vegetarian restaurant in all New England. Common Ground served as "both a business model for cooperative decisions and ownership and a gathering place for dinners and 'long, long meetings' that eventually led to the formation of a local Brattleboro food-buying collective: the embryonic Brattleboro Food Co-op," Christine Holderness wrote for the co-op's fortieth anniversary in 2016. People still miss the Common Ground and swoon with the memory of its yogurt-tahini salad dressing.

John Douglas described how the restaurant ran: "We brought in people from different communes each day to cook dinner and run the restaurant. We did that for several years, getting milk at dawn, cooking stews, or figuring out what was left from the day before. Somehow it seemed to work," he said. Of course, he was busy with his documentary films for much of this time, so his perspective may be more positive than others. But, despite what sounds like a recipe for chaos, the restaurant persisted, serving wholesome food with generous dollops of liberal politics for thirty-seven years. But times changed, as did people's tastes and habits—along with the ability to hold such an enterprise together. Over the years, the restaurant went through several difficult chapters, reorganizing, reopening, and eventually closing for good in 2007. In 2008, the Twelve Tribes Communities purchased the building. The Twelve Tribes is a religious group that began in Tennessee then moved to Island Pond in Vermont's Northeast Kingdom in the late 1970s. The group came under the scrutiny of Vermont state officials in 1984 over discipline and other practices involving children of members. Now claiming fifty settlements or groups in nine countries, the messianic community, which resembles the hippies in its preference for whole food, communal living, and homespun clothing, announced plans to reopen Common Ground, but as of 2017 it had not.

The building that once housed the Back Home Café in Rutland, another storied restaurant from the hippie era, was also bought by the Twelve Tribes years after it had closed. As with Common Ground, some fans of the two restaurants considered it anathema that a group that operated under a hierarchical structure in which men had authority over women and all adults had some level of authority over the children would own these two iconic counterculture restaurants. Unlike with Common Ground, the Twelve Tribes had success in Rutland with their Back Home Again Restaurant, which morphed into the Yellow Deli and a hostel they opened in some of the buildings once associated with the Back Home and its owner Will Patten.

Patten's story is a link to Scott Nearing and the earlier counterculture settlement along Pikes Falls in Winhall. His parents, influenced by the Nearings' experiment, had moved to the mountain town of Shrewsbury in Rutland County from Newark, New Jersey, in 1939. Patten attended Shrewsbury's one-room schoolhouse, Rutland High School, and Johns Hopkins University, graduating in 1967 before moving to Berkeley to fight the "other war," his term for the war against the Vietnam War. There, he experimented with drugs but found they weren't his thing, instead recalling the time as one of trying to understand why governments continued to try to solve problems and challenges using war rather than collaboration. In part to understand the world a little better, he went on a tour of Europe with no particular return date in mind. He quickly fell in love with café life where strangers became acquaintances over coffee or a glass of wine, sharing the conversation of the day and slowly, civilly, becoming friends.

By the time he got to Scandinavia a few months later and saw birch trees, he knew it was time to go home. He'd missed Vermont and the seasons. "I realized that rhythm was deeply engrained in me," he recalled. Back home in 1970, he quickly realized there were hundreds of hippies living in Brandon, Middletown Springs, Shrewsbury, and other towns in Rutland County, hippies who had no comfortable gathering place. And so, he opened the Back Home Café on the expansive second floor of a commercial building on Center Street in Rutland's handsome downtown, loving the double meaning of its name: that he was back home and that the place itself could be a kind of home for others.

The Back Home Café became a communal touchstone for hundreds of hippies and non-hippies alike. You climbed a long flight of stairs and turned left across from where Kathleen Murphy, later Will's wife, ran a secondhand clothing store called Gypsy's. There would be Arthur Patten, father of Will, greeting customers with his wise, smiling eyes, impressive eyebrows, and white beard, sporting a dashiki complete with some sort of hippie medallion hanging mid-chest.

It was hard to find a seat at lunchtime as many business people and even the portly Rutland mayor Gilbert Godnick frequented the place, "Gilly" once quipping that the only reason one would climb the double flight of stairs was for the food. But few came to dinner, leading Patten to hire Maurice "Mo" Cyr to create a dinner menu, help cook it and arrange the evening's entertainment. Cyr had hair almost to his waist and no culinary training, but he succeeded. At the time, other than the Back Home Café, amateur softball games sponsored by various businesses were among the few places where hippies and straight residents found themselves in one another's company. This led to the infamous softball game between the city police and Back Home staff and regulars to raise money for a local ice hockey association; the game was affectionately referred to as the Fuzz versus the Fuzzies. Cyr still speaks with joy about the Fuzzies beating the Fuzz in the tenth inning, the game tied until Patten hit a single past the second baseman, driving in the winning run.

Cyr, who grew up in Thomaston, Connecticut, and graduated from Providence College before moving to Vermont in 1972, might still be cooking but for a car accident. While he was traveling with a girlfriend in 1977, a woman

Wearing their Back Home Café T-shirts, the Fuzzies take on the Fuzz for a cause. The newspaper caption for this photo said, "What appears to be an unlikely meeting is really a pre-game handshake between the leaders of two of the city's finest softball teams. Representing 'The Fuzz' at left are State Trooper Stephen Ynchko and City Patrolman John Tuepker. Representing 'The Fuzzies' at right are Robert Peltak and Maurice 'Mo' Cyr. The game's proceeds benefitted the Rutland Amateur Hockey Association."
Courtesy of Rutland Herald

driver coming in the opposite direction passed two cars before ramming into his vehicle head-on. The woman driver died while Cyr and his girlfriend were thrown from the car, surviving but injured. For months, Cyr had daily headaches, headaches that never went away until he tried being treated by a chiropractor, found relief and his purpose. Now a longtime chiropractor in Rutland, he said some of his patients call him Doctor Cyr and some still call him Mo. "We've both blended in *and* changed Vermont," he said. "My favorite thing I like to tell people about Vermont is that the reason hitchhiking is legal in Vermont is because Governor Salmon got hassled by police for hitchhiking when his car broke down on the way to his wedding. He refused to sign a bill against hitchhiking. That's Vermont."

Rutland native Claire Clarino had grown up in her nonnie's kitchen and garden, absorbing the instinctual flavors of her Italian family's version of garden to table. In the early 1970s, while in college at UVM, she became a vegetarian and began teaching herself about healthy foraging, eating, and cooking with Euell Gibbons' *Stalking the Wild Asparagus*, Frances Moore Lappé's *Diet for a Small Planet*, and Jean Hewitt's *New York Times Natural Foods Cookbook*. Then she "made a $3.95 purchase that changed my life," she recalled, referring to Edward Brown's *Tassajara Bread Book*, discovering the art of making bread "as meditation, as a total fulfilling and rewarding experience." Among the book's messages that she remembered decades later was this: "It's just you and the dough—ripening, maturing, baking, blossoming together."

She soon became part of the Back Home crew, first as a waitress and later as a line cook where she, Neal Vargas, and John Petrone, who purchased the Back Home after Patten opened Murphy's, another iconic Rutland restaurant, cranked out sinful open-faced Reubens and giant burgers, baked ziti and broiled fish, humungous salads and vegetarian sandwiches made with sour cream, cucumbers, and sprouts, homemade date-nut bread with cream cheese. "Everything had sprouts, many of which were growing in mason jars in the back room," she recalled, not daring to think how they got past the health inspectors. In her third incarnation at the Back Home, Clarino, then married with two young children, worked as a baker with another Rutland native, Dale Mangieri Gray. Their carrot cake and Aunt Clem's chocolate cake are legendary.

As Clarino described, the Back Home was home away from home for hundreds of hippies and non-hippies alike: "People raised their kids there. Benefits were held for good causes. The Farmer's Market was born there."

As her description of the Back Home suggested, the histories of Vermont's organic farms, farmers' markets, and food co-ops are entwined. They evolved simultaneously, at times independent of one another and at others in concert, starting in the mid-1960s with buyers' clubs and small co-ops who ordered the whole wheat flour and brown rice, peanut butter made just from peanuts, and dried fruit they'd grown accustomed to coming from college towns and cities. While they could still buy raw milk from the farmer down the road, the rice and naturally dried raisins had to be ordered through mail-order suppliers such as Paul and Betty Keene's Walnut Acres. The arrival of the Walnut Acres product catalogue with their stories about farm life and recipes was cause for celebration. As the newcomers met others looking for these hard-to-get products, they began ordering together to save money and shipping costs.

A pivotal moment in Vermont's food revolution occurred on April 9, 1966, when a small macrobiotic and natural-foods store opened on Newbury Street in Boston, perhaps the first such store in the United States. By 1969, Erewhon Foods had expanded into a wholesale business, paving the way for members of buyers' clubs and small food co-ops to order in bulk. Its location was close enough to drive to, eliminating shipping charges.

"What fun the co-op meetings were," Diane Gottlieb, a licensed psychologist who came to Vermont in 1971 from New York City with her husband, Charlie, also a psychologist, recalled. The two were committed feminists who chose Vermont as the place where they would live, raise their child, and work in harmony with their values. Eating healthy was essential to that. But, as Diane pointed out, that didn't mean it couldn't be fun. The buyers' clubs and food co-ops were far from formal organizations but rather evolving groups of people who met to barter—"I'll take a half-pound of your wheat germ if you'll go in on twenty pounds of whole wheat flour with me"—and trade. By ordering with others, a person could purchase products he or she might not have been able to afford or need in large quantity, dried fruit, for example, or carob chips. Once the order was ready for pickup, a few members would carpool, borrow, or rent a truck to retrieve it at the warehouse. Again, there would be a gathering, the work shared as the load was divvied up. In this way, ever-expanding circles of like-minded people grew, welcoming neighbors who might not otherwise have much exchange with the hippies in their town. Good food at a reasonable price went a long way toward making friends. Sometimes there would be a potluck. Sometimes, people would bring instruments and sit around and sing after the ordering. Young parents helped one another with nursing and sleeping problems and traded recipes on homemade baby food. But beyond their social, economic, and educational value, these first co-ops were also political statements, albeit ones wrapped in the nonthreatening appeal of plump Thompson raisins and roasted cashews. At their core, even the smallest food co-op or buyers' club held to the philosophy—indeed, for some, almost a religion—centered on the sanctity of food. Lappé's *Diet for a Small Planet* and George Ohsawa's books on macrobiotics brought together the idea of food as the foundation of health and happiness with the belief that each individual was responsible to care as fully as possible for the planet. But while they were making that personal statement, the members of these small co-ops were making another, whether they acknowledged it or not: They were not investing in their communities. Indeed, they were doing the opposite of buying local. For, while the farmers' markets and storefront co-ops that grew out of the original buyers' clubs and early back-to-the-land movement provided opportunities for jobs, community building, and activism, not to mention keeping money local, the smaller buyers' clubs were economically subversive. By going directly to the warehouse or distributor, the buyers' club and co-op members were taking their money out of state for the purpose of bringing what they saw as better food in. Thus, it was essential to Vermont's economy as well as to the relationship between the counterculture and the existing culture that the buyers' clubs evolved into storefront co-ops, and that organic farming, farmers' markets, community-supported agriculture programs, farm-to-table restaurants, and other food-related activities were blended into the general society over the course of the past forty or so years. Without that evolution, Vermont's agricultural health and economy might look much different today.

* * *

As the small, often home-based food co-ops proliferated in the mid-1970s, the New England Peoples Co-op (NEPCOOP) was created to coordinate eight food co-ops in Vermont and New Hampshire. Each regional group would distribute order sheets to individual families, then collate the orders and submit them to NEPCOOP, with the Plainfield Co-op serving as the central organization. NEPCOOP eventually hired Carl Gamba, owner of the Loaves and Fishes Trucking Company headquartered in the Northeast Kingdom, to drive a tractor-trailer to Boston and New York warehouses to collect the food and haul it back to Vermont, according to Charles Adams. Adams, now of Newport, Rhode Island, wrote a history of how the various co-ops and buyers' clubs coordinated their efforts as part of the Middlebury Co-op's fortieth anniversary in 2016. Gamba or another driver "would drive around to each of the co-ops from Bennington in the south to Derby Center in the north dropping off foodstuffs. Each co-op provided labor to assist with the pickups and deliveries in rotating order," Adams explained.

NEPCOOP had been spearheaded by Samuel Kaymen, later the cofounder of Stonyfield yogurt in Wilton, New Hampshire. NEPCOOP was centered in a storefront in Lebanon, New Hampshire called the (Don't Just Talk About It,) Do It Store, which served as a regional clubhouse and supply center for antiwar, women's, and other social groups. Robert Houriet calls Kaymen a "prophet" who realized while living on a farm in upstate New York that a movement or revolution could not grow out of a negative but had to emanate from a shared positive ideal. It wasn't enough to be in the country simply because the city was a mess; each person, he realized, needed a reason to be there, something they could do to contribute to the greater good. Creating a network that supported healthy agriculture while providing smoother access to healthy ingredients struck him as something the Northeast needed.

Houriet and Kaymen met in Barton, where Kaymen was starting to organize people into food co-ops and farmers into organic farming associations. At the time, Houriet, no longer living at Frog Run commune, was looking for a focus. He too had come to the realization that "If we were to have self-sufficient communities, we had to form a larger cooperative movement. I had become a farmer in the radical sense. Organic farming became a political purpose," he recalled in an oral history recorded at the University of Massachusetts–Amherst.

By 1973, informational meetings were being held in various parts of Vermont and along the Connecticut River towns of New Hampshire, Massachusetts, and Connecticut, linking organic farmers on both sides of the river with food co-ops, day care centers and progressive groups in New York City who wanted fresh, organic produce from Vermont. Houriet took on the job of writing the group's newsletter and sometimes going on the pickup and delivery trips. He recalled the time he arrived at one city warehouse in the wee hours of the morning to find a hundred people waiting. They "all cheered like we had pulled off some kind of guerilla operation. They gave us the power salute," he recalled. Power salute or not, these were fourteen- to sixteen-hour days of grueling work, driving from farm to farm, loading produce, then more driving to the Bowery and other destinations, more unloading, and finally driving back to Vermont. With little money, no real staff, and the vagaries of weather and crops, people were getting burned out. And by then, also, Kaymen had become involved in developing Stonyfield yogurt. Houriet, who was living in the Do It Store by then, was close to burnout. At a meeting at a Grange hall in Canaan, New Hampshire, he suggested abandoning the New York project and organizing the Vermont and New Hampshire farmers around the idea of "local food for local markets." It was the locavore idea, launched in 1973, and the beginning of NOFA, the Northeast Organic Farming Association. In retrospect, it was a no-brainer: local food for local consumption. It was Houriet who saw it.

For the next few years, Houriet put his attention to grant writing as he helped small farmers' markets start up in Brattleboro, Rutland, Montpelier, Burlington and in towns along the Connecticut River in both New Hampshire and Vermont, and in the Northeast Kingdom. Forty years later, in 2016,

the Vermont Department of Agriculture, Food, and Markets, while reporting that Vermont's agricultural economy was the largest of any state in New
England at $776 million, boasted ninety farmers' markets that provided more
fresh local food in 2015 than had any other state per capita. Additionally, its
583 certified organic farms (a 2011 figure) also represented more than any
other state per capita.

This didn't happen overnight, of course. The Rutland Farmers' Market,
one of the first, had a less than promising beginning, held initially on the
lawn of the Unitarian Universalist Church in downtown Rutland and later
in "Gilly's Gully," a pit on Wales Street named for Godnick. Godnick wasn't
crazy about a bunch of hippies selling their organic crops downtown. He
fought efforts by Andy Snyder, the market manager, to locate the market in a
more appropriate location. But Snyder persevered.

Snyder had been hired to help grow vegetables as the agricultural director
for the Whipple Hollow Cannery in 1976. The cannery was one of several innovative projects funded through the surfeit of national grants and programs
available at the time, through organizations as diverse as the Volunteers in
Service to America to the Office of Economic Opportunity. These grants
often challenged recipients to develop self-sustaining enterprises to help
low-income people become independent. States also received funds through
the Comprehensive Education and Training Act to develop programs to
help people get back to work.

Bread and Law Task Force managed several of these grant programs. In
one, a $75,000 grant from the Campaign for Human Development aimed
to establish and train staff at three canneries, the Whipple Hollow Cannery
in West Rutland, the Northeast Kingdom Co-operative Cannery in Barton,
and the Cherry Hill Community Cannery in Barre. The idea was simple:
people could be more self-sufficient if they had the tools to grow and preserve
healthy food. Christine Anderson, a young college graduate who had grown
up in Rutland, was hired as the Whipple Hollow production supervisor. She
had studied science at Cornell but otherwise had no experience in food preservation. "It was rather intimidating," she recalled, especially her first-ever
plane trip from Burlington to Rochester, New York, for training organized by
the USDA in 1976. The most essential element to learn was how to use retort
pressure cookers to sterilize canned food and how to teach the skill to others.

John Squires, a farmer from an old Tinmouth family, was "incredibly
helpful and supportive," allowing the growers to use his land to grow tomatoes and cabbage; a property owner in Castleton let the cadre of hippies pick

a thousand bushels of apples. The Whipple Hollow canners made sauer-kraut, applesauce, apple butter, and tomato sauce and sold it at the nascent farmers' markets. Squires, a legend in Rutland County, liked to tease the back-to-the-landers about their obsession with growing organic food. He had a bumper sticker made that said, Organic in My Mind. But, like Harry Thompson of Cabot, Squires was patron saint to the young hippie farmers in Rutland County and taught them so much, such as the suggestion to keep a stack of paper bags handy to put over young tomato plants when there was a frost warning. The canneries struggled, but the skills Snyder and Anderson learned at the cannery, from growing to preserving, helped them as together they turned Fire Hill Farm in Florence into a productive farm and joined with dozens of others to make the Rutland County Farmers' Market grow into a parallel success. Snyder built up the number of farmers participating in the market and the diversity of offerings by visiting area farmers and en-couraging them to join the market. He was always urging them to try growing something new, incrementally improving the variety available at the market. Meanwhile, he lobbied downtown merchants and friends at the *Rutland Daily Herald* to support a permanent location for the market, arguing the move would help the market to grow and attract customers into the down-town area, creating business for everyone. That argument eventually made its way to the Rutland board of aldermen where the board chairman, Walter Moore, had been Anderson's English teacher at Mount St. Joseph Academy. He wasn't so keen on the hippie market, but Anderson had been a good stu-dent and with his vote, the new location got approved.

"I understood that this wasn't just about selling cabbage; the market was to be an event, a place to meet, a place to go, with music, dance, street the-ater, art taking place, and the beginning of the farmers' market movement as a way to remind people once again where their food comes from, to see the person who made it," Snyder explained. To fully appreciate this, picture Sny-der at the time, fully bearded, gregarious, a born talker, his and Anderson's stand decorated with sunflowers, always a big chunk of Crowley cheese for sale and a crock of homemade pickles as crunchy as ones they sell in New York delis, another crock with sauerkraut, piles of gorgeous vegetables, and Snyder rapping and rhapsodizing about their excellence. By the time Snyder left to pursue his interest in politics, the market was the largest in Vermont and one of the largest in northern New England.

Snyder comes by his agricultural roots by an unlikely path. He had grown up in Harlem, Washington Heights, and the East Village in a household

Andy Snyder at the Rutland County Farmers' Market in the early 1970s, one of the first and most successful farmers' markets in Vermont.
Courtesy of Andy Snyder

in which color, religion, and social status were inconsequential. One of his earliest influences was Camp Hurley in the Catskills, run by activist singers Pete Seeger and Janis Ian's families. The camp was full of red-diaper babies, the term for children of parents who had Communist sympathies, about to become the next generation of agitators. Snyder's father, Murry Snyder, was something of a celebrity at the time, as he was a leading promoter of the idea that stuttering was an emotional condition not a physical disability. In 1968, he got talked into buying the Florence property by a coworker whose brother, Frank Punderson, was starting out in business. The plea that he give the kid a break was accompanied by the suggestion that Murry deserved a country reprieve. As it turned out, Punderson became one of the region's top sellers, and Murry Snyder was "like a pig in shit, forty-eight years old, and just loving life on a farm," Andy recalled.

He was attending Adelphi at the time, and was an antiwar activist and draft counselor who, among other actions, led a demonstration that closed down traffic on the New York Thruway after President Nixon approved the bombing of Cambodia. Days after graduation, he moved to Vermont and got his first job—like so many others he'd soon become friends with—at the Brandon Training School.

In the intervening years, Snyder has served on the Vermont legislature and worked for the Vermont Department of Education in intergovernmental affairs. Upon retirement, he returned to an old passion, working with clay, creating his signature pottery in his MudPuppy studio located in a renovated camp between two lakes—Sunrise and Sunset—in Orwell. His favorite memories, however, are of those Saturday mornings hawking pickles and peas.

✳ ✳ ✳

West Rutland farmer Greg Cox ushered the Rutland County Farmers' Market into its next phase: becoming the first year-round market with a winter building, the Vermont Farmers Food Center, equipped with a commercial kitchen, space for educational programs, and community dinners. Where else could you get a full meal, salad to dessert, and all organically grown by local farmers, for $7?

If anyone had told Cox when he first began dreaming of being a farmer that he would become an integral part of Rutland County's economy, he would have called them a "wonderful but delusional dreamer." It's not just he who has helped buoy the county: Cox is part of a network of organic farmers who support one another through internship and sabbatical programs while providing Vermont-grown produce, meat, poultry, and other products year-round to food shelves and programs that serve hundreds of homeless people, seniors, and low-income families. In 2017, the market installed two large greenhouses adjacent to its winter headquarters, funded in part by a grant from Rutland City Rotary. Local school children participate in a program that allows them to grow a bit of their own food and prepare it in the kitchen at the food center.

As a boy, Cox fell in love with nature "just about instantly" when his family moved from Queens to King's Park on Long Island, where their housing development was located next to a bird sanctuary. He loved helping local farmers and watching the seasons unfurl through bird migrations and other seasonal changes, but finally acquiesced to his parents' demand that he go to college. He chose Johnson State College in northern Vermont as much because it was located in the country as for its proximity to the Canadian border. His brother had served in Vietnam and begged him not to follow, to do anything to avoid the draft.

"I had never seen anything so beautiful, just amazing," Cox recalled of the drive north. At Johnson, he embraced the opportunity to continue playing outside in nature, hiking and skiing and working for local farmers. A sociology professor, George Warren, became his draft advisor. Cox had a bad number: 95. That meant he would likely be drafted for military duty in Vietnam. Warren coached Cox how to follow a high salt diet, which led him to hyperventilate prior to his physical and earned him a 4-F deferment. It was Warren also who urged him not to become a teacher, considering education "the reproductive organ of societal conformity," but rather to "seek self-realization." Cox already knew what he wanted to do and it wasn't teach. That had been his parents' dream for him. He wanted to farm.

For close to a decade, he worked shoveling shit and raising vegetables for other farmers in the summer and shoveling snow at Killington Ski Area in the winter; he cooked at the Back Home Café, and later was caretaker for an upscale farm. All the while, he was learning and saving money for his own piece of paradise. In the mid-1980s, he bought Boardman Hill Farm in West Rutland and began growing anything that could be raised in Vermont's unpredictable climate. In between, there was a failed marriage and then a successful one to a local woman named Gaye who shared his love of the land, and kids.

Even when he struggled to make ends meet, Cox ascribed to the theory that "Agriculture needs to be part of the economic engine of the future." His efforts in making that dream a reality were acknowledged when in 2016 Cox became the first farmer recognized as Businessman of the Year by the Rutland Region Chamber of Commerce. Cox, appropriately, blushed so hard that his face turned beet red when the surprise award was announced.

But the award was well deserved as the market, housed in an old factory building in the winter, and showcased in the center of the city's downtown in summer, is among the bright spots in a community that has seen too many businesses come and go.

＊ ＊ ＊

As with other counterculture kids, Joey Klein was fortunate to meet individuals who helped shape him at an early age. Paul and Dorothea Stockwell were among the first. The Stockwells were retired professionals who had bought one of Vermont's oldest farms, Heifer Hill in West Brattleboro, in the 1950s; a decade or so later, they opened it up to young people as a place to live and learn about organic farming. Over the years, Heifer Hill's one hundred acres of forest, pasture, and buildings have been a potter's commune, a residential high school, and the Bonnyvale Environmental Education Center, which celebrated its twenty-fifth anniversary in 2016. Klein, then a recent graduate from Marlboro College, "was profoundly influenced by Paul who was a rugged individualist; the Stockwells became my role models." He and Betsy Ziegler were married at Heifer Hill. Today, their Littlewood Farm in Plainfield is one of the little gems of central Vermont but the road to successful farming was not easy. Their first venture, a farm in Williamstown, was a study in battling the elements: they found the location "too bony, too cold, too high up, too windy." In 1987, they found the land that became Littlewood Farm. In short order, Klein discovered that "If you show any interest in farming, the old-timers will check you out." Phil Winter, a dairy farmer and rock-rib Republican state legislator, befriended the couple as did Walter Smith of Grovewood Farm, "a mentor to many of us."

Klein had met Houriet as Houriet was making his tour of communes and hippie farms, recruiting farmers to join NOFA, the organic farmers' association. At a meeting at the Common Ground restaurant, Houriet signed up seventy-five members who pledged to work for the new organization. From that moment on, Klein embraced the idea of Vermont farmers connected to one another and to the greater economy, and became an unpaid advocate for NOFA. During the fifteen years he worked as a salesman with Karl Hammer's Vermont Compost Company, as he traveled from one farm to another, Klein sang the organization's praises and got to know Cox and Snyder and other small organic growers throughout the Northeast, connections that have in turn sustained him through the years and strengthened NOFA.

But he credited Houriet with making NOFA successful and securing its link to Vermont's farmers' markets. "Robert brought an SDS approach to NOFA," Klein recalled. "His idea was, you've got to talk to a lot of people, reach out. The vision he had of organic farming as something political and even revolutionary got articulated over the years through all the successes and failures. It is at the absolute foundational root of the foodie thing now. NOFA did it, getting farmer's markets off the ground, working to support organic dairying, fruit production, making it possible to get people of similar interest to talk to one another, and learn from each other."

The success of these efforts should not be measured just in the twelve hundred members of NOFA throughout Vermont, the 589 farms and processors who meet USDA national organic program standards, and the 122,825 acres of certified organic farmland in Vermont in 2017, but also in the hundreds of other organic farmers throughout the Northeast and beyond who have been mentored through NOFA and its member farmers. Along with educational conferences, NOFA helps farmers with financial planning and assistance, runs regional workshops, and provides a full array of support for new farmers. Both in conjunction with NOFA and independently, hundreds of young people who want to get into farming have spent weeks and years on Vermont farms through formal and informal internship programs; some are now successful Vermont farmers. And, again, those efforts have spread beyond Vermont's borders. Dozens, perhaps hundreds of Vermont farmers and producers now sell their wares commercially, that Made in Vermont label proudly displayed.

"I've learned a lot about how Vermonters are ahead of the curve, even when it seems they are behind it," Klein said. "Small is beautiful is not really a party line; here, it crosses party lines. Across the state, farming has been at the root of the grassroots building of an alternative economy."

He noted that while he, like so many others, came to Vermont to drop out of society, he has served on one town committee or another for decades while his wife has long served on the Plainfield select board. He also noted that Vermont's lieutenant governor, David Zuckerman, a longhaired organic farmer, ran and won as a Progressive Democrat.

Resistance to the dominant paradigm may have been the motto when these young people began their experiment in organic farming and food preparation but, as Cox observed, the organic movement and its multitude of partners are essential now. "Seeing our success, the way we have become an integral part of Vermont's agricultural economy while providing wholesome food to literally thousands, that is the cream on the milk. We came here not knowing much, although we thought we knew everything. Vermont taught us. We've passed what people like Farmer John and so many others taught us on to other farmers. We've helped transform the way people think of food, and the health of food, and the health of farming. It's been a pretty good deal for all of us and Vermont too, a lesson for the rest of the world."

* * *

While all this was going on, the state's food co-ops were also evolving from small buyers' clubs and home-based food co-ops to storefront co-ops run by employees rather than volunteers. The long and quirky history of the Middlebury Co-op illustrates the "butterfly effect" inherent in this progression —the theory that one action will cause other actions and impacts that in turn will effect change elsewhere and so on. In this case, it was an invitation to neighbors of an experimental environmental center in Ripton that set in motion steps that not only led to the creation of the Middlebury Food Co-op but to an experiment in which Vermonters grew and milled their own grain with the dream of becoming independent from corporate producers.

In 1969, a group of wealthy landowners and politicians that included Laurance Rockefeller created an environmental camp called the Vermont Environmental Education Center in response to the passage of the state's landmark environmental-protection legislation, Act 250. The law created a complicated process for reviewing the environmental impact of large projects on the surrounding communities and the environment. The investors believed in it, but they worried that it might prove unpopular with the populace. They believed Vermonters had to be educated about and committed to environmental protection if Act 250 was to succeed and envisioned the center as a way to make ordinary people partners in the law's enforcement, not by just educating them, but by showing the interrelationship between humans and the planet. Thus, for example, in 1971, the center offered a course to Middlebury, Goddard, Bennington, and Williams College students in Contemporary Human Ecology that included hands-on activities in the woods as well as lectures by ecologists. Through a contract with the Vermont Department of Education, teachers were offered workshops and given tools to bring environmental education into their classrooms. Youngsters were exposed to ecology through outdoor activities at the center. Not only did the staff want to eat healthy food, but they also wanted to serve healthy food to their attendees as another form of education. They created a buyers' club for that purpose, inviting neighbors to join in purchasing whole food in bulk from Erewhon and elsewhere.

The center had been funded through an unusual source, a two-year $150,000 grant from the New England Regional Commission. Vermont attorney David Cowles of Lincoln worked as a caretaker at the center in his early twenties and recalled that "the people who ran it were pretty liberal, professors from all over. With their long hair and beards, there was always a conflict when the straitlaced suits from the commission came to visit," but the commissioners seemed to like the food.

The idea of the food co-op resonated with Cowles from the beginning, coming from old Vermont stock where people were used to sharing and bartering. When the center closed after just a few years in operation, he took over the buyers' club, moving it to his home in Ripton. From there it moved

Charles Adams was proud of the title "miller" when the Middlebury Food Co-op established a grain-milling operation in New Haven. *Photo by Paul Ralston; courtesy of Charles Adams*

to Middlebury College where a student, David Tier, increased participation greatly by inviting other students to join. To meet the demand, Tier rented a barn on Route 7 south of New Haven where distribution became more manageable. Tier handed coordination duties off to Charles Adams when he opened a bike shop in Middlebury. Under Adams's management, the co-op moved to a building adjacent to the old Middlebury train station where it began offering storefront sales.

Meanwhile, a joint project had been created between NOFA and NEPCOOP called Beans and Grains, aimed at making Vermont independent from national markets. NEPCOOP, the New England People's Co-op, hired Greensboro farmer David Allen to grow oats and Francis Angier, an Addison County farmer, to grow wheat. Initially, the crops were milled in Canada but that proved a disaster when ten tons of oats were ruined when the miller failed to remove the hulls. The Vermont co-ops then purchased a Meadows thirty-inch stone mill from Erewhon that operated in a back room at the Plainfield Co-op. They named their mill Audrey. "All the flours and cornmeal distributed by the Vermont co-ops and buyers' clubs were milled by Henry Tewksbury," Adams recalled. In 1977, the Middlebury Co-op took over the milling business. "A large barn on South Street in New Haven that used to be a chicken farm was rented, steam cleaned, and painted. A loading bay was built, office area enclosed, three-phase power service installed, the mill moved and set up, staff hired, and operations begun. Ellen Temple was the warehouse manager, and I was the miller."

To meet the demand for grain, more Vermonters began growing wheat, something that hadn't occurred in decades. Despite difficult soil and weather conditions, there was so much enthusiasm for Vermont being independent

Filling the grain silo.
Photo by Charles Adams

of outside growers that "the mill operation expanded with the purchase of Vermont-grown wheat in bulk, the construction of a grain storage silo, grain elevator, and purchase of a commercial seed cleaner [from French's mustard]." Sadly, the mill, like the canneries, floundered without enough volume to make the operation profitable. Additionally, disagreements arose over the advisability of purchasing grain from more commercial growers who might not adhere to strict organic procedures. After three years, the project was abandoned.

"I still think it was a shame," Adams said. "We really felt we could create a state within a state and get more control over our own food sources by co-operating with each other. But idealism dissipated after a few years" at least it terms of the flour mill. "I'm still so proud to say once I was a miller."

Nonetheless, the Middlebury Co-op, like so many around the state, prospered, in 2016 reporting 4,500 members, 70 employees, and sales of $13 million, 35 percent of which came from local producers. By 2017, it was expanding again.

The story of Burlington's food co-op is also impressive. Larry Kupferman, the director of Burlington's Community and Economic Development Office from 2007 to 2012, told the state historical society how the Onion River Co-op initially grew from a buyers' group to a storefront on North Winooski

Avenue serving about a hundred buying groups. The operation was held to-gether with promises and trust. "We had no money. . . . The whole basis was that people would pre-order, and we would use that to buy. We would pay cash and we would go to New York City and Boston and pick up all of these things. One year we tallied it up and it was a million dollars in sales. How did we do that? But somehow we bought this property on Archibald Street. We were building an alternative economy."

Forty years later, that food co-op begun as a subversive act to build an al-ternative economy had evolved into Burlington's City Market, where both organic and conventional food is sold, a kind of traditional food store cum member-owned food co-op. By 2016, City Market's co-op side boasted more than $38 million a year in business, the largest sales volume of any single-store food co-op in the country.

A revolution indeed.

Entrepreneurship— Hippie-Style

A common theme emerges when you talk to Vermonters who were part of the counterculture generation about the relationship between their work and living in Vermont. It doesn't seem to matter whether it's making poetry or pottery, massive reels for the cable and wire industry, designing a better bra for active women, or finding a way to keep the sheep breeding business alive by making the equivalent of artisanal wool. David Budbill, the Zen poet who spent fifty years working and living at the hermitage he and his wife, the painter Lois Eby, built in Wolcott, put it this way: "There's this deep connection for me between what I am and what I do and where I do it. I'm lucky to have been able to do it in such a remarkable place. I do not take it for granted."

Jerry Greenfield, cofounder of Ben & Jerry's Homemade Ice Cream, put it in business terms: "When we started we called ourselves 'Vermont's finest all-natural ice cream.' We made the decision to use Vermont milk and cream and be associated with Vermont. From a business point of view, it was a fortunate thing because Vermont has such a great reputation. It sells the product. Better still, we get to live here."

Yet, a study of innovative Vermont businesses founded in the last few decades by the generation of progressives, counterculturists, and hippies suggests that, along with the good feelings that come from doing work you love in a caring, responsible manner in a location that also sustains you, come the same travails of traditional business and the same pitfalls. For Budbill and Eby, who needed to earn enough to sustain themselves and their family while growing their own food and cutting wood for heat, it may have been possible to adhere strictly to the values that brought them to Vermont. But, as Greenfield and his partner Ben Cohen, or Alan Newman, first of Gardener's Supply and Seventh Generation, then of Magic Hat Brewery, and now part of the Marijuana Collaborative, discovered, cavalier hippie ideas and practices must be balanced with sound business practices and clear monitoring of the bottom line.

Nonetheless, and despite its rural nature, Vermont's entrepreneurial spirit is recognized widely. The state ranked second in a 2015 study by the Kauffman Foundation of the best states for entrepreneurs and start-ups. A subsequent article provided a list of familiar Vermont-based companies that grew out of the movements of the 1960s and '70s as proof of that ranking. They included the usual entries: Gardener's Supply, Ben & Jerry's, Green Mountain Coffee Roasters, Seventh Generation, Magic Hat Brewery, Autumn Harp, and many more. And, while the founders of these companies no longer control them, all grew out of what Lisa Lindahl, a founder of Jogbra, the first successful sports bra for women, called "the creative, freeing" environment that was part and parcel of the counterculture in Vermont.

Cecile Betit, a retired professor, author, and researcher who has followed the socially responsible business movement in Vermont and beyond, believes the baby-boom generation took risks in creating businesses, both large and small, and were willing to tackle ventures they knew absolutely nothing about, from starting an organic farm to transforming a run-down waterfront into a gem of urban renewal, not so much to reject their parents and their values, but rather to "*embrace* what our parents preached. What many in the sixties generation saw was that their parents talked about equality and justice and individual rights but they were not living what they preached. Taking what our parents said—that we could do anything—and then doing it, believing that there were no restrictions," created an atmosphere in which taking risk was not such a scary proposition. "Our President Kennedy had dreamed of putting a man on the moon," she said. For a generation, "the cosmos was at the doorstep."

The baby-boom generation also "had the opportunity—the luxury—to question how do we want the world to be. We had the ability to process like few generations before. During the sixties, the influence of Buddhism, transcendental meditation, even drugs like LSD, provided an opening into deeper thought. The boundary of possibility was not fixed. That was the gift Bernie Sanders, Ben and Jerry, many of those people experienced either through psychedelics, study, meditation, or simply the sentiment that was pervasive, that we can construct our own reality."

Betit, who grew up in Bennington, noted that Vermont has long provided rich territory for creatively minded entrepreneurs. She learned this growing up in a home where her parents "lived a life made by hand." Her father, who grew up on a farm, could make anything, often adapting one tool to serve a better purpose. "He observed early on that the sixties people were also willing to make a life made by hand," she said. In this way, "Vermonters were hippies before they knew one, that's what my father always knew. He loved my hippie friends." Her own story is one of constant invention. After graduating from Emmanuel College in Boston in 1965, she became one of the first white teachers working in North Philadelphia before earning a doctorate at Temple University and launching a long career as a college professor and administrator, researcher, speaker, and writer who is currently exploring what she calls "corporate citizenship."

The idea that commerce can be a vehicle for social change has been part of Vermont's business culture since at least the 1940s, when Lyman Wood moved from New York to Burlington and subsequently founded Garden Way, the mail-order gardening supply business. Wood's goal was to "live the garden way of life" in contrast to work done simply for profit. He was the author of *The Have More Plan*, a 1944 pamphlet that instructed the post-wartime population about how to live off the land. In the 1960s he purchased the Troy-Bilt rototiller company and expanded Garden Way into publishing, retail sales, and other ventures, in the process becoming "a mentor to younger do-gooder entrepreneurs, including John Sortino, founder of Vermont Teddy Bear, and Will Raap of Gardener's Supply," according to Jess McCuan, writing for Inc.com, the business website. Vermont fostered this entrepreneurial spirit in the 1970s by "doling out loans to would-be business owners, and socially oriented private venture groups, such as Northern Vermont Lending Partners and the Vermont Food Venture Center, soon followed suit. . . . Since then, Vermont has become as much a brand as an address. Businesses like Green Mountain Coffee Roasters, based in Waterbury, and Orvis, an outdoor gear retailer in Manchester, make direct reference to the state's landscape in their marketing materials," McCuan observed.

McCuan recognized the work of Ben Cohen and Jerry Greenfield who, in 1990, helped found Vermont Businesses for Social Responsibility, the largest and oldest state group of its kind with more than 750 members in 640 companies in 2017. According to VBSR's website, its founders "believed businesses have as much responsibility to workers, communities and the environment as they do to being financially successful."

It's an assertion Bill Carris and his father, Henry, put into action, an example of how the old way of doing business resonated with the new. Almost from the moment he returned to Vermont after military duty, Bill Carris began work to transform Carris Reels, an international company headquartered in Rutland that makes reels for wire and cable, from a family-owned corporation to an employee-owned and governed enterprise. He and his father had been influenced by the philosophy of personal responsibility and community activism both had been exposed to as campers—a generation apart—at Camp Killooleet in Hancock, long operated by Pete Seeger's brother John.

Instilled with the values of shared wealth and shared responsibility espoused at Killooleet, Henry, who founded Carris Reels in 1951, was one of the first Vermonters to offer profit-sharing options to his employees; he made a point of employing people with disabilities and supported local arts programs, believing that a business prospers when it invests in the communities where it's located. Bill Carris grew up with those values, augmented by Killooleet's mandate to fight poverty and inequality whenever possible. Threatened by the draft, he enlisted in the army hoping to avoid being sent to Vietnam; his gamble worked and he spent his tour of duty in Germany. He returned to Rutland with his wife, Barbara, one child, and another on the way, determined to expand his father's work and philosophy with the goal of eventually putting ownership of Carris Reels in the hands of the employees. After he assumed company leadership in 1980, however, he faced economic challenges, including a devastating fire in 1981 and a severe recession. Nonetheless, he carried on with his plan, just more slowly. Since the company had many plants around the country, this was particularly daunting. It took twenty years, but Carris was convinced "it was just the right thing to do. It was the employees who were creating the capital and the family was getting the full value out of that. We had to make it right." Carris subsequently served Rutland County as a Vermont senator from 2006 to 2012. He remains particularly proud that Vermont has "one of the highest number [per capita] of employee-owned businesses in the country, companies of all sizes." Among them are large corporations like Carris Reels, Gardener's Supply, and King Arthur Flour, as well as small endeavors like Green Mountain Spinnery in Putney.

✳ ✳ ✳

Founded by progressives who in the 1970s set out with one goal—to create a company that would serve a social purpose—Green Mountain Spinnery is one of the few artisan wool companies in the country that uses no bleach or other environmentally harmful ingredients in its processes. It may be the only woolen mill in the country that is a worker-owned cooperative. Their 100 percent wool yarn is spun exclusively from New England fleece.

Like Bill Carris, David Ritchie, one of the Spinnery's founders, was relieved to avoid the Vietnam War by serving in Germany after graduation from Miami University of Ohio. Like Carris, Ritchie would not have called himself a hippie, but he embraced much of the counterculture mandate to make the world a better place. Having avoided war, Ritchie felt compelled to be more than grateful and enrolled in Vermont's School for International Training in Brattleboro in 1970 to prepare for a career in humanitarian work around the world.

After an internship in Ghana and a teaching job in Harlem, he began to think more closely about the message one of his professors, Norm Wilson, had stressed. Wilson, a Quaker, had been recruited in 1956 to teach in a graduate program created by Antioch College in Putney. The program was designed to prepare future teachers to approach social studies and history differently—to explore with students the economic, environmental, and social causes of world conflict and to get them thinking about possible solutions at an early age. The idea was revolutionary in that it postulated that a teacher's job was more than simply to present subject matter but also to use their classes as workshops for stimulating social activism. Wilson taught a similar course at SIT where he introduced the idea of making the world a better place by working in one's own community. This idea stayed with Ritchie in New York as he discovered he really missed Vermont. When he and his wife at the time returned, he took a job as codirector of Morningside House, a halfway home for people with developmental disabilities. After Wilson died, Ritchie attended a weeklong seminar held in Wilson's honor in which his ideas were explored more fully. Some attendees then formed a study group to move from theory to action.

Another member of the group, Bob Mills, had been impressed with the ideas of economist E. F. Schumacher, whose 1973 book, *Small Is Beautiful*, warned that globalization was unsustainable, that it would only bring First World problems to Third World countries. Schumacher postulated the idea of village-based economics in which people produced as much as they could close to home, relying as much as possible on renewable energy and local materials. Today, we call that locavore.

This idea resonated with the group, and they began thinking of a business they might create that would be of local use while not putting undue stress on the environment. It was in these sessions that Ritchie became close with Wilson's widow, Claire Wilson, and her friend Libby Mills, wife of Bob Mills. Bob and Libby Mills were teachers at the Putney School where Libby had created its weaving department and Bob had introduced environmentalism and ecology into the curriculum. Claire Wilson and Bob and Libby Mills were at least fifteen years older than Ritchie and his former wife, Diana, yet they embraced the young couple and their idealistic values. Indeed, Claire and Libby, who had met through their interest in fiber crafts and weaving, were thrilled that so many young people were becoming interested in environmental protection. "We liked the hippies," Claire said.

While Ritchie had demonstrated against the Vietnam War and against the Seabrook Nuclear Power Plant in New Hampshire, Libby Mills and Claire Wilson had taken the idea of demonstrating to another plane. They had joined the Clamshell Alliance with the express purpose of getting arrested. They were concerned that average Americans and government officials were dismissive toward the young demonstrators' concerns about nuclear power plants; they thought their presence as "older, middle-class women" might bring more legitimacy to the protests. Thus, in May 1977, when more than 2,000 protestors occupied the Seabrook site, the two women were among the 1,414 arrested and subsequently held for weeks after refusing bail. Their gambit proved successful as they and their views became the subject of news stories that went around the world. "You talk about the counterculture," Libby Mills said. "We were left of left."

Over the course of their discussions, the group considered possible endeavors that might allow them to "think globally but act locally." Nothing stuck until Claire Wilson realized the yarn she used "was coming from Scotland, Great Britain, Scandinavia, and even New Zealand, and meanwhile sheep were being raised in Vermont." At that time, Vermont's sheep industry was in decline and so were the mills that turned wool into yarn. Because there was little demand for Vermont wool, it was simply being wasted. "Foolishly, we thought, 'Let's see what we could do about this problem right here,'" she said. Now, starting a woolen mill was about the last thing that Ritchie had in mind when he envisioned a job that would make the world a better place. But, as the group studied the issue—the waste of wool from local breeders, the lack of American (never mind Vermont-produced) yarn, and the environmentally questionable processes used in commercial woolen mills—it became apparent that here was their contribution to the world.

They bought an old gas station, cleaned and expanded it, bought several vintage milling machines, hired people who knew how to run them, and began the process of convincing sheep farmers to save their wool for processing. That was often Ritchie's job, going to sheep farmers and asking them to take part in their endeavor. Some were suspicious, he said, and many thought the project unrealistic, but over time they convinced the breeders to trust them, and many increased their herds.

Also, from the beginning, they envisioned a company that would be employee-owned and operated. Thus, along with the work they already had taken on came countless meetings in which they ironed out bylaws, one person, one vote. All these decades later, the company employs thirteen people and is known for its fine yarn and patterns, designed by none other than Claire Wilson and Libby Mills. Today, also, Green Mountain Spinnery remains one of the few woolen mills producing 100 percent wool yarn, much of it from Vermont sheep, and processed without bleach, mothproofing, or other harmful chemicals. Ritchie is the only founder still working at the mill. For him the work is part and parcel of his pleasure in living in Vermont, of being part of a small community, of doing something useful and beautiful. "Something significant came out of that time, deep relationships with the land and the people," he said, noting that it was better to do his service in Vermont than anywhere else, to be a small part of a movement that "has made Vermont a place people know and admire for its values, for being committed to doing what's right."

* * *

T-shirts? Unlike producing artisanal wool on antique equipment, screen-printing T-shirts as a way to make money was a no-brainer. But while many counterculture entrepreneurs tried silk-screening, printing, or otherwise making cash with one of the generation's most ubiquitous items of clothing, Wayne Turiansky excelled with T-shirt designs that spoke to the generation's enjoyment of topical messages and quirky sayings, whether it was the Anita Sucks Navels offering created to mock Florida citrus spokesperson and pop singer Anita Bryant's antigay campaign, or the Vermont Ain't Flat classic sporting a bicyclist approaching a challenging, curvaceous hill that, not coincidentally, wound uphill across the chest.

Turiansky and his former wife, Kathryn, moved to Salisbury in 1972 when she got a job at the Vermont Achievement Center, a residential center in Rutland for young people with disabilities then known as the Vermont Association for the Crippled. Answering an ad in the Rutland Herald, they found themselves renting the Barnstone house in Salisbury where so many other hippies, back-to-the-landers, and feminists lived before and after them, instantly part of a network of like-minded people. Turiansky went to work for Democratic presidential candidate George McGovern's campaign, along with a young David Wolk, the Rutland native and future president of Castleton University, then joined the hippies working at the Brandon Training School.

A "born Democrat," Turiansky grew up on Long Island, flunked out of Bard the year he discovered LSD, then graduated from New Hampshire's Franconia College, from which he discovered Vermont, falling in love with the state on his first visit. Laid off after just one year working as a teacher at Fair Haven Union High School, he decided to go to graduate school in Florida. It was there that Turiansky's Amalgamated Culture Works T-shirt business was born with the Anita Sucks T-shirt and others with iconic messages. Back in Vermont, Turiansky—known to his friends as Crunch Debris, the meaning of which is too convoluted to explain—opened the Emperor of Ice Cream in downtown Rutland, where you could get ice cream *and* live music, an instant but short-lived success before delving fully into the T-shirt business. Some lean years followed: long hours selling shirts on the bridge outside Fenway Park and at fairs and farmers' markets within a few hours' drive. Printing was done in the barn that happened to be the couple's home in Wallingford. But at some point—and Turiansky has given up on figuring out how or why—the T-shirts began to have a cult following. Perhaps it was their wit, such as the classic sporting a cartoon of President Ronald Reagan and his wife above a slogan that read, "You say Reagan, I say Raygun; let's call the whole thing off." The shirt, produced to deride Reagan's Strategic Defense Initiative, often referred to facetiously as Star Wars, sold well in magazines like *Mother Jones*, *Mad* magazine, and *National Lampoon*. Each advertisement prominently announced the company's quirky name, Amalgamated Culture Works, and its equally odd motto, "Specialists in replacement parts for a decaying society."

By 1982, Turiansky's Vermont-themed shirts were selling in more than one hundred stores, requiring him to rent production space in downtown Rutland and hire employees. A few years later, Turiansky moved the company to its current production center in Burlington, where his custom designs and charity discounts have increased the brand's cachet. From 1981 when the company sold $33,000 worth of T-shirts to 2016, Amalgamated Culture Works is now a $1.5 million business with nine employees and progressive benefits

Wayne Turiansky, founder of Amalgamated Culture Works, in the Emperor of Ice Cream Days.
Courtesy of Wayne Turiansky

that reflect Turiansky's belief that "If you treat your staff well, in all ways, you will be rewarded in the end." He has remained the sole proprietor.

An avid bicyclist who divides his time between Vermont and Montreal, he attributed his success and happiness to Vermont. "It's not even a question as to whether the counterculture changed Vermont," he said, "but the change was more the other way. We came pissed off at what was happening to our generation being sacrificed in Vietnam by the Masters of War, and all of a sudden we were not angry any more because we were accepted by Vermonters. I can't remember anyone telling me to get a haircut." He found comfort living in a place where billboards were prohibited and even the Republicans had the sense to protect the environment through laws like Act 250. "It's a rational place, and a transcendent place," he said. "That's why we wound up here."

* * *

Lisa Lindahl's success was also a no-brainer: she's just amazed no one had thought of it before her. It began in 1975 when her sister complained that she loved jogging but couldn't find a bra that was comfortable, one that would keep her breasts from chafing when she ran. Lindahl, then a graduate student at the University of Vermont, had recently taken up jogging with the same complaint. As it turned out, Lindahl's childhood friend Polly Smith happened to be in town working as costume designer for the Burlington Shakespeare Festival. On a whim, Lindahl solicited Smith's help in designing a comfortable sports bra. They were having little success until Lindahl's former husband quipped something like, "What you need is a jockstrap for your breasts." The two women quickly sewed two jockstraps together using the sewing machine in the costume shop at UVM's Royall Tyler Theatre—and voilà—after several alterations, the course of women's exercise was transformed, and a multimillion dollar business first called Jockbra was created. After Lindahl incorporated Jogbra in 1977, she sent equal shares to Smith and Hinda Miller, also a costume designer who became Lindahl's longtime business partner. Considered the first commercially successful bra for active women, Jogbra was sold to Playtex in 1990. "It was all part of the playfulness and sense of exploration and invention of the times," Lindahl said. "You got an idea and you tried it. I wasn't into drugs because I have epilepsy, but I was certainly into mind-expansion and reinvention. It was a time when you had the sense that most anything was possible."

The women have gone on to other successful endeavors. Miller became a Vermont state senator and business consultant who ran for Burlington mayor and became a member of the Vermont Cannabis Collective. Smith has won seven Emmy awards for her work as a costume designer for *The Muppet Show* and *Sesame Street*. And Lindahl, after helping to design a compression garment for breast cancer patients and long serving as the vice president of the board of the Epilepsy Society of America, authored the book *True Beauty*, an exploration of "true" beauty—using the Aristotelian idea that wherever you look, there was beauty—and how to put that knowledge of beauty into actions that would benefit the world.

A bronzed example of an early Jogbra is displayed near the Royall Tyler Theatre's costume shop at UVM, while another is displayed at the Metropolitan Museum of Art in New York. Two others were featured in a Smithsonian National Museum of Art exhibit of items that helped women gain greater independence. In naming the invention of Jogbra and Title IX, the law that opened up athletics for girls and women, as major milestones in women's liberation, the Smithsonian said, "Until the Jogbra's appearance in 1977, incalculable numbers of women were too discouraged to participate in impact sports such as running or aerobics because of the discomfort or embarrassment."

* * *

"I couldn't have done it without psychedelics. They took me from Katy Gibbs to marching with Daniel Ellsberg, listening to Jimi Hendrix, and hanging out with freaks in Copley Square," Melinda Moulton said as prelude to the story of how she evolved from a student at Gibbs's "secretarial school" to a hippie transplant in Vermont to cofounder of one of the most successful and purposefully sustainable development companies in Vermont. In the process, she helped shepherd Burlington's waterfront from a toxic, petroleum-polluted dumpsite for abandoned boats, its shoreline littered with a rat-infested granary, decaying fuel tanks, and dying businesses, to a successful marriage between commercial use, art, recreation, tourism, and nature.

But not without challenges. Of course, if there's one thing you learn about Moulton within minutes, it's that she's a no-holds-barred woman, proud of her hippie past and comfortable saying that it was her lack of experience, her "naiveté," that helped launch her career. She's also far from self-conscious about her education at Katherine Gibbs College, often dismissed as simply a finishing school for girls looking for a husband. Yes, "we wore pillbox hats and gloves," she said, but Katy Gibbs, as Moulton affectionately called her alma mater, was about more than manners. She remembered its founder as a woman who instilled organizational and management skills in students and promoted the idea that women would make great executives. "I've never had an assistant. I answer my own phone because I'm the best assistant there is," she said. "Katy Gibbs taught me well." Believe that but believe this more: Moulton is the kind of person who can wring the most benefit out of just about any situation.

She had learned the rudiments of the building trade growing up in Allentown, Pennsylvania, where she trailed her father, a developer, on the job after her mother died when she was twelve. She wanted to be a doctor but he enrolled her in Katherine Gibbs in Boston. As soon as she graduated, she abandoned pillbox hats and gloves, instead embracing the dress and culture of the sixties. Hippie to her core, she was working for a famous Harvard microbiologist when she met Rick Moulton, an adventurer who had shot films about surfing in Hawaii with the appealing names *Freedoms* and *Oceans*. They spent the summer with ten other people in Westford, not far from the Canadian border. Their bed was a hammock hung in a sugar shack. When it came time for Rick to return to Denver to finish his degree, she moved with him. There, the first of their two children was born. It was sixteen years before they married. In Denver, they found the water undrinkable and the landscape harsh. They returned to Vermont and bought a "ten-acre hayfield in the shadow of Camel's Hump" in Huntington with money Moulton had inherited from her grandmother. Having grown up in a stone house, she insisted they build one of their own, using the slip-form method reminiscent of Scott Nearing's simple buildings. She talked a farmer into letting her pick fieldstones off his land in Starksboro, thirty-six truckloads with her son on her back, then hauled them in her battered truck to Huntington. Perhaps they spent more on pot and beer than on the house that summer because by October, when there was six inches of snow on the ground, there was still no roof on the structure. By Easter, the house was complete enough to move into, and six years of homesteading and parenting began. All the while, Rick developed his documentary film business, including the award-winning *Legends of American Skiing*. By the time their daughter started school, Moulton, like Steve Sherrill and so many other counterculture kids then raising children, realized the family needed insurance and consistent income.

In 1983, Bernie Sanders began his second term as mayor of Burlington, and the Alden Waterfront Corporation founded by Lisa Steele and her former husband began looking for an operations manager. Steele had purchased a majority of the available property that could be commercially developed along the waterfront and needed help creating a development plan for the property. With essentially no experience, Moulton got the job. For three years, she educated herself on market and budget projections and other unfamiliar subjects while the development proposal, the $100 million Alden Plan, was prepared. Controversial from the start, in 1985 voters soundly defeated a bond proposal to bring the plan to fruition. Residents considered its inclusion of retail stores, high-end condos, a parking garage, offices, and a seven-story hotel anathema to their concept of revitalization. Sanders had backed the plan, one that many of his supporters thought was not much of an improvement over a previous plan he had fought against. Indeed, the voters' rejection could have derailed Sanders' political ambitions, but the story wasn't over yet even though Moulton and Lisa Steele were so devastated they initially abandoned the project. Moulton took a job as marketing director for Lake Champlain Chocolates, while Steele tried to tidy up the loose ends of the failed endeavor. Even that was an overwhelming task. One day she called Moulton for help. Moulton agreed to come back, but only if they would try to do it again—and right this time. That was exactly what Steele wanted to hear. They named their new company Main Street Landing and moved into the old Union Station at One Main Street.

"We created a new master plan based on localism, affordability, lots of green space, a focus on the arts, putting the 1960s values ahead of accepted business practices," Moulton explained. "As with the thinking during the hippie and freak movements, we began with the idea that anything is possible and sometimes not knowing what you can't do is a wonderful, freeing thing. We didn't have the Internet back then. We couldn't just look it up. We didn't have a model to build on. We just had such unhappiness with the status quo, with rules that didn't make sense, with restrictions that cramped creativity, with what hadn't worked, that we chose to operate differently" the second time around. When they applied that approach to the project, putting goals and values first, such as setting strict green principles for design and construction, they found themselves in relatively new territory. "We had to discover how to do it. And we did."

That's where the lessons from taking psychedelics came in. They helped Moulton understand the complexity and interactivity of the world, and led her to embrace possibility. She and Steele assembled a team of architects to help with the designs, met with community members to gather viewpoints and created a twenty-five-year plan for the property. And, rather than accept common practices, they made green values the bottom line, beginning with the renovation of Union Station. When engineers advised windows that didn't open — cheaper, they were told — they insisted on windows that did, used as much recycled material as possible, banned petroleum-based products and toxic paints and carpeting from the building. This was, of course, just before the epidemic of "sick buildings" that couldn't breathe and were full of chemicals from carpeting and prefab cubicles. As for the wider project of managing the waterfront renovation, the property is generally considered a successful blend of uses. It boasts a community boathouse, sailing center, and science museum, a fishing pier, an eight-mile bike path, and acres of public beach and parkland with a minimum of small-scale commercial development.

Moulton wore her hippie dress, a splash of blues and mini, of course, to the Vermont Historical Society's 2016 conference, where organizers showcased the society's two-year project to capture the stories of the hippies and freaks and back-to-the-landers who came to Vermont. Moulton was among those who told her story, warts and all. Of course, happy endings go a long way toward being open. Toward the end of the daylong conference and in response to hearing about all the accomplishments the counterculture generation had brought to Vermont, one attendee complained that the world still faced many of the same problems that the hippies had identified and that, despite their efforts, there was still war and injustice and a bad election going on. Moulton was the one to respond. "I'll tell you what I tell my children," she said. "I'm sorry we didn't make it right for you. The world is coming back to a lot of things that frightened me as a young person. We tried to turn it the other way. The problem was we were just a small part of a large generation. We were never the controlling group of our generation."

But, in Vermont, she said, "We have a chance. We still have a chance."

As she pointed out, in creating new businesses that bring jobs into Vermont without putting undue stress on the environment—jobs like those created by Don Mayer at Small Dog Electronics, or Dave Sellers's sustainable architectural ventures in Warren, and Will Raap's Gardener's Supply and Intervale Center for growing and educating people about healthy eating in Burlington—Vermont continues to lead the way in innovation.

Ever the hippie optimist.

* * *

Talk about a long, strange trip. Few business owners profited more from the idea of Vermont as a hippie haven than Ben Cohen and Jerry Greenfield, the world-famous creators of Ben & Jerry's Homemade Ice Cream. Even today, the level of their success baffles the two men, and they know they owe much of it to the early failures that led them to Vermont. As Greenfield put it, "We were latecomers to the scene but we fit right in with Vermont and the times. It didn't take long to realize this was the right place for what we wanted to do." Greenfield was speaking in the partners' downtown Burlington office where the conference room is called the Cookie Dough Room, a picture of Bernie Sanders is on the wall, casual Friday is every day, and it is still a place where people could bring their values to work.

"If you open up the mind, the opportunity to address both profits and social conditions are limitless. It's a process of innovation," Greenfield said, summarizing what could be the company's mantra, one that resonated with Moulton's ideas about possibility. For Ben and Jerry, though, it didn't hurt that their product was really, really delicious. Simply put, their success was built upon producing something people loved enough and were willing to pay a little more for, especially as they were vaguely aware that they were supporting a business that took care of its employees and the environment. But don't give them too much credit. There was much about their success that was just a little bit shit blind luck and a lot of being in the right place at the right time.

Ben Cohen and Jerry Greenfield of Ben & Jerry's Homemade Ice Cream.
Photo by Erin Zimmer; courtesy of Jerry Greenfield

In many ways.

The two men were born just four days apart in 1951 at the same Brooklyn hospital but didn't meet until gym class in junior high where they both got yelled at for running the mile too slow and were ordered to do it again. Greenfield knew he and Cohen would be friends when he heard Cohen yell out, "Hey coach, if I didn't do it in under seven minutes the first time, I'm sure not going to the second."

After college, while Greenfield tried to get into medical school, Cohen worked at a school for at-risk kids in upstate New York. The school was close to Burlington and he found himself visiting frequently and loving the city's vibe. When med school didn't work out for Greenfield, the two decided to go into business together. Since they'd both had stints scooping ice cream and still loved ice cream, they settled on the idea of opening an ice-cream business featuring homemade ice cream. They split the cost of a $5 correspondence course in ice-cream making from Penn State and began looking for a college town in the South without an ice-cream shop. Finding none but convinced that ice cream and college town were a natural union, they kept looking north—all the way to Vermont. It turned out that Burlington, with its five area colleges, had no ice-cream parlor. Greenfield had never been to Vermont and fell in love instantly, but discovered the true meaning of cold when the two rented a summerhouse on Lake Champlain for the winter. The house was fairly isolated as well. As they worked on their plan, they took jobs working for Caryl Stewart, who had opened the Bennington Potters North store in 1974.

During the 1977 Christmas season, Stewart decided shoppers needed a warm reprieve and hired Cohen and Greenfield to serve hot drinks and cookies to anyone wandering in. "Money wasn't the important thing for her —or us," Greenfield recalled. Indeed, the job gave them something more important than money, a way to meet local people while staying warm. "We made fresh eggnog every morning, made cookies in a toaster oven. If you told us a joke and we laughed, you got a drink. It was easy to make us laugh."

Their venture began in 1978 with the rental of an old garage for $12,000, with $4,000 of it borrowed. Within a few years, the word was out, and they had outgrown their second home in an old spool-and-bobbin mill on South Champlain Street. About then, they also began opening franchise stores. Will Patten's in Rutland was the second in Vermont. Will had been an early devotee, served Ben & Jerry's ice cream at the Back Home whenever Ben delivered some in his old Volkswagen.

The garage where Ben & Jerry's began.
Courtesy of Jerry Greenfield

As they grew, Greenfield and Cohen were determined to keep social consciousness central to their business model through something they called linked prosperity. "As the community prospers, we prosper," Greenfield said, echoing the Carris Reels motto. Thus, to thank Vermont and Vermont customers while raising money for a new manufacturing plant, they created a Vermont-only stock option in 1984. Simultaneously, they established the Ben & Jerry's Foundation under which 7.5 percent of the company's annual pretax profits would fund community-based projects.

They were already buying their five core ingredients—sugar, cocoa, bananas, coffee, and vanilla—from fair-trade-certified companies and using packaging that passed strict environmental standards. Then along came Monsanto's bovine growth hormone, an injection given to cows to increase milk production. Farmers enjoyed getting more production from their cows but some consumers were wary of milk from hormone-treated cows. Monsanto didn't mean to give the men a gift but, after Cohen and Greenfield announced they would use no milk from cows that had been treated with growth hormone, the popularity of their ice cream increased dramatically. That was only the first volley in the debate over genetic modification of food products, one that has repeatedly put Vermont in the national spotlight.

The controversy occurred alongside President Reagan's recognition of Ben & Jerry's Homemade Ice Cream as small business of the year; the introduction of Cherry Garcia, Wavy Gravy, and Phish Food ice-cream flavors; free concerts and free cone days. Through its foundations, the company helped dozens of community action groups and encouraged other sustainable businesses. It was a partner in Farm Aid, for example, and championed the Children's Defense Fund campaign.

In all, an amazing trip.

In 2000, all that threatened to melt into memory when lessening stock returns led to the company's acquisition by Unilever, one of the world's largest corporations with more than four hundred brands, for $48 million. While the partners negotiated the best deal they could, many supporters were devastated. Yet, it does seem remarkable that a company the size of Unilever would agree to the founders' progressive demands, especially as many stockholders wanted the deal. Unilever could have played hardball. Instead, the stockholders were made whole while Unilever pledged to support the Ben & Jerry's Foundation and maintain its structure under which employees were the ones who chose what projects to support. Unilever committed to continue donating 7.5 percent of Ben & Jerry's profits to the fund while also pledging $5 million of its own money to it. They donated yet another $5 million to help minority-owned businesses and for support of poor neighborhoods. Yet another $5 million was distributed among employees, whose jobs Unilever said would not be reduced. For lovers of Chunky Monkey and Chubby Hubby, Unilever committed to not altering the way the ice cream was made. That must have been some negotiation that Cohen and Greenfield pulled off, but they've not spoken much about the details.

Greenfield remained president of the Ben & Jerry's Foundation, which has four trustees. However, "the trustees are essentially a rubber stamp in terms of who gets the grants," he explained, as it's a committee of employees that actually reviews and decides the allocation. "They do the work that brings in the money and so they ought to be the ones making the decisions." Cohen chairs a committee that oversees Unilever's policies and procedures, helping the company make sound, sustainable decisions.

Here's another example of the idea postulated in Pollak's hippie invasion story—how changes made in a small state could stimulate change in the wider world. "We're both very concerned about the corrupting influence of money on the political situation. In a way, we can concentrate even more of our efforts on issues we are concerned with, and we've had an impact on Unilever, such a huge company," Greenfield said.

One cause got them arrested on April 19, 2016, as, sporting Bernie for President signs, they joined hundreds of Democracy Awakening protesters demanding a fair hearing on President Obama's Supreme Court nominee and the overturning of Citizens United. Within the company, Greenfield has been involved in an initiative addressing climate change, while Cohen has dedicated himself to the issue of mandatory labeling of products containing GMOs, an effort that led Vermont to pass the first-in-the-nation law requiring labeling of GMO-modified ingredients. That law was subsequently nullified by a less specific and, for supporters, less useful federal law.

And while the new jobs allow them to "essentially do whatever we want, which of course is pretty far out, I think we'll remain constructive," Greenfield said. "It's just in our nature."

* * *

A few years ago, Patten, who began his career by bringing people together at the Back Home Café, created a similar space for residents of Hinesburg, the town he moved to when he launched his career as Ben & Jerry's director of retail sales, overseeing six hundred franchises around the world. He subsequently was executive director of Vermont Businesses for Social Responsibility, helping that organization's membership grow. One day, sitting in the Bobcat Café, a gathering place for residents in nearby Bristol, it dawned on Kathleen and him that Hinesburg needed a place like the old Back Home. With a $200,000 investment and $500 shares to local investors, they renovated a long-closed factory in the center of town into the Hinesburg Public House, serving "hearty, healthy, made-from-scratch and locally sourced Vermont food." Their version of giving back not only focuses on buying Vermont produce and meat but extends to Kathleen's volunteer efforts with Vermont Works for Women and as a mentor to incarcerated women prisoners.

Occasionally, they go for long sailing trips together, each time "knowing that when we sail out of here, we will see beautiful places, but we'll never see a more beautiful place," Kathleen said. "That's because our heart is here."

* * *

For some counterculture entrepreneurs, making a Vermont dream a reality took patience, hard work—and courage. Marcy and Andy Tanger of Mount Holly set their eyes on owning a Vermont country store and living in a place in synch with their political views but waited until they had enough money to survive the uncertainties of a new business in a new location before taking the leap. For five years, from 1972 to 1977, Marcy worked sixty deadening hours a week at a Pennsylvania insurance company, saving every penny while the couple lived off Andy's paycheck.

"I needed that security because my childhood was so messed up," she said. Marcy had spent her first years in Liberia and then Peru, accompanying her father Marvin Allison, the celebrated paleopathologist known for his research into the diseases of antiquity in humans and animals and their applications for modern man. He examined pre-Columbian mummies in Chile, ancient human remains in Africa, and a 5,300-year-old frozen Neolithic mummy discovered in the Italian Alps, all while treating local people, sometimes as many as one hundred a day, at his various clinics.

In Liberia, the family lived on a rubber-tree plantation; in Peru, in an oil-company town at the most western point of all South America. Marcy spoke the local languages, not English. "My first language was Grebo," the language of Liberia, she said. In Peru, she translated Spanish for the family. Suddenly, when she was six, her father sent her and her mother to the States and married a Peruvian woman. While her father and his new family led a comfortable life as he traveled and later taught at various universities, she and her mother struggled in a series of homes from Pennsylvania to Florida. The two moved so often she attended twelve schools before graduating from high school where she found herself a champion of her black classmates. Her love affair with Vermont began the summer of her twelfth year when she accompanied her father, stepmother, and two stepsisters to Quebec, all of them stuffed in a vw Beetle. She captured Vermont's gorgeous panoramas on her Brownie camera, the photos cherished still.

Andy spent a year researching possibilities before they purchased the Perkinsville General Store, which was established in 1837. On moving day in early May 1977, the couple had to stop on the Vermont border to put on their winter coats and awoke the next morning from sleeping on the floor to the reality of the work ahead. "Every square inch had to be done over, the entire store," she recalled. "We took carpentry courses while working twelve hours a day. For me, a lot of what I did came from my life living in Third World countries where you learn self-sufficiency. In Africa, my father went hunting once a week. There were nineteen people in our household. He hunted with and for them. In Peru, also, people lived with us and helped out. For me, they were our family and we were part of the community. I wanted to move to Vermont for that." When Governor Richard Snelling stopped by to visit, Marcy knew she was in a place far different from Pennsylvania.

The Tangers quickly became part of their community, not just in the village of Perkinsville with its population of just over a hundred people, but statewide, as they became friends with customers, vendors, and other small storeowners. In 1987, after ten years as storeowners and recognizing the impact of convenience stores moving into the area, they sold their store and moved to Mount Holly with their two toddlers, living in a tent and then the basement as they built their new home.

Andy became a rural mail deliverer while Marcy raised their two young children and became a fulltime political activist, over the years campaigning for local and national progressives running for office, working locally on environmental issues, and offering her home as a way station for the children of Guatemalan refugees so the children could attend the Mount Holly school. The family had been given sanctuary at the Weston Priory in the early 1980s but arranging transportation between the priory and Mount Holly was often difficult. When Senator Bernie Sanders urged people to fight the Citizens United ruling, she helped sixty-nine Vermont towns get a motion to that effect on town-meeting ballots.

Locally, she successfully campaigned for a $10,000 grant to help weatherize buildings in her town, winning the national Dorothy Richardson Resident Leadership Award in 2014 from NeighborWorks America and NeighborWorks of Western Vermont. More recently, working with Roland Marks, also of Mount Holly, she successfully found partners in a solar project located on Greg Cox's Boardman Hill farm in West Rutland. Vermont is now home to hundreds of solar arrays in which many owners or participants sell their renewable energy credits to other utility companies. In contrast, partners in the Boardman Hill project all agreed not to sell their renewable energy credits, making the project 100 percent green.

"I really wanted to make a difference in this world," she said. "In Vermont, we discovered a way to have security through hard work *and* make a difference in a place that's small enough that you can have an impact, and people see that and it encourages them to also make choices that benefit the world."

Political Transformation

Let's flash back to 1961 to the University of Chicago where members of the radical civil rights group the Congress of Racial Equality have discovered that the university was turning away black students attempting to rent its apartments. The university leadership explains that the situation had grown from long-entrenched housing policies and they were doing their very best to address the problem. A scruffy New Yorker stands up at a heated meeting about the issue to declare, "It is an intolerable situation when Negro and white students of the university cannot live together in university-owned apartments."

The young man was Bernie Sanders, chairman of U of C's chapter of CORE, living away from Brooklyn and his parents' three-and-a-half-room apartment for the first time. A serious student—although his grades didn't always reflect that—somewhat nerdish, and always passionate, as when he helped to organize the first civil rights sit-in in Chicago history, Sanders had been arrested as part of his antiwar activities and joined the Young People's Socialist League. Just a few years later, he was in Vermont, campaigning for national office on a platform that included an end to compulsory education, legalization of drugs, and a guaranteed minimum wage.

Given this history, who in the intervening years could imagine that this fervent activist with unmanageable hair and a sometimes irascible personality would be seen fifty-five years later dancing on television with the lesbian comedian Ellen DeGeneres as a serious candidate for president of the United States?

Sanders's popularity in the 2016 and 2020 presidential races was almost as remarkable as his rise to power in Vermont, where, after four unsuccessful races for national office as a candidate with the antiwar Liberty Union Party in the 1970s, he stunned the pundits in 1980 by beating Democratic incumbent Gordon Paquette to become mayor of Vermont's largest city, Burlington. From there, Sanders went on to defeat a young and popular Republican, incumbent Peter Smith, for Vermont's lone seat in the U.S. House of Representatives and then was elected U.S. senator, a position he has held since 2006.

But while his popularity as a presidential candidate had much to do with the mood of the country as its divisions along economic, class, racial, and gender lines became more apparent, in Vermont, almost more than anything else, Sanders's success illustrated something else entirely. In an odd way it explained why the counterculture took root in what was once considered one of America's most conservative states. From the standpoint of many Vermonters who tend to be socially liberal and fiscally conservative, Sanders's championing of the little guy, his humble economic background, and his willingness to disagree with the Democratic, Republican, and even the Progressive party cemented his reputation as an independent thinker. Throughout his terms, he has remained accessible to constituents, holding town meetings statewide where his support for veterans, workers, and health reform have held center stage.

* * *

The transformation of Vermont from red to blue, albeit with many moderate and conservative Republicans in the mix, was certainly due to the impact of young out-of-staters and Vermonters from the baby-boom generation. But it should also be noted that Republicans helped bring about this evolution—or devolution if you happen to think Vermont has been bankrupted financially and morally since the 1960s.

For, while Sanders was still organizing sit-ins and studying radical politics at the University of Chicago, a crew of forward-thinking Vermont politicians on both sides of the aisle was challenging the status quo, eventually upending 108 years of Republican dominance. In 1962, just a few years before the hippie invasion, members of the so-called Aiken-Gibson wing, named for two popular politicians who had been governors and U.S. senators, George Aiken and Ernest W. Gibson Jr., were feuding with F. Ray Keyser Jr., who was running as an incumbent for governor. Aiken and Gibson supported Phil Hoff, the Democratic candidate, but neither could bring themselves to actually vote for the Democrat ticket. They got around that by "creating" two additional parties—Independent and Independent/Democrat—with Hoff the candidate in both.

A handsome and energetic legislator from Burlington, Hoff was a lawyer who had grown up in Turners Falls, Massachusetts. He was one of the more articulate members of the "young Turks," a group of eleven Republicans and a few Democrats who were shaking things up in Montpelier. Their ideas had begun to resonate with voters who felt it was time for Vermont to move forward. The support of Aiken and Gibson increased Hoff's legitimacy, so much so that, when the votes were tallied, the two new "parties" put Hoff over the 50 percent mark, a shocking development for a state that had elected a Republican to its highest state office since the party formed in 1854.

Hoff was reelected twice, in 1964 and 1966, and pursued sweeping initiatives in education and civil rights. He was the first Democratic governor to oppose the Vietnam War, leading to a rift with President Johnson, none of which was lost on those members of the counterculture looking for a place to settle. Hoff had become increasingly distressed about racism and inequality in the inner cities while worrying that Vermont youths needed more exposure to people of color. He brought his concerns to New York City mayor John Lindsay and, together, they founded the Vermont–New York Youth Project, a summer program that brought 300 minority students to Vermont to study, work, and play with 300 white Vermont kids. The program, which doubled Vermont's black population, revealed an embarrassing level of bigotry within Vermont and an undercurrent of simmering anger among the black students. Tensions were sometimes high during the program's second year, after which it was not continued by Hoff's successor, Deane Davis. Hoff was aware of inequity for women as well, and created the Vermont Commission on the Status of Women, one of the first of such organizations in the nation. He endorsed Robert Kennedy for president, then campaigned for Eugene McCarthy after Kennedy's assassination. These stands, viewed radical by many Vermonters, may have led to his defeat in 1970 when he ran for the U.S. Senate. Yet, the changes he brought to Vermont, along with those promulgated by Davis from 1969 to 1973, were essential elements in the counterculture's flowering in Vermont. Without them, the hippies might have encountered an entirely different state.

Davis, a lifelong Vermonter and Republican lawyer, had been National Life Insurance Company's chief counsel and president. Governor when the *Playboy* article appeared, he successfully calmed local fears. But it was also during his terms of office that perennially divisive laws, oddly still associated more with the liberal newcomers than with Republicans, were passed. Paramount in these was Act 250, the state's pioneering land-use regulation that

Davis saw as an enticement rather than deterrent to business growth, given its protections of Vermont's aesthetic character.

Historian Garrison Nelson observed that, as the nation became more conservative and Vermont more liberal, even longtime Republicans were influenced by the newcomers and the ideas they promulgated. Living in Shrewsbury, a community with a healthy mix of old Vermonters and new, young liberals, had helped shape the views of U.S. senator James M. Jeffords, the scion of an old Republican family who in 2001 gave up the longest continuously held Republican seat in the U.S. Senate to protest President George W. Bush's education budget. Years before that, from 1975 to 1987, journalist and book publisher Steven Carlson, who grew up on the New Hamburger commune in Plainfield, had been Jeffords's chief aide.

The continued support in Vermont for U.S. senator Patrick Leahy, often described as among the most liberal members of the Senate, and more recently for Peter Welch, a left-leaning Democrat, the state's lone representative in Congress, show the power of the Democrats and Independents in Vermont.

Reflecting back, without the influx of the newcomers, it was unlikely that Madeleine M. Kunin would have won election as Vermont's first and only female governor, and questionable whether Howard Dean would have won reelection after being named governor with the sudden death of Republican Richard Snelling. Snelling was a popular moderate who, nonetheless, lost a try for the U.S. Senate against Leahy before winning his fifth term as governor, during which he died of a heart attack in 1991.

* * *

Put another way, while the more radical elements of the counterculture may have wanted to take over the state, it was the infiltration of less radical hippies and people sympathetic to their causes into every aspect of Vermont life, as parents and neighbors, teachers and carpenters, social workers and counselors, lawyers and bakers—and voters—that incrementally brought about the liberalization of Vermont. Arborist Eldred French provides a good example. He had no intention of being a politician when he moved to Vermont in the early 1970s, but spent four years as a Vermont legislator and two as state senator, serving on the Judiciary Committee when many of the state's most controversial recent laws were passed. In many ways, he and his wife Lily are the quintessential counterculture couple, their stories encapsulating the stereotypes of the era and its impact on Vermont while contradicting the usual labels. For while they sampled the temptations of the times, lived itinerant lives before marrying, embraced the back-to-the-land lifestyle, initially homeschooled their daughters, and remain dedicated to liberal causes, the two were fundamentally too industrious to be called hippies, although their neighbors probably saw them that way in their first years in Shrewsbury.

In Avon, Connecticut, Eldred attended Huckleberry Hill Elementary School, excelled in sports, was a good student, and accepted that, like his father and older brother, he would join the military after college. But when he tried to join ROTC at Tufts, he was deemed ineligible due to a heart murmur. "By the time I was a sophomore, I was so happy to have this piece of paper to show my draft board. I felt some guilt that I didn't have to go to Vietnam but not that I did not have to die," he said.

He's typical of his generation in Vermont in that he pursued a variety of avocations—teacher, shipmate, bartender, arborist, town-meeting moderator, and community church trustee—before being elected to the Vermont house. Lily has been a school speech pathologist and founded a paper-recycling business that she and Eldred ran long before recycling became de rigueur. While Lily came to Vermont to get an advanced certificate in environmental protection at Goddard, and stayed even though the program had been abandoned, Eldred has deep roots in Vermont. His grandmother owned a house in Chippenhook and later Shrewsbury and, from age eight to sixteen, he spent each summer at Camp Najerog on Lake Raponda in Wilmington. "I can remember driving up, how the landscape would change, the smell of manure, the openness," he said. At camp, "I went haying. I worked in a garden, milked, and showed goats. I was actually showman of the year one year. I even did theater there. It was heaven."

After college and a year circumnavigating the globe on a research ship, he was invited by the ship's captain in 1971 to work as an arborist in New Zealand. Needing a crash course in tree safety, he heard of an old Vermont tree man, a straitlaced old Swede named Hilmer Johnson of Proctor, who might need help. When Eldred showed up at his house, Johnson took a skeptical look at his wild Afro, but perked up when Eldred announced, "I want to learn as much as I can. I don't care what you pay me." Eight months later, he was in New Zealand as the Watergate hearings were being held, harvesting wood. He lasted a year. "Our news was their news. I wanted to be in the place where the news was being made," he said. Returning, he moved into his grandmother's house, discovering an old sauna attached to the house, met Dick Brigham, a young scamp from an old Shrewsbury family who welcomed him

Arborist Eldred French of Shrewsbury became a Vermont legislator—state representative and senator—and community church trustee, none of which were on his radar when he moved into his grandmother's house in Shrewsbury in 1973.
Courtesy of Eldred French

with homemade white lightning and a woodstove for the sauna. "I was immediately taken under their wing," he said of the Brigham family and other multigenerational families in town. "I felt like I'd lived there all my life. It was a turnkey operation as a social scene. I smoked a lot of homegrown and had long hair but I was industrious. When I met Will Patten, I was introduced to the whole Rutland group, a lot of hippies, and tended bar at the old Back Home Café five days a week. The rest is history. Now, we're all each other's children's godfathers and we're grandfathers." At seventy-one in 2017, the founder of Acorn Tree Service was still climbing trees, along with his partner, Rob Barker of Wallingford, another member of the counterculture who has long served as a town selectman.

"I was a city girl," Lily French said, describing how living in Vermont changed her. "Now I could never live anywhere else. The quality of food and life and air and everything is so different you can never go back. I didn't know the difference between an annual and a perennial; now, I'm a gardener. My mother didn't can. Now, I can and freeze and there are weeks when we only eat food grown in Shrewsbury. You don't buy grocery-store meat anymore."

Even though Eldred lost his senate seat in 2014 after Republicans targeted him as vulnerable, he remains high on Vermont's citizen legislature. "When you are in the legislature and see the way Vermont does things, the way each person is essential to the process, to be there during the marriage-equality vote, for example, it was life-changing. I put my neck on the line right away," he said, recalling that when he was interviewed to replace a retiring senator, "I was clear how I would vote on the issue. I never cast a vote that wasn't in my heart. I think that's true of most Vermont politicians. There's not the impetus and pressure to vote party over conscience here. That's a rare and wonderful thing."

* * *

On the other hand, Bernie Sanders did have political aspirations from an early age. It was the antiwar Liberty Union party that gave him the opportunity to run for office. The party was founded in 1970 in an old seventeen-room farmhouse in West Rupert owned by former U.S. congressman William H. Meyer, a Democrat. That's right: While Hoff is acknowledged for breaking Republican control of the state's highest office, Meyer, a professional forester instrumental in founding the Vermont Natural Resources Council in 1963, had been elected to the U.S. Congress in 1958 as a Democrat. He served just one term, as his refusal to soften his stands on national issues—he advocated nuclear arms control and opposed the draft—led to four subsequent losses as a Democrat and, in 1972, as the nascent Liberty Union Party's candidate.

Sanders had the energy and commitment the party needed desperately as another of Liberty Union's founders, the perennial candidate Peter Diamondstone, was often in a state of disarray, so much so that within a few years Sanders became Liberty Union party chairman. By 1974, the party had garnered at least 5 percent of the vote, thus qualifying for major party status, but its candidates hadn't come close to winning elections. By 1976, Sanders had concluded that the party was at a dead end, and began running as an Independent or Social Democrat, first as mayor of Burlington and subsequently as U.S. congressman and senator.

Since the formation of Liberty Union, Vermont has seen many left-leaning third parties, including the Citizens Party, which was associated with presidential candidate Barry Commoner. Among other third parties have been the Rainbow Coalition, which grew out of support for the Reverend Jesse Jackson Sr.'s presidential bid, and the Natural Law party, which grew out of the Transcendental Meditation movement, as well as the Small Is

Beautiful Party, the Marijuana Party, the Green Party, the Vermont Grass-roots Party, and others. Fracturing of left-leaning parties hindered the candidates' chance of success, however, until statewide candidates took a chapter from the Aiken/Gibson book and began running as Progressive/Democrat. By 2017, using this tactic, Vermont had the most Progressives and Progressive-endorsed politicians serving in elected positions per capita of any state in the union, and organic farmer Dave Zuckerman, a Progressive, was elected lieutenant governor. But here's the interesting thing: Vermont has simultaneously been among the most balanced of states in terms of electing governors, with elections since Hoff usually going to a candidate of the opposite major party every few terms. It's gone like this: Phil Hoff, D; Deane Davis, R; Thomas Salmon, D; Richard Snelling, R; Madeleine Kunin, D; Snelling, R; Howard Dean, D; Jim Douglas, R; Peter Shumlin, D; Phil Scott, R. Of these, Davis, Shumlin, and Scott are native Vermonters. When it comes to the top state office, Vermonters apparently don't want it controlled by any one party for too long.

✳ ✳ ✳

One could argue that the early success of progressive candidates occurred because the young political activists recognized early on something Vermont politicians and political bodies had been ignoring, the fact that the state economy was in serious decline with as many as 85,000 Vermonters living at the poverty level by the late 1970s. As Greg Guma, author of *The People's Republic: Vermont and the Sanders Revolution*, pointed out, in reaching out to low-income people during his unsuccessful bids for national office and his successful campaign for Burlington mayor, Sanders brought many disenfranchised Vermonters into the political debate. Darcy G. Richardson, author of *Bernie: A Lifelong Crusade against Wall Street & Wealth*, agreed. "Vermont's worsening economy and growing distrust of established institutions, combined with its small scale, made the state fertile territory for the emergence of a third political party," he wrote. By stressing economic disparity and support for labor, Progressives were able to introduce other perhaps less palatable issues to a population that was generally quite patriotic and homogeneously white, campaign issues such as peace, health reform, and racial justice. How else to explain how the most rural and second-whitest state in the union, normally strong indicators of Republican strength, was President Obama's second-strongest state, surpassed only by his birth state of Hawaii.

Even though the national media tried to paint Sanders as a Vermont hippie, he was an activist, not a hippie. Sanders didn't care for marijuana, trying it only twice by his own account. Often, he was too serious for some of his commune friends, driving them crazy with endless political talk. Rather, he was hungry for conversation that might lead to political action, activism emanating from, as he put it, the knowledge that his "father's whole family was killed by Hitler."

Born September 8, 1941, in the Flatbush neighborhood of Brooklyn, he grew up lower-middle-class. His mother, Dorothy, the daughter of Polish immigrants, worked as a housewife, and his father, Eli, who'd immigrated to the United States from Poland, sold paint. After college, inspired by the promotional brochures he and his brother had encountered in their youth, he brought his first wife to Vermont where the two found eighty-five acres in Middlesex costing $2,500 in 1964. The property was thick woodland with just one building, a sugar shack with a dirt floor. They spent a few summers there before divorcing in 1966.

Two years later, he bought another property complete with an A-frame building in Stannard, a town *Mother Jones* writer Tim Murphy artfully described as "a tiny hamlet with no paved roads in the buckle of the commune belt." That summer, his son Levi was born.

Sanders's first jobs in Vermont included researching property records for the Vermont Department of Taxes and helping people apply for food stamps for the nonprofit anti-poverty group, the Bread and Law Task Force. He had applied for conscientious objector status, but the only grounds for being granted such a deferment were religious. "There's nothing about being Jewish that says you can't shoot a gun," Sanders told Russell Banks in a 1980 profile. While his deferral was denied, after numerous hearings and an FBI investigation, time was in Sanders's favor. At twenty-six, the various tactics resulted in Sanders simply being too old to be drafted. The Banks piece written during Sanders's third term as mayor is superlatively entertaining and insightful, albeit brutally honest with descriptions like this: "His tangled, prematurely gray hair is unfashionably long and looks permanently uncombed. He wears thick glasses of the plastic horn-rimmed variety preferred by serious graduate students in the 1950s, a striped short-sleeved shirt with the tail flapping over the baggy seat of dark brown corduroy trousers. His shoes are the kind of orange, moccasin-toed work shoes made in Taiwan and sold at K-Mart. On the basis of appearance alone . . . the mayor looks like a maverick in an eastern-university philosophy department who persists in embarrassing his colleagues, making them wish they'd never tenured him."

Bernie Sanders campaigning for mayor of Burlington.
Courtesy of Rutland Herald

Sanders's political life in Vermont began at Goddard College in 1971, at a meeting organized by Diamondstone. With Levi on his lap, Sanders raised his hand when the desperate call came for someone to run as the Liberty Union candidate for the U.S. Senate. In those early years, Sanders bombarded newspapers and radio news organizations with press releases focusing on workers' rights, sounding pretty much the same as when he ran for president. He also made celluloid filmstrips on historic subjects he felt were being ignored; these he sold door-to-door and to schools and libraries. There were fifteen in all, including a biography of Eugene V. Debs, the early twentieth-century Socialist. He also tried his hand at freelance journalism, writing what became rather embarrassing articles about men's sexual fantasies and the causes of cancer. None of this paid very well.

In one article entitled "The Revolution Is Life Versus Death," Sanders described the dreadfulness of a moronic, nine-to-five office job in which one's creative spirit would be sucked dry, leading to "suicide, nervous breakdown, cancer, sexual deadness, heart attack, alcoholism, senility at 50. Slow death, fast death. DEATH." Not exactly a formula for attracting support from farmers, factory workers, carpenters, and loggers whose long days for little pay left little time for contemplating their creative spirit.

It was a random meeting with Richard Sugarman, a religion professor at the University of Vermont that led to success. Sugarman came to UVM from Yale to teach philosophy, a part-time job that led to a tenured position and his creation of the Living/Learning Center where he has held court over the intervening years, part philosopher, part counselor—to both students and faculty. For twenty years he also directed the university's Integrated Humanities Program for first-year students. His influence on UVM students and on Vermont youth and the resulting impact on Burlington politics and elections cannot be underestimated. He seemed to be universally appreciated, winning all three of the teaching awards UVM offers, gaining accolades from students, faculty, and alumni alike over the decades.

Sanders and Sugarman met in 1976 on a train traveling from New York to Vermont. By then, Sanders had made the Queen City home. The two discovered they had much in common, ideologically and politically. Like Sanders, Sugarman was particularly upset that city employees couldn't afford to live in Burlington. Sanders was vaguely aware that Burlington was being run by a Democratic machine that wasn't much different from a Republican machine, one that favored those well entrenched in the business community, closed to new ideas and to including students in the city's power structure.

Sugarman urged Sanders to run against the incumbent mayor in the March 1981 election. He had studied Sanders's numbers in his statewide races, noting that, while his best showing was only 6 percent of the total votes, most of those votes had come from Burlington. He convinced Sanders that the campaign had to be about "things people care about," such as the health of neighborhoods, snow removal, and street paving. When his advice brought Sanders his first political success, Sugarman asked Sanders what was in it for him. Sanders's reply: "You get to be commissioner of reality," Sugarman recalled, laughing. "I've held that position ever since."

The Burlington establishment was far from happy with Sanders's election. During his first term, the establishment maintained control through their majority on the thirteen-member city council. But a few liberals had won positions on the board, including Terry Bouricius, the first city counselor elected from the Citizens Party. These outliers joined forces in what they termed the Progressive Coalition (the forerunner of Vermont's statewide Progressive Party). The coalition was able to maintain enough seats to keep the council from overriding Sanders's vetoes and helped him achieve a few of his earliest goals, such as forming a community-housing trust fund. With each subsequent election, Sanders's support grew, as did his margin of victory. *U.S. News & World Report* named him one of the nation's best mayors in 1988.

That popularity may have been attributable to his neurosis in following Sugarman's advice about taking care of the little things. Sanders was known for staying up all night during snowstorms, even going out to ride the plows. His wife, Jane O'Meara Sanders, whom he married in 1988 after a long courtship, raising her three children as his own, told NPR another sweet story, that of Sanders's resolve to bring baseball to the economically depressed Old North End neighborhood of Burlington. At that time, she headed the city's youth agency. Because there weren't enough kids to make up several teams, the North End team had kids aged six to sixteen. "It became the most compassionate and supportive place," she said. In that interview, she also talked about Sanders's love of Vermont, a love she shared, and said the most difficult part of his national success has been their having to spend so much time away from Vermont.

Coincidentally, Jane Sanders was raised traditional Irish-Catholic in a neighborhood just fifteen blocks from where Sanders grew up. Nine years younger, they didn't meet until Sanders's first victory party. She'd already been impressed, having arranged a debate between him and Paquette, hearing in his comments sentiments similar to everything she'd ever believed in. When he won, she volunteered to be on Sanders's task force on youth and, subsequently, from 1981 to 1990, headed the Mayor's Youth Office.

The official version of Sanders's tenure as mayor of Burlington is that he revitalized Burlington's shabby downtown and the Lake Champlain waterfront, fighting plans by developer Tony Pomerleau to convert the city's waterfront land into expensive condominiums, offices, and hotels, successfully spearheading instead a mixed-use area that includes a gorgeous, much-used public park complete with bike paths, all within walking distance of the popular Church Street Marketplace.

That's the short version, and not exactly accurate. Greg Guma, a progressive journalist and activist who ran unsuccessfully as an independent for Burlington mayor in 2015, pointed out that, before there was the waterfront deal Sanders likes to tout, he had supported the Steele project, a proposal that would have allowed considerable development of that precious Lake Champlain waterfront. Progressives and Democrats rebelled against what they considered a disastrous pact, forcing Sanders to renegotiate the deal with the help of Moulton and Steele, leading to the result he is now so proud of.

This and other actions over the years alienated Sanders from some of his former associates both in and outside of Vermont. Although Guma, for example, has voted consistently for Sanders and supported him in the presidential race, he criticized what he considered Sanders's obsession with workers' and veterans' rights to the detriment of other social issues such as the environment, women's issues, and peace initiatives.

And, although he has more recently been embraced by Vermont Democrats, Sanders has often angered the state party and its political leaders. For example, between his third and fourth terms as mayor, in 1986, he ran for governor as an Independent in a race that nearly cost Kunin the election. Then, again in 1988, Sanders ran as an Independent in a three-way race for the U.S. House against the popular young Republican Peter Smith, who had been lieutenant governor and founding president of the Community College of Vermont, and Democrat Paul Poirier, then a state representative. Sanders beat Poirier, while Smith commanded the lead with 41 percent of the vote over Sanders's 38 percent. Sanders's defeat of Poirier indicated that Vermonters were willing to support third-party candidates, even Socialists, but there was much political blowback from his running against a Democrat. Pundits suggested Sanders had blown his chance for national office.

History has an odd way of rearranging expectations. Smith was young, attractive, smart, and well spoken but he made a fatal mistake during his first term. As a candidate, he had promised to oppose all forms of gun control, gaining the backing of the National Rifle Association. Yet, as a rookie congressman, after hearing firsthand testimony from people affected by gun violence, Smith had an epiphany about gun violence in America and co-sponsored a bill that would have banned the sale of some assault weapons. He argued that it was a reasonable position: Who needs assault weapons to hunt in the woods?

The NRA was so outraged at what it considered his treasonous act that it vowed to defeat him. In that election, Sanders campaigned against national mandatory waiting periods for the sale of handguns, saying the issue should be decided state by state. The position resulted in his being the only Vermont candidate the NRA actively supported in 1990, spending as much as $20,000 on his campaign. Sanders felt safe in taking his position on the waiting-period issue, believing his more progressive positions protected him from being rejected by liberals, while it cemented his popularity with hunters and NRA supporters. This kind of quid pro quo continued to benefit him as he won every congressional race since then, and in 2006 ran successfully for U.S. Senate.

Despite success as a political outsider, the man who gave Sanders his first chance at politics became estranged from him. Diamondstone, who lost his home and the entire archive of the Liberty Union Party in a house fire in 2012, and was very ill when interviewed in 2015, said, "Even if Bernie was the candidate—and he very well could be—I won't vote for him. He's not a socialist any more. You can't be a socialist and say you're out to save the middle class. Socialists want to destroy all classes."

* * *

As Sanders's victory in Burlington suggests, the full impact of the countercul-turists on Vermont politics wasn't felt until fifteen or twenty years after their arrival. By then, many former hippies were serving on town committees and running for statewide offices. With the election of Howard Dean and Demo-cratic control of both houses in the legislature in the 1990s, that impact came to maturity, leading to contentious battles that pitted conservatives against liberals, with Vermont's passage of the civil union law the most divisive. In 2000, in response to a Vermont Supreme Court ruling, the legislature ap-proved civil union legislation, which stopped just short of making same-sex marriage legal. The following November's election became a referendum on civil unions, with the legislature and governorship at stake. Polls showed Vermonters were equally divided on the issue. Opponents organized under the slogan Take Back Vermont. Vermont's Catholic bishop Kenneth Angell actively campaigned against the law, urging Catholics to vote their "informed consciences." Six incumbents who had supported civil unions, five Repub-licans and one Democrat, lost their primaries. In the 2000 general election, Dean won reelection for the fifth time, becoming the second-longest-serving governor of Vermont with only Thomas Chittenden, the first gov-ernor of Vermont, exceeding him. Nonetheless, the fallout from civil unions caused Democrats to lose control of the Vermont house for the first time in fourteen years.

Ruth Dwyer, a conservative Republican from Thetford, had opposed Dean in 1998 and again in 2000. Dwyer had served on the Thetford school board and two terms in the Vermont house. Relatively unknown statewide before the 1998 campaign, Dwyer did quite well, earning 41 percent of the vote to Dean's comfortable win at 56 percent. In the 2000 election, she ad-opted the mantle of the Take Back Vermont movement with the same result, defeat. Dean garnered 50 percent of the votes, Dwyer 38 percent. Surprising the pundits, Anthony Pollina, a Progressive, came in third with almost 10 percent of the vote.

Dwyer took her loss hard as she believed she had been railroaded by the "liberal press." The experience was so disheartening that she said she would never again seek public office other than animal control officer. Indeed, she believed "it's too late to save Vermont. What we learned is that there aren't enough real Vermonters in the state to win." By real Vermonters, she didn't necessarily mean lifelong residents as opposed to newcomers with liberal ideas. Rather, she defined "real Vermonters" as independent people who "don't take government handouts, mind their own business, and want to hold on to the values that made this country." After her loss, she said she canceled her newspaper subscriptions and Internet service and got rid of her cell phone, and even avoided watching television. "I'm not alone. Many of us who believe in traditional values just can't stand to see what's happened to Vermont or the country we love. Vermont in particular has been taken over by the liberals, the educated professionals who think their values are more important than ours, even though their values are a joke. They highjacked Vermont and turned it into a material and craven place."

Her relative popularity foreshadowed the direction the country—and Vermont to a lesser degree—was headed. An Ohio native, Dwyer moved to Shelburne as a young girl. There, she adored going to football rallies, intercollegiate games, and taking part in other activities associated with UVM. The family subsequently moved to a farm in Thetford, where she graduated from Thetford Academy in 1976. When she enrolled at UVM, she envisioned it would be the way she remembered. She discovered within a few days that the college had changed. "UVM had become a hotbed of hippie radicalism," she said, which prompts the question of what she might have thought of Goddard or other more liberal schools. Nonetheless, a cherished dream was shattered. She lasted a year, returning home heartbroken and angry.

Dwyer subsequently felt Thetford had been highjacked as well. "I've lived forty-five years on this farm. This is where I feel I belong, except if I were to choose where I belong it wouldn't be Vermont. Thetford was a perfect place to watch the changes because they put the interstate in and Thetford suddenly became a bedroom community for Dartmouth and the hospital. All of a sudden, dairy farmers were replaced by highly educated, eloquent people who feel so superior to the local people, and this is the interesting part, they want to be accepted by the local people but they can't be because they don't share their values."

To illustrate her point, she told a story from when she was on the local school board and prepared to offer an amendment to level-fund the school budget rather than raise taxes for programs the "liberals" were promoting. Several longtime residents had pledged to speak out in favor of her position, but when the time came, "the teachers who wanted to raise the budget all jumped to their feet and accused me of being the equivalent of a mass murderer; not one of those people who promised to support me stood up. In that charged atmosphere, they were not willing to be humiliated."

She acknowledged that the political activists, back-to-the-landers, and urban professionals whom she felt changed her Vermont for the worse were open about their ideas from the beginning and had incrementally brought their goals to fruition. She also acknowledged that there had been ample opportunity for those of opposing views to counter their efforts. But she expressed a sentiment that became important in the 2016 presidential election, a sense that liberals talked down to them, using terms like "tolerance" and "diversity" as code words for suggesting that anyone who opposed them was morally inferior. "I don't like being made to feel that I'm inferior because I see moral issues differently. The irony is that the people who came here espousing freedom turned into the controllers. They won, we lost."

* * *

Be that as it may, after the 2002 election, a more moderate and well-known Republican, Jim Douglas—the same Jim Douglas who had headed Middlebury College's Republican Club—followed Dean. In doing so, he had campaigned against the former lieutenant governor under Dean, Doug Racine, emphasizing his belief that liberals under Dean had gone too far. While his statements were never as vitriolic as Dwyer's, his past experience as state treasurer, his campaign promise to bring jobs to Vermont, and his promise to fight efforts to legalize gay marriage resonated with the Take Back Vermont crowd. Neither candidate won 50 percent of the vote, sending the decision to the legislature, which selected Douglas who had 3 percentage points over Racine, a clear indication of how divided the state was on these issues.

Douglas went on to serve four terms, winning easily, although in 2008 his closest challenger in a three-way race was Pollina. The Progressive candidate had garnered 32 percent of the vote, outpacing Democrat Gaye Symington. That race again illustrated the divisions in Vermont, suggesting that Progressives could challenge both Democrats and Republicans. Pollina, of course, was well known to Vermonters as Sanders's longtime campaign manager.

In 2009, over Douglas's veto, the Vermont legislature passed the Marriage Equality Act, 100–49 in the house and 23–5 in the senate, perhaps leading to his decision not to seek reelection. More recently Douglas sounded nostalgic for a simpler and more conservative time as he lamented the changes that have occurred since he moved to Vermont from Springfield, Massachusetts, as a college student, changes he attributed to not just the counterculture generation but to their children and others who were influenced by counterculture values. The problem, he said, was that the "political majority wants to spend more money than we can afford and tax the rich, but there's fewer of them to tax," resulting in a "very high tax burden on the average person who's simultaneously finding it hard to get a job and a place to live." He suggested that unrealistic values, values borne out of hippie idealism, have kept Vermont from attracting businesses. And, he said, while Chittenden County has prospered and influenced the way decisions are made in Vermont, much of the state is "suffering. Idealism is great, but it doesn't feed the kids or pay for school and town budgets."

Bill Schubart of Hinesburg suggested that liberals might benefit from being more sympathetic to people like Dwyer who feel their version of Vermont had been destroyed. Schubart, who leans to the left, has led a most interesting life. An author and founder with his brother of Philo Records, which produced folk and classical albums, at age twenty-six he became the youngest chair of the Vermont Arts Council, serving in that capacity again at age forty-one. Like Dwyer, he was born elsewhere (New York City) and moved to Vermont while quite young, living in Morrisville with his rather independent mom after his father died in World War II prior to his birth. "What these [Take Back Vermont] people are responding to, I think, is the pace of change. More good than bad came out of the opening up of Vermont through migration, the interstate highways, all the elements that led to what we are today, including the counterculture's impact. There are elements, however, that do make me sad. I feel sad about the erosion of the cohesive element of our downtowns, some of which were civic, business, cultural, and religious institutions that held us together. The cultural ones are persisting but much of the rest is gone," he observed, suggesting that newcomers who hadn't grown up in Vermont communities where life revolved around church and community events didn't place the same value on these institutions simply because they were not theirs, and inadvertently failed to support them or support them sufficiently. The changes the Take Back Vermont supporters detested may have come to Vermont with or without the hippies, but they may have hastened them. Nonetheless, he added wryly, "You can't stop what they call progress."

Creativity

Painter Kathleen Kolb began nurturing her homesteading fantasy as a young girl reading Laura Ingalls Wilder's *Little House on the Prairie*. "I wanted that kind of rural adventure, that test against nature she writes about. I made fairy houses and loved moss almost more than anything," Kolb recalled from her home situated high on a rise surrounded by the higher ridges of Lincoln, a property where moss grows soft and emerald on a rock outside her door.

Decades after that childhood fantasy, Kolb is among Vermont's most successful painters, her material the landscape that attracted her and so many from her generation to Vermont in the first place. Along with stunning paintings of mountains, villages, and wildflowers, Kolb's work celebrates the people who have long worked those woods—loggers, mill operators, and foresters. As such, she is among the literally hundreds of people "from away" who found a place where they could pursue their creative endeavors while making a living, whether it was from crafts like weaving and pottery, as part of a network of musicians keeping the oldest of America's musical offerings alive, or people fashioning buildings and furniture with tools and techniques of the past reimagined for today.

Schubart, the Vermont Arts Council chair who brought youth into the organization, observed that "Vermont's art and cultural scene was enriched by those who came here beginning in the 1970s," expanding the cultural landscape and, in some cases providing cultural opportunities that weren't previously available. Schubart should know. Along with chairing the Vermont Arts Council board, he also served as a board member of the Vermont Symphony Orchestra and founding chair of the Vermont Folklife Center. He helped the Vermont Humanities Council become a self-standing organization and has assisted on a half dozen other cultural and community organizations over the decades. His own creative endeavors have included his work to keep roots music alive through Philo Records, his many novels, and thoughtful essays on contemporary life.

Schubart observed that many Vermont artists associated with the counterculture like Kolb or Woody Jackson, the painter of Holstein cows set against Vermont mountains and city landscapes who lived in the nineteenth-century clapboard colonial in Addison that housed a commune he moved into after graduating from Middlebury College, elevate professions like logging and farming in their art. In so doing, they are part of the state's long history of using Vermont itself as subject matter while reminding us of the practical partnership between man and nature.

Likewise, Vermont artisans have elevated old-time crafts to something both practical and beautiful. "When I was a kid, there weren't art-crafts people. People made tools. They made utilitarian things. If they were beautiful, that was an added bonus. But with this influx [of the counterculture], crafts morphed from utilitarian to aesthetic and everything in between. In my view, a very healthy thing that happened," Schubart said.

When Schubart joined the arts council, state funding went to two organizations, the vso and the Lane Series of concerts at uvm. One of his first acts was to democratize the allocations, giving grants that, for example, supported bluegrass, folk, jazz, and other musical performers and festivals, "opening up the idea that the arts council was there for everybody's art forms."

For Kolb and thousands of other Vermont artists, writers, musicians, and craftspeople, the support of organizations like the Vermont Council on the Arts and the Vermont Council on the Humanities has often made the difference between failure and success. Kolb knew that supporting herself from her art or living off the land would be financially difficult. While she nurtured her back-to-the-land fantasy in Cleveland where she grew up, when she enrolled at the Rhode Island School of Design she studied "weaving and pottery so I could make cloth and dishes. I thought, I'll be homesteading and might need them." Simultaneously, however, she took classes in watercolor painting and illustration so she'd have a fallback profession for earning money.

A former RISD student, Tim Fisher, got her attention when he introduced himself by saying, "I'm homesteading in Vermont." His wasn't the farm she had envisioned in her fantasies but, when she joined a group of friends visiting Fisher, she was taken in by "a grand old elm tree, its huge expanse comforting, and beyond it a sky full of stars. I felt so at home."

Fisher had grown up in Africa, one of four boys whose parents worked for the Foreign Service. Between two-year stints in D.C., they lived in Ethiopia, Rhodesia (now Zimbabwe), Nyasaland (now Malawi), and Uganda. His love affair with Vermont began his senior year at the Putney School. Fisher had always wanted to build a house, and at Putney, that dream returned. He wrote his brothers, who expressed interest in such a venture. Fisher rode his bicycle around southern Vermont searching for land they could afford, failing until a relative in Greensboro remarked that land in the Northeast Kingdom was selling for around $100 an acre, a bargain compared to land in southern Vermont. The brothers found the perfect property and, in 1968, Fisher was hired to tear down an old horse barn which he and his brothers used to build their first house, complete with eight-by-eight-inch beams, and situated atop a hill near a spring with beautiful water. It was their base for five years, the place they could gather together as they traveled, worked, and finished school. Unfortunately, the remote location proved to be its downfall when a fire broke out and the firemen couldn't get equipment up the hill.

But there were more dilapidated buildings to repurpose, and the second house he built was the one Kolb came to live in when she and Fisher married two years after their meeting. For someone who loved history, the Northeast Kingdom of the early 1970s seemed "almost frozen in time." Not that her family necessarily understood this step back into history. "I remember my grandmother saying, 'She could have had anything. Why give her silver, what's she going to do with it?'"

Fisher was fascinated with the slip-form structures Scott and Helen Nearing had built—simple mortar-and-stone houses constructed in stages by pouring cement around rocks positioned between forms and held together with rebar—and he began experimenting with the form. Meanwhile, the couple was actually homesteading: raising sheep, chickens, and vegetables, cutting their own wood, and making maple syrup on a commercial scale. Between the demands of work they worked on their art—Fisher carving wooden sculptures with hand tools and Kolb painting the landscape that surrounded her.

Life in the Kingdom could be lonely. "There weren't many people. We went to Hardwick once a week and that was my social life," Kolb recalled. That began to change with the influx of other hippies. "We could see the strong sense of outsiders and insiders; we lived in a community with a lot of summer people, a lot of interesting and educated people, but the divide was there. We weren't part of the summer community [but] we had entrée to it."

She came to understand the ways in which newcomer and old-timer were

Kathleen Kolb and the Fisher family in the kitchen, equipped with the necessities of homesteading: a wood-burning cookstove, cast-iron frying pans, and canning jars. *Left to right*: Brooksie Stanton, Jonathan Fisher, Kathleen Kolb, Timothy Fisher, Tony Fisher.
Courtesy of Kathleen Kolb

kept separate. For example, there was no access to Caspian Lake unless you owned property on it, and much of it was owned by out-of-staters. "We lived there full-time, so we knew what it was to gut it out in the winter. I had a lot of respect and romanticized the life and work of the people who had been there for generations. I admired them, people like Lewis and Nancy Hill, a fifth-generation Greensboro family; they ran nurseries, a berry operation, grew fruit trees, and hosta plants. Always so interesting. Lewis wrote a lot of books. He had an eighth-grade education but he was smart as anyone. I remember him saying, 'It's a good thing you all came. We missed a generation.' Lewis nailed it. He had a humble and appreciative attitude, not a Take Back Vermont attitude. He understood there was a problem [with a declining population in the region]. But we also understood that we were outsiders and always would be, even though I haven't lived in a house with backup heat in years.

"Philosophically, I wanted to respect the environment. I didn't want to change it; I wanted to be part of it. I've seen less of that over the years. I think now people want change without being sensitive to the fact that there's something here that determines the quality of the place. It's fragile. I remember the older women who did the hot lunch program at the school. I didn't want them to turn into something else, to be cooking out of the *New York Times* or the natural-food cookbook. But we created change in spite of ourselves."

That thinking may explain why her work often counters the idea that harvesting wood for human use is bad for the environment. She celebrates those whose practices reflect a balance between forest management and harvesting wood for fuel and furniture, buildings and paper, a position she's proud to defend.

As it turned out, Greensboro provided a kind of serendipity she benefited from. That summer community included a fairly sophisticated contingent from Princeton University along with professionals from New York and Boston. Among them were artists Claire and Eugene Fern. Eugene had taught at the Art Students League in New York City and New York Community College, but suffered a heart attack and wanted a less stressful life. In 1975, the couple moved to East Hardwick, built a little house, an art studio, and then a gallery, where Kolb had her first show.

In 1975 there wasn't a lot of entertainment in the Kingdom. The Ferns' gallery attracted people, people who wanted a piece of the Northeast Kingdom for their walls. And, because it was the Northeast Kingdom, the Ferns wanted to keep the artwork affordable. "That's how I began to get my name out, selling work for not very much. It was all about place and the affection for place, the farms and landscapes of that area," she said. Editor Tom Slayton noticed her work and celebrated it in *Vermont Life* magazine, which brought more attention and other shows.

That isolation may have kept the couple together, for, after their oldest child came of school age and they moved to Cornwall, the relationship began to fray. They rented for a year while Fisher renovated what both refer to as Kolb's dream home, taking apart and reconstructing an 1806 post-and-beam building. He found two ancient barns complete with slate roofs, had them moved across the frozen property in winter, and then the couple had their early American homestead, complete with two period barns.

When they divorced a few years later, Fisher sold the house and built a six-sided slip-form stone house next door. There, he too has pursued his art, creating whimsical, two- and three-dimensional painted pieces, structures composed of fiber and paper, and large woodcarvings. The couple have remained friends and raised their kids together. Fisher said both counterculture and back-to-the-land tags applied to him. He grows much of his vegetables, as does Kolb. As a builder, he observed that "Vermont has much more red tape and it's more expensive to live here than when we came. There are more permits required, not that I oppose that because the population has doubled and we need some protections. Vermont is a gorgeous place. I'm still in love with it."

While the Lincoln home where she eventually settled is surrounded by gorgeous mountains, she remained nostalgic about her time in the Northeast Kingdom. "It was a little museum of the past when we arrived. That was part of what I loved about it. I thought we had an opportunity to escape some of the mistakes that had happened in other parts of the country, but I do think there's been some consciousness, eye-opening for me, of how much change occurred between 1960 and 1975 and continues into today, some good and some bad, and there are always threats to the environment and the economy that have to be thought out carefully. I'm hopeful we can solve our problems, move forward without losing what is so precious to us. It won't happen unless we consciously work toward that, however, working together."

* * *

A sense of possibility, of making a difference, and a wealth of fresh material that had not been explored in the arts drew screenwriter and filmmaker Jay Craven to Vermont. When he met Howard Frank Mosher, the author of eleven novels set in the Northeast Kingdom, novels that celebrated the remnants of the self-ruling, self-reliant hill people living there, he knew the two would be a perfect match. Mosher too had once been a newcomer to the Kingdom, a lover of wilderness and ornery characters whose novels chronicled the time before the coming of the interstate and the counterculture. Craven has made five of Mosher's books into films, in the process bringing Mosher's celebrations of old Vermont to the big screen while garnering international acclaim himself.

Craven might at any time have returned to New York City, where he had made his first documentary film on the International House, an experiment in cross-cultural living connected to Columbia University. But he was enchanted by Vermont and its people and, within a few years, felt committed to the place that offered an artist the rare opportunity to belong to and contribute to the communities where they worked. He had learned the power of visual art as a tool for political consciousness-raising during his years on the forefront of the antiwar movement. The antiwar activist and political science professor Howard Zinn had been his mentor at BU where Craven was student-body president his junior year. He also became close with David Dellinger, whom he met in the autumn of 1970 after another Chicago Seven defendant, Rennie Davis, asked him to join a delegation of student leaders traveling to North and South Vietnam to negotiate with Vietnamese students. Craven agreed, but he had to be approved by Dellinger, the project's organizer. At their meeting, Dellinger asked Craven to commit to helping him organize a national antiwar demonstration planned for the coming May.

Craven and the other delegation leaders showed their ingenuity when the U.S. State Department blocked them from entering South Vietnam. They flew instead to North Vietnam by way of Laos, met with North and South Vietnamese, then flew to Paris for a press conference where they presented what came to be called the Peoples Peace Treaty. Upon returning to the states, Craven kept his agreement with Dellinger, traveling the country to garner support for the 1971 May Day action, three days of protest that led to the largest mass arrest of demonstrators—12,625 people—in U.S. history. American disapproval of Nixon and the war increased as millions saw television and documentary accounts of peaceful protesters being beaten and tear-gassed by police and military troops, many rousted from sleep in tent cities they'd set up near the Capitol for the May Day action.

As the antiwar movement climaxed and Nixon's presidency unraveled, on October 30, 1973, the night of the Saturday Night Massacre, so-named for Nixon's attempt to fire independent special prosecutor Archibald Cox and the resulting resignation of several top cabinet members, Craven turned to his girlfriend of the time, Patty Oldenburg Mucha, and announced it was time to get out of New York. What followed is a useful illustration of the ways in which progressive elements within New York's cultural scene had quickly become integrated into Vermont.

Mucha had been the wife of sculptor Claes Oldenburg, known for his large installations of public art, usually replicas of everyday objects. A poet and artist who once sang in a band with Andy Warhol, she traveled in circles that included Bob Dylan, John Lennon, and Abbie Hoffman. Getting out of New York translated into a visit to Kenward Elmslie, the writer, performer, and publisher who was Joseph Pulitzer's grandson. Elmslie lived at Maple Corners in East Calais, an area popular with the counterculture and innovative artists and writers. He commanded the couple to spend the next few days visiting real estate agents in Morrisville, Hardwick, and St. Johnsbury where in no time they found an old farmhouse slumping on the side of a hill with forty acres of beautiful land and bought it. The house was heated with a wood furnace, needing lots and lots of fuel. That first summer in Vermont, Craven borrowed a truck from a neighboring dairy farmer and took to the woods, but on his third day of logging, the truck's brakes gave out and he went careening down a very steep hill, baled out, broke his arm and spent his first winter in Vermont nursing a broken arm and researching Vermont history.

A year later, after he and Mucha broke up, Craven rented the oldest house in Danville for $50 a month. The catch: he had agreed to fix the ancient horsehair plaster walls in return for reduced rent, a nasty task. Meanwhile, he got a job teaching at the alternative Peacham School. He became aware that Vermonters had limited access to films, particularly older classics, and in May 1975 founded Catamount Arts, using it as a vehicle to show European and American film classics that he rented and showed in town halls, church basements, and colleges, traveling the state with a 16-mm film projector in the back of his Plymouth Valiant to bring these classics, along with more current independent films, to people who had no other access to them. At the Peacham School, he taught kids not only how to look at movies but how to make them; that was until 1979 when a bookkeeper embezzled $15,000 and the school closed. He renewed his energies in Catamount Arts, converting a second-story loft in St. Johnsbury and then the historic Post Office building in St. Johnsbury into a community center for films and performing art, a cafe, gallery, and school arts programs. Simultaneously, he earned a master's degree from Goddard, taught at area colleges, and produced two important documentary films. The first, *Dawn of the People*, was produced with Burlington filmmakers Doreen Kraft, the longtime director of Burlington City Arts, and Robin Lloyd, an activist with the Women's International League for Peace and Freedom. The documentary tells the story of how 65,000 Nicaraguan students went into remote regions of their country to teach reading and writing skills. Pete Seeger performed at Burlington's Memorial Auditorium to raise money for the film, whose purpose was not only to celebrate the Nicaraguan movement but also raise consciousness about the power of ordinary people to bring change to their own communities.

Craven's second documentary, *Gayleen*, profiled the self-taught artist Gayleen Aiken of Barre, who had been discovered by another New York transplant to Vermont, the artist Don Sunseri. Sunseri had left New York's

Jay Craven on the set
for *High Water*.
Courtesy of Jay Craven

progressive Little Red School House to move to West Glover in 1974. There, he discovered a wealth of untrained native artists whose work he began to promote. Sunseri went on to found GRACE (Grass Roots Art and Community Effort), an art workshop for the elderly and people with disabilities; it in turn became a national model for programs to help people with limited access express themselves through art. Craven's documentary brought international recognition to Gayleen Aiken and other grassroots artists who worked with the materials available to them, crayons and cardboard, for example, and paint straight from the tube.

All the while, however, Craven's goal had been to make narrative films. He hadn't found his material until he read Mosher's novel *Disappearances* and *Where the Rivers Flow North*. *Disappearances* was already optioned, but *Rivers*, a short story and novella collection, presented the opportunity to make a small film centered on one story from the collection as a way to gain financial and community support for something more challenging. The thirty-four-minute film based on the story "High Water" opened in St. Johnsbury with eight hundred people, including Governor Kunin, in attendance. Over the summer, he showed the short film in sixty-two towns and at numerous film festivals where it won award after award, putting him on the national map and helping him raise the money to produce *Where the Rivers Flow North*. As with most of his films, the *Rivers'* cast was composed of average Vermonters along with celebrities like Rip Torn, Michael J. Fox, Trent Williams, and Tantoo Cardinal. Governor Howard Dean made a cameo appearance.

The rest is history: three other movies made from Mosher's books and eleven films in all, recognized with an Emmy, and recognition from the

On the shoot for *Disappearances*, Howard Frank Mosher's first novel made into a film by Jay Craven. *Left to right*, Gary Farmer, Kris Kristofferson, and Jay Craven.
Courtesy of Jay Craven

Cannes International Film Festival, the Sundance Film Festival, the Producers' Guild of America, and others.

"A sense of possibility is what drew me to Vermont, the opportunity to be part of a community and make a difference. As a community organizer who really didn't have anything to offer other than the arts, that appealed to me. It required reciprocity," he said, explaining his commitment to Vermont. Simultaneously, however, he lamented that it had become "more difficult for young artists as it became more expensive to live in Vermont, but not as expensive as elsewhere. I'm waiting to see who is going to continue what we started. I wish we could see another wave of young people in Vermont. But I'm encouraged" through watching his sons — Jasper, an investigative reporter, and Sasha, a film editor — along with other new Vermonters making a difference. He's also buoyed by the important themes explored by his film students and alums at Marlboro College, where he was a tenured professor for twenty years before moving on to teach at Sarah Lawrence College.

"Vermont provided me with a platform to act on a vision and make it happen. I am the recipient of so much good will. All of us were," he said of the counterculture generation. "What we discovered was, if you serve your community here, your community gives back. How many places can you say that about?"

* * *

Potter Susan Leader and old-time music fiddler John Specker's story blends aspects of America's history as radical as the Nearing experiment in Pikes Falls with some of the country's earliest musical and artistic traditions. Leader is the younger daughter of Herb and Marion Leader who homesteaded with the Nearings a few years before her birth. Unlike other participants in the Nearings' social experiment, Herb Leader was a native Vermonter. He had grown up in Bennington, the son of eastern European immigrants who fled Europe in 1908. Leader described her grandfather, a rabbi in Poland, as "the only rabbi and kosher butcher in the area, a jack-of-all-trades who did what he had to do to survive with five kids. He salvaged a lot of old railroad ties, bought and sold whatever could be turned into a profit, and ended up owning farms and a tenement building in the middle of the town; it's now the senior center."

Her father "would have been your regular Vermont guy except he went to City College in New York in the thirties and became radicalized." Later, he fell under the influence of Helen and Scott Nearing. The story goes that he heard Scott Nearing splitting wood while hiking the Long Trail, followed the sound and struck up a conversation. In short order, he and his new bride, who'd been raised a labor Zionist, moved into a tent on land owned by another of the Pikes Falls settlers.

"He came to believe like them that it was better not to make money because it would just go to the war machine," Susan said of her father. A few years before she was born, her parents had traveled with their oldest daughter to Palestine for the 1948 establishment of Israel, staying through the war with the Arab League before returning to Pikes Falls. "I grew up with the myth about the perfect commune and the perfect lifestyle. It fed nicely into the sixties," she said.

After Pikes Falls, the Leaders bought land in Andover, a parcel of which she inherited. "We loved our place and had a strong family life. Money was a dirty word growing up but we believed we were very rich," she said. Nonetheless, the family "had a very uncomfortable relationship with the town. My father was a conscientious objector. As vegetarians, we might as well have been from Mars. If you didn't eat meat, you were offending mother and apple pie. Just being Jewish, forget it! I failed to form relationships with other kids."

Despite a master's degree in education, her father was blacklisted everywhere he applied and fired from UVM for his political leanings. Thus, "he earned a living hauling milk so we all had milk, and he worked as a janitor at a sawmill in Weston. He sold old books in his barn and rented cabins he built to hoboes and hermits for $10 a month. My parents homesteaded; they had to be self-sufficient," she said. That ended after her father sustained a benign brain tumor and, although he survived an operation, he couldn't work and the family needed to take welfare from the town. It was humiliating and unsustainable.

By fifth grade, the family found it necessary to spend the school year at Leader's grandmother's home in northeastern Massachusetts but they returned to the Vermont property on weekends and summers. When time came for college in 1969, Leader chose Antioch, where she fell in love with Japanese pottery, traveled to Japan to study with master potters, and lived in a "pottery village" for a year and a half. "It was a meditative kind of experience. Japanese pottery seemed like the ultimate expression of freedom in the natural world," she said. When she returned, she followed the hippie pattern, hitchhiking around the country, hanging out in Berkeley, farming with mules in Tennessee, and "making a pilgrimage" to Jugtown, North Carolina, to learn from the multigenerational family of potters there.

By the mid-1970s, "I had almost given up that I would ever feel comfortable living in Vermont. I was just in seventh heaven to find my people here," she said, referring to hippies like musician John Specker whom she met when she returned to her parents' land. "That was when I realized I could live here too."

Specker had grown up in Queens where his older brother had turned him on to a never-ending selection of "doo-wop, Elvis, Chuck Berry, Little Richard, the blues, and Dylan. At an early age I developed an RBA, a rural black attitude," he recalled, laughing. He began playing violin in school band, but at the Philadelphia College of Art switched to guitar, having observed that it was the guitar players who got the girls. Then he discovered hillbilly music and the Band's *Music from Big Pink* album, which led him to traditional old-time music and the fiddle. After college, he moved to Ithaca, where he developed a personalized style of playing fiddle and singing that combined the strict melody of old-time music with foot-stomping, grins and grimaces, whispers and shouts. He had quite a following for several years before moving to Vermont in the mid-1970s.

Specker wasn't the only hippie musician interested in old-time music, a genre played primarily on acoustic instruments, usually guitars, fiddles, and banjos, and often accompanied by clogging and square dancing. It's the music most rural people listened to prior to the mid-1920s, but it had nearly disappeared outside of Appalachia before being resurrected by folksingers and troubadours drawn to its rich blend of Anglo-Saxon and African-American ingredients, including musicians like Specker and his friend George Ainley of Perkinsville.

The two met in Cambridge, Massachusetts, as they made the circuit to music festivals around the country where they could learn from and play with older practitioners. Ainley, a Connecticut native and 1970 Dartmouth graduate, was a muscular, sinewy young man with an instinctual understanding of the fiddle; he bought his first one the year he graduated from Dartmouth, in a hardware store of all places, but his proficiency grew rapidly. In the 1970s, he loosely managed a modified fiddle-player-based apple-picking crew in Vermont that Specker joined. They harvested apples on the Scott Farm in Brattleboro, the former estate of Rudyard Kipling, and played old-time music at night. Specker crashed with Ainley and his wife, Julie, then moved nearby to a cottage located next door to Tamar Hennessey, the daughter of Catholic activist Dorothy Day. In the way that the world sometimes feels very small, Day had been a friend and supporter of the Nearings. These connections eventually brought Susan Leader and Specker together.

When they became a couple, they moved into a commune in Perkinsville called Peregrine's Rest that was managed by Ahmet Baycu, himself a banjo maker and player and old-time-music archivist. For Leader, the kaleidoscope of young and talented people with ideas not all that dissimilar from her parents' was a welcome change from the alienation she had felt growing up in nearby Andover.

After they married, the couple lived in one of the woodchoppers' cabins her father had dragged down from the mountain. There, two daughters were born as the couple developed their crafts. While Specker performed in various bands and as a single artist, demand for Leader's hand-thrown, majolica glazed pottery, decorated with original sponge designs and fired in an earthen kiln she made herself, grew. She developed a successful mail-order business, and the couple eventually built a more comfortable home. The one-room cabin became Leader's studio. As farmers' markets and craft shows expanded throughout the state, she found a way to have direct contact with her customers, selling at markets located within fifty miles of home, including Norwich, Dorset, Ludlow, and Londonderry. "These markets are amazing," she said. "They serve the same purpose they do in any third-world country, a tribal community where countless home-based businesses are thriving, along with small organic farmers, all of us meeting and serving local customers and tourists."

In this old photo, Susan Leader stands with her brother Emmett Leader atop the clay oven she made on her parents' property in Andover. Her parents were part of the utopian experiment along Pikes Falls in the 1940s and later bought property in Andover where she grew up. There her family's beliefs and vegetarian diet made her an outsider until she met and became friends with the musicians who lived on a nearby commune.

Courtesy of Susan Leader

The irony that Leader went all the way to Japan searching for a community where she could produce traditional pottery "only to return home and practice it in my own backyard" did not escape her. "I was convinced I'd have to go somewhere else to feel at home. Vermont has changed and Andover as well. When my father helped start the Democratic Party in Andover, it was a radical thing to do. It was not easy growing up here, but now I have a deeply abiding love for this place. And that I make art from its clay is a beautiful thing."

* * *

In their book *Vermonters at Their Craft*, Catharine Wright and Nancy Means Wright celebrate the Vermont craftspeople whose "work is in the tradition of old-time craftsmanship, joined with a fine art sensibility." They noted that half of the twenty-four artisans they profiled were not native Vermonters. Rather, like Kolb, Jackson, and woodcut artist Mary Azarian, they came "up-country . . . as part of (if they didn't realize it then) the 'back to the land' movement. In a sense, these migrants made up the first generation of contemporary craftspeople in Vermont (and elsewhere)—a subculture that dared to pursue handcrafts in the face of an anonymous industrial machine."

They write, also, that many were self-taught; they "came to their craft by accident, or through an affinity for their material. They were attracted to the solitude that allowed them to experiment, and the chance to be their own boss."

Azarian, a woodcut printmaker, grew up on her grandfather's small farm outside Washington, D.C., where she fell in love with gardening, drawing, and painting, and exploring the woods and fields on her pony, Patsy. She made her first relief print in fourth grade, carving into the ubiquitous linoleum blocks of grammar school art class, and was hooked. At Smith College, she studied printmaking "with one of the great twentieth-century printmakers, Leonard Baskin."

She and her husband Tom lived near Smith after graduation, then began looking for land to farm and raise a family. There was no way she could return to her native Virginia, which was "being paved over with asphalt." Just as Elmslie sent Craven to the Kingdom, a realtor in southern Vermont sent the couple to Hardwick with the advice that the further north they went the better their chances of finding land they could afford. "It was a shot in the dark," she said of their first farm in Cabot, where the couple's three sons helped them farm with horses, make maple syrup commercially, and tend chickens, a Jersey milk cow, and sheep.

She and Tom Azarian were "more than not part of the counterculture," as members of an early co-op and opponents of the Vietnam War, but farming took up most of their energies. They found few mentors in Cabot. "We lived in a town that was very suspicious of outsiders and associated us with Goddard, even though we were not really part of the college," she said. "But as time went on, people became more tolerant. Still, it was not easy. I have no fond memories of that town." Sociability and a more comfortable setting came when they moved to a farm in East Calais.

After teaching at a one-room schoolhouse in Walden, Azarian secured a job as an art teacher for the district that required her to drive to each of the district's four schools for a one-hour art lesson once a week. It wasn't particularly useful to the students, she felt, nor satisfying for her. She began to hope she might make a living with her woodcuts, first printing with black ink, then adding color by hand until discovering an old Vanderbilt press she called the "Rolls Royce of proof presses."

"Slowly and randomly" she began illustrating books. She compared the first, *The Wild Flavor*, written by Marilyn Kluger in 1973, to Euell Gibbons's *Stalking the Wild Asparagus*, folksy and unpretentious. Other books fol-

An early woodcut by Mary Azarian.
Courtesy of Mary Azarian

lowed, more than fifty in the intervening years, including *Snowflake Bentley*, which won the 1999 Caldecott Award for the best children's picture book of the year. Later, she returned to black-and-white prints made on Japanese *washi*, a kind of handmade paper.

Despite the initial suspicion of some outsiders, as time progressed, "I found the people tolerant and kindhearted, and I still feel that way," she said. "All things considered, I can't imagine living anywhere else."

Nancy Edwards's life has blended lessons from old-time craftsmanship, homecrafts, and self-sustainability with ancient disciplines from the East. A weaver, spinner, Reiki practitioner and hospice volunteer, her journey to Vermont was fairly helter-skelter, but once she landed, she recognized the opportunity that homecrafts, healing arts, and meditation provided for living a good and useful life while helping others. Edwards calls herself an accidental tourist to the sixties and seventies. She didn't mean to drive her parents crazy back home in Hellertown, Pennsylvania, by joining the ragtag pilgrims who went off to the Woodstock Music Festival, by taking up hitchhiking, crashing at Goddard, and rejecting the life of ease her folks had envisioned for her. "It was the sixties and I just happened to be there," she said. At Harcum Junior College, where her parents had sent her to find a rich husband from Villanova, she took art classes out of interest, not with the sense that she'd need to support herself. In 1968, as a volunteer with a church program in Chicago, she saw poor blacks living in slums and Black Panthers being gassed as they marched for equality. Her world began to open up as she recognized the disparities in American society. She wandered from coast to coast, taking part in peace marches, and, in 1969, while visiting a friend in the hills of Pennsylvania, heard about a concert in the woods. "We had hunting knives strapped to our thighs. We were into this earth-mother look; it was part of our costume," she recalled of the outfit she wore to Woodstock, a life-changing experience. Back home, and feeling trapped, she decided to visit a friend at Goddard, joining the many who lived there for free for a short spell. That was another eye-opening experience.

"My parents were ripping their hair out. But for me, the sky was the limit. Everybody was doing it with everybody. So, you're constantly making choices. I was aware of the need to make sure I was doing something out of choice and was really careful with drugs, which was a good thing, of course. In retrospect, the back-to-the-land movement was a funny thing to come out of it all because [farming] was really hard work and traditional and not much up until that had been."

The next adventure was a visit to the Tyler School of Art where she found her focus in heritage arts, especially textiles, bought a loom, and began studying weaving. She met her future husband, Steve Edwards, who was finishing college in Philadelphia. When he moved to upstate New York to teach pottery and leather craft at the Thousand Island Museum Craft School, he asked her to come along. Two weeks after she declined, they almost eloped, but couldn't punish their parents that way, and had a formal wedding.

At the craft school, Emily Post—not the author of etiquette books but the school's founder, a woman dedicated to preserving traditional art and supporting artists and artisans—took Edwards under her wing. "She made a deal that I could have a scholarship for the winter if I'd teach weaving to the locals in the summer. I got an amazing crash course in weaving." The couple lived and taught at Thousand Island for several years—their first son was born there—but longed to join the back-to-the-land movement in Vermont. Steve applied to every school in Vermont and, in 1974, got accepted to teach art at Rock Point School, an alternative program in Burlington for students with educational and social challenges. Nancy taught pottery at night, all the while looking for land they could afford, finally finding the perfect property in Monkton. With an FHA loan, they moved into a bare shell of a building that Steve built a house around. Over the next decade, Steve worked various jobs before joining Garden Way, the company Lyman Wood had founded around Troy Bilt rototillers and other tools. Wood was the promoter of the *Have More Plan*, a 1944 booklet offering ideas on how to live off the land. The Edwards were devotees; their motto was "If it could be made, we'd make it ourselves." They raised their own food and learned how to put food by, Edwards canning hundreds of jars of fruit, jam, sauces, and vegetables each fall. She designed and sewed their clothing, learned to spin, and opened a weaving business, Fuller Mountain Weaving, making shawls and jackets and blankets for the family and customers who appreciated her blending of old-time patterns with less traditional colors. Her clothing was featured and sold at the Frog Hollow State Craft Center, art shows, and privately. On the side, she taught weaving to others. It took seven years to finish their house, during which time another son was born. They'd probably be on that property until the end, she said, but when much of the Troy Bilt business moved to Troy, New York, they had to move as well. They found a way to stay in Vermont by buying an 1820 home in Old Bennington not far from Troy, and set to restoring it, bottom up, by hand. In Bennington, she partnered with another weaver, studied Buddhism at the Zen Center of Santa Fe and Reiki and acupuncture at the Karuna Reiki Center in England.

Edwards has multiple sclerosis, and as she aged, she closed her commercial weaving business and her Reiki practice. Ever the optimist, however, she said, "MS was a kind of blessing. It made me not put everything off," describing the pilgrimages she has made to sites considered sacred in Buddhism, holy places located in India, Thailand, and Bali. Like the poet David Budbill, she reflected that Vermont was a Buddhist place. "It's not only nurturing but you learn soon enough that you can't control outside elements like weather. You learn to slow down, to think, to accept, to appreciate."

She also began to think about end-of-life issues and the benefits she'd been given. Her parents died when she was in her thirties, and she and her husband had helped them die at home. The women in her mother's life were with her at the end. "It was like Ruth and Naomi from the Bible. I felt like we had midwifed her. That stayed with me, midwifing someone into the next stage," she said. And thus, she became a hospice volunteer, choosing to be with people in the last weeks and days of life. "Sometimes I just sit there, silent. Sometimes I sing. It's what the person wants and needs, that's how I try to be with them," she explained.

In their late sixties, the couple decided to return to the self-sufficient lifestyle they'd set out to follow when they moved to Vermont. In 2017, they sold their house in Old Bennington and moved to a half-acre property in

Cornwall where Steve helped build an eco-conscious house complete with a nine-foot counter designed for canning. "The grounding for me began with coming to Vermont. It was fertile ground for both political openness and arts and crafts, but all of that done with Yankee ingenuity. We hippies took it and the love for the land and added another dimension. I love that it's difficult to live here. It means that the people who live here really want to live here, that we're a part of an intentional community. How fortunate that it happened that way. From weaving to canning to accepting the cycles of life, it's all part of the same journey. Vermonters know that."

* * *

Music has always kept company with war, but in the 1960s and '70s the soundtrack was more likely to express opposition than support for the battle and addressed other causes and ideals of the day: racial equality, love for the planet, sexual freedom, and consciousness-raising through drugs and meditation. The soundtrack came to Vermont hippies living in remote areas, often without television reception or radio options, through vinyl, CHOM, a Montreal FM radio station, WRMC with Brian Collamore, later a Republican senator from Rutland, at the mic, and other alternative radio stations. When one of the icons of the music scene came to Vermont—usually to Goddard, Middlebury, or Burlington—nearly everyone who could get there (or knew about it) showed up. But, mostly music was local. Schubart pointed out that almost every town in Vermont could boast a local band featuring a combination of musicians from old Vermont families and newcomers with counterculture roots, groups playing bluegrass, folk, and country music in which common themes such as the vicissitudes of the working person were accompanied by acoustic instruments.

Some towns in Vermont seem to have attracted more than their share of these musicians along with artists, writers, craftspeople, and other practitioners of arts and crafts from the baby-boom generation: Burlington, of course, in part because of Ben & Jerry's and the many colleges located there; towns around Brattleboro where the commune movement was strong; and, of course, Plainfield due to Goddard College. Shrewsbury in Rutland County ranks high among these communities that seemed to have welcomed the coming of the hippies. It now boasts an impressive number of creative residents.

Psychologist and musician Paul Sgalia attributes Shrewsbury's comfortable blend of old and new Vermont and its wealth of creativity in part to the long existence there of Spring Lake Ranch where he worked for several decades. The farm-based treatment center for people with emotional and addiction issues was founded in 1932 by Wayne and Elizabeth Sarcka who believed in the therapeutic value of outdoor work and play. Over the years, the farm attracted forward-thinking people to work there. Many settled in the region, as did clients who came for treatment and support and decided to stay. They, in turn, attracted others with an arts and musical bent who shared the idea of work as therapy, especially if the work placed one outside in nature.

Along with Sgalia and his wife, Victoria Arthur, a teacher, vocalist, and musician, Shrewsbury is home to Mark "Catfish" Hamilton, a pilot and fiddler; his wife Licia Gambino Hamilton, a teacher, flutist, fiddler, and square-dance caller; potter Maya Zelkin; artist Grace Brigham; Gerry Martin, a craftsman specializing in wooden bowls and vessels; poet Joan Aleshire; Nancy Bell, an artist and Conservation Fund New England director; Ahmet Baycu, the instrument maker, banjo player, and music archivist; and many others.

Sgalia credited four siblings, Marion, Marjorie, Glendon, and Gordon Pierce, with setting a tone of welcome for newcomers to the town. The Pierce siblings long operated Pierce's General Store, a repository of old Vermont with its antique cash register, penny candy, and woodstove. After the last of the Pierce siblings died, a community trust was established to keep the store operating. There, several times a week, one or another of the local musicians might offer a free concert on the porch.

That cordiality goes deep, Sgalia said, describing concerts and benefits organized quickly and efficiently over the years for local and global causes, from neighbors whose business had burned down to aid for flood victims in Haiti. "I hadn't been in a community where I could notice so much willingness to interact and connect between the old-timers and the young folks until I came to Shrewsbury; there was a real nice ebb and flow already there when I arrived. It felt a bit new to me because of where I'd come from; there was nothing like a town-wide picnic where locals played together," he observed, adding, "Shrewsbury is a sweet place."

Sgalia's earliest memories of Vermont began at 4:30 Friday afternoons when his father would close up his dentist office and the family would pack up the car and head north from Dover, New Jersey, to arrive in Dorset six hours later and fall asleep in a tent pitched on a wooden platform. He'd awake to dad making pancakes over a Coleman stove. There would be hunting and fishing and skiing with other friends and their families. Eventually, a cabin got built on the property on Mount Tom Road. At Lehigh University, Sgalia wasn't interested in fraternity life. Instead, he studied and got serious about playing guitar. He fell in love with folk music with its emphasis on racial equality and peace. He graduated in 1974 and moved to Vermont the next year, earned a master's degree, eventually secured a job at Spring Lake Ranch and moved to Shrewsbury. There, he began playing with Tom Mitchell, a legendary guitar, autoharp, recorder, and kazoo player who formed many bands over the years. Sgalia joined one called Workman's Compensation, followed by the Saltash Serenaders, an eclectic folk ensemble of Mitchell, Sgalia, Arthur on vocals and guitar, and Steve Spensley from Pittsford on fiddle and guitar. They played at nursing homes, on local radio shows, and at farmers' markets, or joined with old-time fiddlers like another local legend, Maynard Welch. There might be a dozen or more musicians from their twenties to their eighties in a room. Other times, Arthur and Sgalia would join various bluegrass bands that included Baycu on banjo, Jim Warren on dobro, and Dan Tyminski, a bluegrass musician who grew up in West Rutland and later played with Allison Kraus and Union Station.

Sgalia and Arthur had met in downtown Rutland when he was playing at the Back Home Café and she was waitressing at Murphy's. One night the band invited musicians to join them. Arthur stepped in with her guitar and amazing voice and soon she was part of the ever-evolving musical offerings in the region. She also joined House Blend, an a cappella group of about twenty singers from Vermont and New Hampshire who specialize in American folk traditions from hill songs of Appalachia to gospel tunes as well as traditional world music.

While Arthur had grown up in Bridgewater, New Jersey, her Vermont roots go deep. Her grandmother was from Florence, graduated from Castleton Normal School, and taught in a one-room schoolhouse before going to Washington to work for FDR. When the children started coming, her grandparents returned to Vermont, settling in Rutland to raise their family. Her father, a Norwich University and Harvard graduate, taught English in New Jersey, but as soon as the school year was out, the family traveled north to the grandparents' home on Killington Avenue. After graduating from Trenton State College, Arthur taught in local schools serving the black community where she discovered her love of a cappella singing and became the only white member of the Trenton All-City Gospel Choir.

Eventually, however, she began to long for Vermont and, when a fortune-

The Saltash Serenaders, *left to right*: Victoria Arthur, Licia Gambino, Tom Mitchell, Mark "Catfish" Hamilton, Paul Sgalia, Steve Spensley.
Photo by Michael Aleshire; courtesy of Victoria Arthur

teller suggested just such a move—punctuating the recommendation with the words, "You'll never look back"—she moved north in 1979. Coming from a long line of teachers, Arthur has taught in Rochester, Randolph, Rutland, and Danby. In joining House Blend, Arthur's history as a performer came full circle back to her years as a young woman singing in inner city New Jersey. Much as that "full-throated spirited singing just really spoke to me," she said, so too has Vermont, a place threaded through her earliest memories, her family's legacy of teaching, and her interest in music from all manner of cultures.

"Moving to Vermont was a way to imbibe in a bit of the counterculture," fellow musician Steve Spensley said. A Dubuque, Iowa, native, Spensley had traveled to Vermont with a college friend in 1967 and met a young local woman named Kim. Over the next year, the two had a "long-distance courtship by letters," as Kim, a teacher, described it. Steve returned the next summer to work with Kim at Camp Betsy Cox, which Kim's aunt, Jean Davies, had founded. The two married at the end of the summer. Following the old adage of not giving up his day job, Spensley has worked as a teacher, wood-cutter, and building and groundskeeper while playing guitar and fiddle with the Saltash Serenaders, the Turkey Mountain Window Smashers, and the Muddy Rhodes Blues Band, along with solo gigs. "I was looking for a simpler, more environmentally conscious way of life and a place to play music," he said of his attraction to Vermont. "What a gift it has been."

And now the couple's daughter, Ellen, and her husband, Matthew Moriarty, both archaeologists, have returned to Vermont from their studies in far-away locales to conduct a dig on property at the base of Lake Champlain where the Abenaki people spent time 11,000 years ago. As Steve observed, that puts "all of our coming here in perspective."

* * *

Sculptor Patrick Farrow, and his wife, the artist Susan Erb Farrow, also met at Spring Lake Ranch, where both worked in the mid-1960s. Patrick is the son of Hollywood actress Maureen O'Sullivan of Tarzan fame and movie director John Villiers Farrow. He too found Vermont and Spring Lake Ranch restorative as he sought to recover from the death of his older brother and the pressures of growing up in the fishbowl of a famous family. Before moving to Vermont, he had been living in New York City, designing posters for the city subway, and "wanted to get as far away from civilization as he could." As the son of one of Hollywood's most successful couples, he'd been educated in strict Catholic boarding schools, traveled the world, met the Beatles, and, like his sister, the actress Mia Farrow, had the opportunity to go into acting himself. He'd actually had a few small parts. But Patrick rejected what he came to see as a numbing social world in which there was no privacy, a quality he considered essential to making art.

Susan first came to Spring Lake Ranch as a student intern studying art at Antioch College and weaving at a Scandinavian craft school in Norway. After college, she returned to New Jersey briefly, but recoiled from the growing suburbs encroaching on the tiny log cabin where she'd grown up with her brother, inventor father, and artist mother. When she returned to work at Spring Lake, she brought a loom she'd purchased in Scandinavia with her. "Vermont was the dream place to go to," she said. "It was seen as the magic state, a beacon," especially for young artists. It didn't take her parents long to follow, moving also to Shrewsbury, where her father, "a dreamer with one hundred patents to his name and no money" bought an old cheese factory he hoped to turn into a school for learning by doing. Soon her brother Peter Erb was also working at Spring Lake, later becoming the center's longtime assistant director.

While their parents might have wanted a big church wedding, in 1966 Patrick and Susan chose to marry at a friend's home with only a few days' notice, causing O'Sullivan—who was starring in a play ironically named "Never Too Late"—to fly into the old Rutland airport in the middle of a January blizzard, arriving just in time for the ceremony. O'Sullivan instantly fell in love with Vermont and later moved to Rutland where she lived with her second husband until shortly before her death, saying she could have been an ambassador for Rutland with its "city creature comforts surrounded by nature." Another Farrow sibling, Tisa, who had acted in several movies herself, also moved to the region.

A self-taught artist, Patrick created metal sculptures using the old lost-wax method, making pieces both large and small, humorous and thoughtful, turning metal into improbable creatures—part animal, part machine—or whimsical scenes. His sculptures were often about balance, such as one called *Circus*, in which two fluid trapeze artists each dangle from just one of their ankles. In *Earlier That Evening*, two humans, their bodies characteristically elongated and freed of gravity, are connected at hand and foot, loosely forming the empty shape of a heart as each steps into the abyss. Another sculpture, *The Pope Goes Shopping*, is comprised of the pope, outfitted with his high miter, pushing an empty shopping cart. Patrick also fashioned graceful jewelry, each piece a miniature sculpture. He was immensely successful for years, with shows in New York galleries and at the Peale Gallery in Danby. He was a fellow in the National Sculpture Society in New York City, where he won numerous awards and was represented in many private and public collections. A theft of dozens of pieces from a New York gallery spoiled him on trusting his work to others, however. That led the couple to purchase a former Catholic church building in Castleton in 1993. They turned the small church, still bearing a Latin phrase painted along its high ceiling and original stained glass windows, into a gallery, studio, and home for themselves and their two daughters. As a curious boy often reprimanded for questioning church doctrine or drawing when he should have been doing his math, he loved the irony of his work being displayed where an altar once stood.

Patrick loved planes and motorcycles. He was instrumental in producing three highly ambitious exhibitions at the Chaffee Art Center in Rutland: a retrospective on the American motorcycle; a half-scale replica of the

The Leash, a larger-than-life bronze sculpture by Patrick Farrow,
at the center of Rutland's historic downtown.
Photo by Donna Wilkins Photography

Vietnam Veterans Memorial wall displayed in Rutland's Main Street Park;
and an aviation exhibition of old planes and memorabilia that included a
World War II trainer airplane.

In 1984, he gave a large bronze sculpture called *The Leash* to Rutland
City. The two-part sculpture features a larger-than-life racing dog straining
against a nonexistent leash tied to a parking meter. His message: resist the
restraints of time and conformity.

Meanwhile, Susan explored art in media as broad as weaving, painting,
drawing, jewelry making, and collage. For years, the couple had the habit
of walking along Old Route 4 in Castleton each morning, Susan collecting
debris and pieces of old metal along the roadside; these made their way onto
black cloth as pictorial narratives, each whimsical and inventive, such as one
of Beethoven with his wild hair made from rusty wire, or Benjamin Franklin
discovering electricity, the story told in roadside detritus.

Together and separately they were community and antiwar activists,
working as environmental activists to stop a trash-incinerator from being
built in Rutland, protesting against the Vietnam, Persian Gulf, and Iraq wars,
and sustaining other artists through their contributions to the Chaffee Art
Center in Rutland, where Susan was long the director and Patrick a tireless

volunteer, and the Frog Hollow Vermont State Craft Center. They were instrumental in bringing Moon Brook Gallery to downtown Rutland and supporting other opportunities for art, poetry, and music in Rutland and beyond.

"Vermont has remained a dream," Susan said. "I've loved it all from the days of the food co-op, divvying up our bushel of bulgur wheat, to now when I've seen some of our grandchildren grow up in Rutland. Vermont feels like a sane plane, a place where the values of the sixties continue, a rare place of sanity in a difficult world."

* * *

"The puppets become the decorating thing around the bread eating," Peter Schumann proclaimed dramatically as he kneaded a mound of dough rising in a much-used wheelbarrow. From there, the dough was shaped into loaves and left to rise again on a sheet of plywood, then baked in the large outdoor brick hearth he had built when he and his wife Elka and their Bread & Puppet Theater came to their farm in Glover in the 1970s. Visitors strolled through the 140-year old hay barn nearby, a warren of rooms and lofts where hundreds of puppets, the veterans of Bread & Puppet's many political actions were housed, along with posters from their various festivals and appearances. Peter took time to talk to the visitors, wiping his dough-encrusted hands on his already much-stained apron, stirring the embers in the oven with the handle of a broken shovel. Inside their farmhouse, Elka was preparing for the couple's upcoming trip to San Francisco where their giant puppets would be the featured performers at an Occupy San Francisco demonstration for fair housing. Peter had already signaled ahead to organizers, requiring them to gather enough bricks to make a sizeable oven so he could bake bread as part of their presentation. The theater's name comes from Schumann's belief that sharing bread with audiences helps create community, and that art is as basic to life as bread. Thus, his homemade, sourdough rye bread is made and passed out at all performances.

"That's my university, baking, oven-making . . . all learned in my years as a refugee," he said, referring to the time that began when his family fled to Poland during the Allied bombing of Germany toward the end of World War II. His and Elka's journey from Europe to Glover, like so many other Vermont stories of the time, interweaves with Scott Nearing's story, and that of the Putney School, and Goddard, and the counterculture.

Elka Schumann, an accomplished graphic artist, is Scott Nearing's granddaughter. Her father, John Scott, is the famous Vermont homesteader's son

Peter Schumann making bread on an outside wood-fired brick oven at home in Glover where he and his wife Elka run the Bread & Puppet Theater and Museum.
Photo by Chuck Clarino

with his first wife. John Scott dropped his surname to have his own identity or because of a falling out with his father; both versions are part of the public record. Scott migrated to Russia in 1932 at age twenty, intrigued by the new Soviet experience. There he lived and worked for five years in Magnitogorsk, an industrial city in Siberia built to rival Pittsburgh. There also he met Maria, Elka's mother. In 1938, he left Siberia to escape arrest. Maria, Elka, and a younger sister later immigrated to the United States. As a girl, Elka lived in New York and Europe after her father became an international journalist for *Time* and other publications. She often visited Scott Nearing in Vermont, and later, Maine, becoming quite close to him. Elka was outspoken in school and didn't have many friends until her senior year when she went to the Putney School, a wonderfully liberating experience that she contrasted to her later years at Bryn Mawr. During her junior year abroad, she met Peter Schumann, and after graduation returned and married him.

The couple came to the United States in 1961, initially living in Claes Oldenburg's old apartment—yes, the sculptor who was the former husband of Jay Craven's former girlfriend. In 1962, Elka was hired to teach Russian at the Putney School while Peter talked his way into offering students a theater workshop. That summer, back in New York, as the Vietnam War ensued, he founded Bread & Puppet and began to join the demonstrations, soon becoming a main attraction with his huge puppets—some ten to fifteen feet high and needing a cadre of volunteers to manage—with Peter leading the throng on ten-foot stilts. This was in-your-face street theater, the puppet effigies representing political figures and the war machine. They performed in countless churches, transforming Christmas and Easter stories into antiwar drama with puppets, attracting antiwar activists and hippies into the circus.

Initially, the couple found life in New York exhilarating but by 1970 they began to tire of the din and, after Elka was robbed at gunpoint, the couple accepted an invitation from Goddard to establish a theater in residence at the college's Cate Farm. The locals weren't impressed when they showed up with their horde of hippie volunteers and followers. "They threw rotten eggs and tomatoes at us," Peter said, "but just once." Soon, "things started changing. On the whole the tolerance was more than the rotten eggs."

In 1974, the Schumanns moved to a farm in Glover that had been purchased by Elka's father. He had sold many tons of gravel from the south end of the property to the company that was building Interstate 91, resulting in a steep, horseshoe-shaped depression. Scott initially thought it should be smoothed out somehow, but Schumann saw its possibilities immediately, realizing that it could serve as an outdoor amphitheater for his puppet shows. The 160-acre property came complete with farmhouse and outbuildings. The Schumanns put in a printing press, turned the old hay barn into a museum, recruited staff and volunteers, and began putting on performances and leading actions on the property and around the world, always accompanied by the request for bricks to build a hearth so there would be bread.

For many summers, Bread & Puppet offered a show every Sunday on the Glover property called the *Domestic Resurrection Circus*. The first was held in 1975. These were full-on affairs with giant puppets manned by dozens, with no subject off-limits. In 1993, one spoof on capitalism included a calf giving birth to a bull market and a balloon representing an industrial capitalist that kept getting larger and larger, never satisfied, until a masked Bernie Sanders

"WHENEVER YOU ARE IN DOUBT. APPLY THE FO
THE POOREST AND THE WEAK
AND ASK YOURSELF IF T
IS GOING TO BE OF A
WILL HE GAIN ANYTHIN
RESTORE HIM TO A CONTROL OVER
AND DESTINY"

MAHATMA GANDHI

IN 1987 MORE PEOPLE BOUGHT BIKES

DEEPLY IMPOVERISHED
NATIONS POUR
PRECIOUS
EXPORT

Puppets and art from
performances fill the Bread
& Puppet Theater Museum.
The museum is a repository of
political theater orchestrated
by Peter and Elka Schumann.

Photos by Yvonne Daley

popped it with a pin. By then a U.S. congressman, Sanders announced, "To-gether, we can create an economy that works for all of us, not just the mil-lionaires." The message never changes.

By 1999, however, the summer events had become so popular that they were unmanageable, and when 30,000 people showed up—so many that followers were camping in neighboring property and one person died during an argument in a campground—Schumann decided to "bring to a close the *Resurrection Circus*. It was pulled apart by its own success. It wasn't ours any-more," he said. The couple and their loyal followers, staff, and volunteers "reclaimed it" by hosting smaller festivals and an annual leaf-peeping pan-cake breakfast, complete with Sacred Harp singing and a new play. In 2016, the show was called *The Gates of Unfinished Life*.

As for an unfinished life, well into his eighties, Peter Schumann continued touring with the troupe although he finally acquiesced and gave up the stilts. Elka, just a few years younger, still swims every morning from early spring into fall, while also presenting puppet shows for children and running the Bread & Puppet printshop and museum. While Peter is the more visible of the couple, many of the literally hundreds of people who have come to their farm as interns, staff, or volunteers consider Elka the heart of the theater.

"People here are such contrasts," Peter Schumann said, reflecting on nearly fifty years living in Vermont's Northeast Kingdom. "There's the bear hunter up the road who lets us use his cider press and Burt Porter, a poet, he participated in the puppets. We wrote a lot of plays together; he's a wonder-ful versifier. . . . It was hard at first; people were suspect of us. I had trouble with the bread. I didn't have the heart to sell it, the bread I learned from my mother. I had a free bread sign I put out, 'FREE Bread.' They wouldn't take it," he said referring to his neighbors. So, he put out another sign. "'Due to inflation, twice as free.' Still they didn't come. That's why the puppet show becomes the decorating thing around the bread eating. You need the circum-stances" to attract people to share bread with. "That worked a little too good. Much too good," he said referring to the *Resurrection Circus*. "It became ev-erything that a market culture produces."

The Kingdom, he said, "is a little different now than when we came and all those hippies, too. It was pretty radically right wing until the nineties. That's the amazing thing. The right is as radical as the left. They might disagree with you, but they let you alone, and when you reach far enough behind your back with the right hand soon enough you are shaking hands with the left. We've all found that out up here, shaking hands, being the neighbors."

Drugs

There's just something Technicolor about Vermont; some might even say the place is downright psychedelic. If you've driven around this beautiful state on a clear, blue-sky day, perhaps in early autumn when the leaves are in full color intermingled with deep green, and the sun is shining sideways so that the trees are airbrushed with light, ablaze with crimson and ochre and colors you don't know the name for, you've a taste of what life looks like on sense-enhancing drugs. Or, it could be a chilly day, each tree and branch magically enshrined in ice, rainbows sparkling as the light turns frost to crystals. And then there's Vermont fog in early morning, the mist low to the ground, masking some physical elements while others remain distinct so that the top of a lamp post or the horizon might seem disembodied, rising from vapor, the real and the illusory in plain view. It was these and myriad other experiences that people who took LSD or smoked marijuana were seeking. For many, Vermont with its luscious, soul-pleasing beauty and remoteness from urban noise and bedlam were the ideal locations for, as one lifelong drug user put it, "taking off the top of my head and letting a lot of unwanted garbage out."

"Call me Lance," he said, "a refugee from traffic, ties, Sunday dinner with the relatives, and sixteen years of bullshit." Lance's Vermont story began the day in 1969 when he ran away from home in suburban Massachusetts, hitch-hiking north with one goal, to become "a professional pot sampler and yearly acolyte of peyote." Today Lance lives in Windsor County where he works as an attorney making a quite lucrative income, having gone to law school in the late 1980s after nearly two decades of "unfocused but joyful success at my goal of not growing up. When my second son was born, however, I realized my days of leisure needed to end."

His flight to Vermont was in part the result of a school viewing of the movie *Reefer Madness,* in which marijuana smokers were shown going insane or driving over pedestrians and leaving the scene of the accident or otherwise wrecking their lives forever. "I'd smoked some pot the summer before they showed the movie in school, to scare us. I got in trouble for making fun of it and eventually it came out that I'd sampled reefer at camp and that led to a lot of questions that would have gotten other people in trouble. I was about to be grounded for a small eternity. No thanks, I said, and headed north. I didn't call my parents for three months and lied about where I was. I regret that still, but I don't regret coming to Vermont. It's been my home for all these years," he said. "And I've smoked pot just about every day of them. It helps me to settle down at the end of the night. Some people have a cocktail; I take a toke. No harm. No foul."

* * *

Not all Vermont residents who identified with the counterculture thought marijuana was harmless. Nancy Edwards, the spinner and weaver who attended lots of parties at Goddard College where people smoked marijuana and dropped acid, said she was too afraid to even try pot. "I was a real hippie but not when it came to drugs. I saw people get really messed up on drugs and I wasn't going to take the chance myself. I'm glad I didn't. I don't feel like I missed a thing."

Wayne Turiansky, the successful owner of Amalgamated Culture Works, the Burlington T-shirt printing and distribution company, described his freshman year at Bard College thus: "You can say I either flunked out or that they eliminated my major, which was psychedelics." Turiansky hasn't smoked pot in so long he can't remember the last time. It makes him nauseous now. Others like him, who enjoyed drugs in their youth, find today's marijuana too strong or their response simply to fall into a stupor. So, as one former user put it, "What's the point?" Most haven't tried psychedelics in years.

One thing is clear, however, a majority of back-to-the-landers, student activists, and other counterculture transplants took part in some drug use in the 1960s and '70s; it was almost a rite of passage. Or, as the keynote speaker at a Vermont Historical Society presentation on the counterculture put it rather glibly, "Chances are if you graduated from college around 1972, you smoked marijuana."

* * *

Steve G. is another longtime Vermonter who had tried a full menu of illegal drugs. His experiences, he said, were spiritual, and showed him that the world is a more complex, sensual and interrelated place than most people know. Ironically, he now lives in suburban Massachusetts and works as a chemist for a medical facility looking for cures for Alzheimer's and other diseases. He rarely uses drugs now, perhaps marijuana occasionally. But he had recently learned about a national trend among young entrepreneurs, computer geeks, and New Age hipsters to come together to experience ayahuasca, a hallucinogenic potion made from boiling the vines of the South American chacruna bush, which contains the psychedelic dimethyltryptamine or DMT, the so-called Jesus drug or God drug. He recalled his own experiments with DMT and other drugs while in grad school and then in Vermont. "DMT was one of the drugs that provided the mystical, mind-expanding experiences we were all seeking from the use of 'drugs,' as different from the merely social uses that pot and the hallucinogens eventually devolved into. I so remember Huxley and his 'doors of perception.' I was looking for ways to step through those doors myself, to see the world fully. I realize hallucinogenic drugs were our salvation from the later devastation of amphetamine, cocaine, and heroin addictions. Those just never had that mystical quality that I was seeking in my youth, so I didn't go down that road," he said, "and because we'd had that mind expansion, or at least I had, there was no interest in drugs that just dulled the mind or were merely physical in nature. Just thinking of that phrase, mind-expanding, makes me long for a time when that was a goal, to expand your mind, not dull it, as seems to be today's goal."

* * *

"Oh, get over it. It's just an herb," Edward Oke O'Brien—who changed his name legally to simply Oke—said when told that many former hippies were reticent to be identified as marijuana users now or decades ago. "By now your reputation has been made, for good or bad, and admitting to smoking a few joints or dropping acid isn't going to change that. Besides, it's basically legal in Vermont now." He was referring to the Vermont law under which possession of up to one ounce of marijuana was considered a civil violation rather than a criminal offense. One of the better known marijuana users of the 1970s whose bust and subsequent legal proceedings were widely reported in the local papers, Oke observed that "getting busted ended my straight career overnight, but it also saved me from a life of chasing money. From that

Oke outside the ski lodge where he was busted by undercover drug officer Paul Lawrence in 1970.
Courtesy of Oke

moment on, I realized I had nothing to lose so no one could take anything away from me. That knowledge has been my biggest asset."

Since his bust in 1970, Oke has essentially lived off the grid. His latest home is in what he calls a "tech-free zone" in the middle of the Chateauguay woods, 60,000 acres of wilderness located within the adjoining towns of Killington, Barnard, Bridgewater, and Stockbridge where his closest neighbors are the birds, a bear, and two cubs. Now in his mid-seventies, Oke sports a white ponytail, a trim beard, and mustache. When he's not working at the Inn at Long Trail in Killington, he goes barefoot, often even in the winter. Before taking the job at Long Trail a few years ago, he lived in another part of the Chateauguay and off the government's grid, claiming no income for nearly three decades after he sent a form to the IRS in 1974 reporting his own death.

"When you have nothing and decide to be poor, your priorities change," he said, cranking up Al Jolson on his Victrola and looking out at the wild violets, mayflowers, and forget-me-nots blooming in abandon outside his doorstep. The sledge propped by the door gave evidence to a different reality —the hard work of getting provisions to his cabin in winter—but Oke had few complaints, other than with the man who busted him and how that man was treated by the state of Vermont.

A rustic cabin in the deep woods was far from the life he envisioned when in 1969 he quit a high-paying, high-profile job at a multimillion-dollar firm in Hartford, Connecticut, to move to Vermont, which he thought was "a green state." He had spent much of his free time in the previous five years at the Killington Ski Resort where he had observed the potential to take his accounting skills to an area rich in money—new money at Killington, old money in Woodstock, and foreign money coming into Vermont at Hawk Mountain. And he was doing quite well, king of the mountain one might say, until undercover drug cop Paul Lawrence busted him on January 20, 1970, at "Oake's Lodge," the misspelled moniker Lawrence used for Oke when seeking a search warrant for the ski lodge Oke had rented on Route 100 in the village of Pittsfield. By "green state," Oke had meant marijuana-friendly. So many people he had met in the area freely used and bought marijuana that he had assumed it was legal or tolerated in Vermont. His well-publicized drug bust put a quick end to that notion. It also soured his business contacts and, for a while, "got me kicked off the mountain."

Lawrence, of course, is among Vermont's most infamous bad cops. From 1967 until he himself was busted in 1974, Lawrence brought drug charges against as many as six hundred people from Brattleboro to Saint Albans in his capacities as both a state and town police officer. As it turned out, many of the drugs Lawrence supposedly confiscated from the accused were ones he had planted, taken from a drug lab in New York or procured illegally. While Lawrence was eventually caught and sent to prison, his reign of false arrests caused "broken lives, broken marriages, broken families. There is a tragedy of unknown proportions beneath the surface of this, " Robert Gensburg, an attorney from St. Johnsbury, wrote in a report issued by a committee created by Governor Thomas Salmon after Lawrence's conviction. As Gensburg noted, at least one of the people whom Lawrence had falsely arrested committed suicide.

On February 26, 1976, Salmon pardoned most of the people convicted of drug offenses based on Lawrence's "intentionally false and perjured affidavits."

The history of Vermont's most famous bad cop reflects the attitudes of many Vermont communities toward hippies and drug users in the 1960s and '70s. It also suggests that Lawrence and his supervisors helped fuel the fear that dangerous drug users were taking over Vermont's rural communities. In retrospect, however, when Lawrence started busting the longhairs and barflies of St. Albans, it wasn't just how many kids were alleged to be selling and using drugs but the kind of drugs they were accused of possessing that should have raised suspicions. Day after day, as Lawrence arrested people for possession of pot, he also alleged they possessed heroin and cocaine, drugs that were rather expensive and fairly unavailable in Vermont at the time. In case after case, the accused got nowhere with their protests that either they were innocent of the charges or that they had possessed only marijuana. Area defense attorneys became so convinced that their clients were telling the truth that they repeatedly wrote to the Vermont Attorney General's office to question Lawrence's methods and allegations, all to no avail.

On the other hand, it's not hard to understand why officials were willing to believe Lawrence. Journalist John Kifner described the conditions that led St. Albans to hire Lawrence, "It was shocking when the changes of the 1960s rippled into this quiet backwater town near the Canadian border. Suddenly, it seemed, there were dirty, longhaired ragged youths drinking beer at all hours in the park in the center of town. At the local high school there was talk of heavy drug use. A young woman died of a drug overdose in the park. It was all a bit much for this town of 8,000."

Still, there was plenty of reason to be suspicious if one wanted to be. Lawrence had been hired by the Vermont State Police as an undercover drug agent in 1968, despite a youthful arrest for illegal possession of liquor and an army discharge that followed three AWOL incidents in just seven months of service. Lawrence was forced to resign from the state police just a few years later after his squad car windshield was shot from the inside while he was alone on patrol. No one, apparently, believed the story he told about surviving a "volley of blasts" aimed at his vehicle after interrupting a warehouse break-in. A subsequent report found that Lawrence had also beaten a handcuffed prisoner with a flashlight. None of that was reflected in his record; rather, Lawrence received an "outstanding" ranking as part of his agreement to resign. Thus, officials in Vergennes and later St. Albans and Burlington were unaware of Lawrence's bad behavior when they hired him. In Vergennes, where he was hired as chief of the city's four-man police force, he lasted just a year after authorities questioned the number of his drug arrests and fielded complaints about his hypervigilant enforcement of speed limits. Again, none of that was made public.

As Vermont journalist Hamilton Davis detailed in his riveting book, *Mocking Justice: America's Biggest Drug Scandal*, it all came to an end after Lawrence's identity was compromised in St. Albans, and he was hired by the Burlington Police Department. There, a young officer, Kevin Bradley, was excited to work undercover with Lawrence, whom he considered a supercop. Bradley became suspicious, however, when every one of Lawrence's drug buys just happened to occur when he was alone. Bradley brought his concerns to then state's attorney Patrick Leahy, who shared the trooper's suspicions. Leahy decided to create a sting to test Lawrence. He hired a special drug investigator from Brooklyn, someone Lawrence would not recognize, and made sure word got out that a big dealer named the Rabbi was selling drugs in downtown Burlington. Days later, as Davis wrote, "Leahy and his colleagues watched from across the street and listened in on a wire as the Rabbi sat down on a park bench and began reading a newspaper." They watched as Lawrence drove by the "pusher," never getting out of the car. Lawrence returned to the station, claiming to have purchased heroin from the Rabbi. To seal their case, Leahy had Lawrence attempt another buy with the same result, whereupon Lawrence was arrested on charges of perjury.

What particularly infuriated Oke and others who had been convicted based on Lawrence's testimony was what they considered a light sentence for the disgraced drug cop, one that was further reduced twice. While Lawrence had faced up to sixteen years in prison, he was sentenced to a minimum of four to eight years, which was reduced by a year before he had served the first year, and reduced again in 1978 when he was place on extended furlough.

Will Patten, the Back Home founder, former Ben & Jerry's executive, and a member of Vermont Businesses for Social Responsibility, had been among Lawrence's victims. At the time, Patten was working for a farmer in Shrewsbury. "It was in the paper, everyone in town knew it. I show up for work with Chan Smith on Lincoln Hill. Chan just says, 'Hey, how you doing?' That's all. The allegations didn't harm me. I was a son of Shrewsbury. He already knew I could work and that was what he judged me on." All the same, Patten sued the state after Lawrence's arrest, and received a cash settlement. "I knew what he charged me with was untrue and I was determined to fight it," he said.

No such luck for Oke. Like many others, he was unable to recoup the fine and legal costs he had accrued. Nonetheless, the executive order signed by Governor Salmon and embossed with the Great Seal of the State of Vermont granting him a "Full and Unconditional Pardon" gives him more than a modicum of pleasure.

As for the impact on Vermont, as Davis wrote, "the affair was much larger than the activities of one man. It was a monstrous miscarriage of justice. It strained the image of law-enforcement in the state, marred the reputation and damaged the careers of many law-enforcement officials, and left a trail of psychological wreckage in the lives of its victims."

* * *

Due to timing, the issue of drug enforcement played an important role in the early careers of several prominent Vermont politicians—and not the one usually associated with the counterculture. Even before the Lawrence case, as Chittenden County State's Attorney, Leahy seemed to show tolerance for marijuana users. He suggested as early as 1968 that prevention was a better investment than punishment. Toward that end, he favored waiving prosecution in order to explore why young people used drugs and learn where the drugs came from. Meanwhile, his counterpart in Washington County, Joseph Palmisano, was calling for more police manpower for drug enforcement and greater penalties for drug users. At that point, Washington County had seen many more drug-related arrests than other more populous and urban places in Vermont, in part because Palmisano had singled out Goddard College as a place where drugs were used and from which they were making their way into the wider community. Palmisano's tactics in going after drug users was criticized by a young James Jeffords when he ran successfully against Palmisano for Vermont attorney general. Jeffords, the son of the chief justice of the Vermont Supreme Court, told voters that environmental protection was more important to the state than staking out college parties. They apparently agreed, as he won in a landslide. A few years later, Leahy's role in busting Lawrence contributed to his successful campaign to become the youngest U.S. senator in Vermont history, a position he has held since 1975.

For those who believe Vermont has been given over to the liberals, however, the machinations the governor and state legislators went through in trying to write, amend, renegotiate, rewrite, and finally approve a marijuana bill in the last few years might suggest otherwise. While Massachusetts and Maine legalized recreational marijuana, Vermont legislators introduced several bills. On May 10, 2017, a joint bill to legalize cannabis, and approved by the entire state legislature, for the first time in U.S. history, was passed. The bill simply allowed possession of an ounce of cannabis. Two weeks later, Governor Phil Scott vetoed the bill and promised to work with the legislature to create one that would meet his concerns about driving while stoned and the accessibility of the drug to minors. In January 2018, a bill passed by both houses was signed into law by the governor.

What made Vermont's recreational bill unusual, and another first in the nation, as Senator Pollina pointed out, was that other states that have legalized recreational use have done so through the referendum process, with voters casting their approval or disapproval of the measure in the anonymity of the polling booth, rather than through the legislative process, in which each elected official's stand is public. Additionally, Vermont became the first state to legalize the possession and growth of small amounts of marijuana just hours after U.S. Attorney General Jeff Sessions removed the federal protections for state-legalized possession and use.

But even for someone like Lance, the issue has become more complicated. As he's aged, he said his views on legalization have come to border on hypocrisy. Despite all his years of illegal use, he wondered whether it was a good idea to legalize marijuana. On one hand, he said he didn't regret his use of pot or hallucinogens, although he hadn't done the latter in decades. "I figure I will drop some acid when I want to spend four hours contemplating my mortality," he said, chuckling. "I've got some in the freezer." At sixty-seven, the father of two clicked off the bad habits he didn't have, all legal. "I rarely drink alcohol. I don't gamble. I quit cigarettes years ago. I figure I'll live to ninety, easy. I still have my brain."

But, as Lance pointed out, 2017's world seemed a lot different than that of 1966, or 1976, for that matter. "Is it us or the world?" he asked. "We felt invincible then and I suppose the kids do now. But I traveled in drug circles. I knew drug dealers. I tried everything that was available, MDA and meth, neither one of which I would recommend, but no one ever offered me heroin. I've often thought booze was more dangerous to health and safety than a little marijuana. Now, like everyone else, I'm reading about heroin and young people dying and I worry that we might send the wrong message when we have so many young people who are in the grips of addiction. So, nah, I'm not sure that pot should be legal. Use my story but don't use my real name."

Days after Governor Scott reluctantly signed the recreational marijuana bill into law, one that allows for possession of up to an ounce of marijuana, two mature and four immature plants, Lance was rethinking his position. "That was my senior citizen coming out," he said of his previous opposition to legalization. "I'm very proud of the Vermont legislature and the careful way they went about crafting the bill. I think it's reasonable. And I particularly liked how they stuck it to Sessions."

Women's Work Reimagined

"Happiness is a baby's laugh or the novelty of a domestic chore as simple as mending. . . . How come a nice girl like you isn't married. . . . Some women fear estrogen may cause nymphomania. . . . A divorcee doesn't belong with married or single people. She's nowhere. . . . No [employer] welcomes the girl who majors in English, history, political science, art or philosophy—the liberal arts." These are among the sentences found in the January 11, 1966, issue of *Look* magazine with its entire fifty-page issue dedicated to "The American Woman." In articles entitled "The Hex on the Single Girl," "Do Men Really Like Women?" and "Is Someone Kidding the College Girl," *Look*, much as *Playboy* had with its article about Vermont's hippie invasion, attempted to explain a country in flux, albeit with a bias toward maintaining the status quo.

While the magazine's content is indicative of the prevalent mind-set, elsewhere in the country in 1966, Ken Kesey was hosting acid-test parties, Muhammad Ali refused to go to war, and Betty Friedan, Shirley Chisholm, and Muriel Fox founded the National Organization for Women. The world was changing, with or without the permission of the psychologists, doctors, mothers, and writers who penned the magazine's articles. Four years previously, President Kennedy had challenged every state to create a Governor's Commission on the Status of Women; Vermont's had been among the first, established in 1964 by Governor Phil Hoff. In the next decades, Vermont would become one of the pioneers in extending legal rights and services to women and children while transforming Vermont's physical and mental health service programs, much of this work brought about not through government intervention but through individual and group efforts by members of the counterculture generation working with other, often older Vermonters with that rare combination of possessing groundbreaking goals and the ability to make them happen.

History books and literature are replete with stories of Vermont women left behind to manage the farm, the business, or the family while husbands went to war, to wander, to wonder, or to find and secure a new and perhaps more promising place. As with those women, a substantial number of hippie women found themselves single mothers after first marriages fell apart and, through need and nature, networked with other women and men to make new lives. Reality can be sobering. Commitment in unity with others, however, was empowering, and in the 1970s, these young women, often working with older mentors like Sister Elizabeth Candon, the president of Trinity College, or Sallie Soule, a feminist from Charlotte, transformed procedures used in childbirth, joined forces to secure women's reproductive rights, organized to open up male-dominated trades to women, and transformed family court to make it more responsive to the needs of the whole family. And then some of these former hippies and activists used what they'd learned to help families as far away as Serbia, Mongolia, and Africa.

This is the broad and optimistic view. The corollary is that, while women have always owned small businesses throughout Vermont, not enough women have found their way to top leadership roles in politics, banking, and business, despite the efforts begun in the 1970s. And, while Vermont women have been fairly well represented in the state legislature, Madeleine Kunin remains Vermont's only female governor. Vermont is one of only two states —Mississippi is the other—that has never elected a woman to the U.S. Congress. Change the Story-VT, a consortium of the Women's Fund, the Vermont Commission on Women, and Vermont Works for Women, presented the conflicting picture of gender equity in its 2017 report. They found that the view of Vermont since the late 1960s as a national pacesetter in the area of women's leadership masks dramatic failures. For example, while 60 percent of the state supreme court justices and 50 percent of public university and college presidents were women in 2017, of the 296 people ever elected to statewide office, only 11 were women and only 8 percent of its highest-grossing companies were woman-led. More alarming, Vermont women were much more likely to live in poverty than Vermont men, especially if they were heads of households with children. One of the questions they will explore as they work to "change the story" was why the movement toward equality so evident from the late 1960s until well into the 1980s lost its steam, leading to what's viewed as stagnation in terms of leadership, pay equity, and other areas in which women's progress is managed.

With that in mind, one answer might be that the counterculture women and men who came and stayed in Vermont were more interested in holistic careers, in helping others rather than promoting themselves as entrepreneurs. Hippies in general weren't all that interested in careers.

The year 1966 was pivotal in the lives of people like Sas Carey, Maureen Dwyer and Patti Whalen, Dr. Emma Ottolenghi, Peggy Luhrs, Dr. Richard Bernstein, Charlie and Diane Gottlieb, Sister Elizabeth Candon, and others. It was the year Carey and her first husband moved to the Northeast Kingdom town of Newark where the locals thought they were beatniks, the year Dwyer began wearing an Afro and decided to become an army nurse, and the year Ottolenghi began planning her move to Vermont. It was the year Candon became president of Trinity College. Whalen, Bernstein, and the Gottliebs were students at colleges far removed from Vermont in 1966. Thanks to those degrees the *Look* magazine writers had dismissed, armed with the ability to think for themselves, the skills to communicate effectively, and the capacity for lifelong learning, they each helped women and families gain greater access to legal services and mental and physical health care in Vermont and, in the case of several, brought these amenities to people far beyond Vermont's borders. Each was motivated by a desire to do good work in the world rather than become rich or powerful. Those were the goals of the era—not competing for wealth—and they thought they were Vermont goals as well.

* * *

In 1970, when the political activists from the Red Clover collective in Putney, members of Earthworks, the farm-based commune in Franklin, and other Vermont communards met to construct together the necessities of the new society—food, education, transportation, and communication—their goals seemed unrealistic given the distances between their individual homes and with their rural locations. It wasn't until many found themselves living nearer one another in Chittenden, Rutland, Windham, and Washington Counties that some of their dreams came to fruition.

The concept of providing free health care and changing the way in which babies came into the world were among the activists' first accomplishments. After residents from Red Clover and Earthworks relocated to Chittenden

County, working with members of the Mount Philo commune located in Charlotte and with Burlington's large youth population, they opened the People's Free Clinic in August 1971 in Burlington's Old North End. It was an immediate success, providing exams and treatment for minor illnesses and injuries, tests for sexually transmitted diseases, and gynecological services. Donations were accepted but never required.

From today's vantage point, in which rules and regulations, certifications, lawsuits, and insurance payments are part and parcel of the "health-care industry," it seems astounding that in 1971 a group of radicals and hippies with limited financial resources and a volunteer medical staff could establish such a health clinic. By the end of its first year, the People's Free Clinic was serving roughly fifty people a week.

Barbara Nolfi helped organize the clinic, reveling in the opportunity to see something tangible come about after the frustrations she experienced when Earthworks disbanded. "It was exhilarating, exciting, rewarding," she said. "Even before we had a location, a few professionals offered their time and trained the volunteers. They donated equipment and supported the clinic financially." Eventually, the clinic made enough money to pay a few staff members; she was one of the first.

Charlotte physician Richard Bernstein volunteered his services. He was attracted to the idea of health care provided "in a nonhierarchical environment. Now you see how forward-thinking it was to imagine you could care for your own with knowledge and proper training, not complex medical stuff, of course, but as a way for people to make health care more affordable, to acknowledge that it is a universal right."

"Things seemed more possible then," Nolfi said, a hint of nostalgia or resignation in her voice. "We served a young population, nothing life-threatening. If someone was really sick, we referred that person to the hospital or another doctor."

Free Vermont also worked with health professionals who were concerned about residents living on Vermont communes and in primitive conditions. Working with UVM doctors and interns and the Burlington Ecumenical Council, they produced the *Home Health Handbook*, which was distributed to communes statewide. It placed an emphasis on sanitation, eating fresh vegetables, and other preventatives. Nolfi and others received training and traveled throughout Vermont to provide basic health care. "After considerable training, some of us became paramedics and the paramedics got more experience and trained others and the docs became good friends," she said.

"Folks thought we weren't practical. That was one of the assumptions back then about us, but we were very practical."

The clinic evolved over the decades, eventually becoming the Community Health Centers of Burlington, which today provides a full range of health and dental care on a sliding payment scale. It's the only Vermont organization that offers free and comprehensive health care for homeless people and, in cooperation with other civic organizations, housing and access to mental health and addiction services. By 2017, its clinics and outreach programs were serving more than 34,000 people in the region.

Not long after the free clinic was established, Nolfi and other women became interested in becoming trained as midwives. To that end, they arranged for "a gynecologist from central Vermont, Thurmond Knight, to do training with us on how to feel the uterus, how to tell how pregnant someone was, teaching us about pregnancy and birth. Knight was very experienced and generous with his time. I learned a lot from him."

Knight was an unusual doctor by any standard. In the early 1970s he was one of few family practitioners who would do home deliveries. Between 1973, when he began accompanying midwives on complicated deliveries, and his retirement in 1988, his efforts helped transform the way babies were born in Vermont. He and pediatrician Lou DiNicola opened the first birthing room in New England at Gifford Medical Center in Randolph—complete with rocking chair, birthing stool, comfortable bed, and shower. They encouraged healthy women to prepare for natural childbirth through classes attended by fathers. They offered workshops and discussed their practices at area hospitals. By the time Knight retired, Gifford had five birthing rooms and was nationally recognized for its approach to birthing, along with the successful rate of breastfeeding among mothers who delivered babies there.

Raven Lang, whose 1972 *Birth Book* became a primer for midwives of the era, also provided the Vermont women with training, traveling from California to "give us a crash course on birthing, five of us, four women and a man. From then on, I started working with births. Doctors and nurses let me into birthing rooms to observe and a lot of people on the communes started asking me to help with their births," Nolfi said. She estimated that she had participated in up to one hundred births between 1973 and 1990 when she retired.

"It was such an empowering time. Women were taking over birth. It was ours. It belonged to us, not the doctors. It changed the way that births happened. Midwives work in hospitals now and it's more common for women to choose to have a natural birth and for the fathers to be part of the birthing. That all came from that meeting we had on the hill," she said. "Imagine that, mostly young people from all over the United States coming here to Vermont, sharing a goal to make a change in the culture, in the way that babies came into the world, not in some sterile environment with strangers all around, but with your loved ones, your family there. Today, that's not considered unnatural. It's how births are done routinely, whether in birthing centers or at home."

Vermont now has as many as twenty licensed home-birth midwives. In 2015, roughly 24 percent of Vermont births were attended by a midwife, primarily in hospitals outfitted with birthing rooms inspired by Gifford. Many have tubs for water-deliveries, while others have an extra bed for a spouse or partner, meals delivered, and rocking chairs.

As for Knight, the demands of delivering babies at all hours of the day and night took its toll. He retired from medicine in 1988 to work as a builder of beautiful violins, violas, and cellos made from wood harvested from his own property.

* * *

While some women were demanding greater freedom in how newborns came into the world, others wanted greater reproductive freedom. Few Vermonters know that Vermont legalized abortion prior to the Supreme Court ruling *Roe v. Wade* or that a Catholic nun helped a group of counterculture activists create the state's first women's health-care center where early abortions were performed. The center resulted from a 1972 court case, *Beecham v. Leahy*, in which a welfare recipient, Jacqueline R., sought an abortion from Doctor Jackson Beecham of St. Johnsbury. Beecham had become increasingly distressed by the number of women who sustained injuries and worse from botched abortions. He agreed that it would be in his patient's physical and mental welfare to abort the fetus. However, her pregnancy did not present a life-threatening condition, the only situation under which a Vermont doctor could legally perform an abortion. At that time, non-life-threatening abortions were legal only in Hawaii and New York. The Vermont woman could not afford to travel. Curiously, Vermont's law had no provision banning a woman from having the procedure while a doctor faced ten to twenty years' imprisonment for performing an abortion. Beecham suggested that his patient sue him in order to test the law.

Patrick Leahy, then a state's attorney, defended the law when it came before the high court. The court ruled that if there were no legal restrictions against a patient receiving a particular medical procedure, the legislature could not deny the right to that procedure. In this backward way, the ruling, issued a year before *Roe v. Wade*, made Vermont the third state to remove all restrictions against access to an abortion.

While some people thought the ruling would lead to doctors providing abortions relatively quickly or that the legislature would address the issue by making abortion illegal for the woman as well as the doctor, neither event happened until activist women like Nolfi and Roz Payne and a Catholic nun joined forces. At the time, as president of Trinity College, a Catholic school, Sister Elizabeth Candon and other clergy members had been meeting to discuss the conflicting issues surrounding women's reproductive rights and the moral issues abortion posed. Candon had grown up on a dairy farm in Pittsford and was especially sympathetic to issues of poverty and the financial and physical burden that unwanted children placed on women and families with meager financial means. When she stepped down from the presidency of Trinity in 1976, Governor Richard Snelling named her secretary of Human Services. In all these roles she often championed progressive ideas, pointing out that her vow as a Sister of Mercy obliged her to "serve the poor, the sick and the uneducated." As a result, she became a proponent of family planning while she also realized that many women became pregnant despite planning and contraceptives, which were not approved of by the Catholic Church. When the U.S. Supreme Court later ruled that states were not required to provide Medicaid payments for elective abortions, Candon, as Human Services secretary, ruled that Vermont would continue to fund the procedures. Of course, this brought considerable criticism upon her, but Candon was not a stereotypical nun. One of her favorite memories was white-water rafting through the Grand Canyon at age seventy-six. A scholar of medieval English language and literature, she taught at least one literature course at Trinity for fifty years, even while serving as college president and DHS secretary. A friend of Goddard College founder Tim Pitkin, Candon's ideas about education had been affected by a trip to Scandinavia that she took with him and his wife in the late 1960s to study nontraditional-aged learners. She introduced these ideas to Vermont as she helped transform the state's education system to help older Vermonters return to college. In 1977, she founded Vermont Women in Higher Education to enhance opportunities for women leaders in Vermont.

* * *

At first, Peggy Luhrs of Burlington was surprised by Candon's involvement in these rather controversial issues, but she soon came to see her as a powerful champion of women's rights and humanitarian goals. Luhrs had become aware of her own feminist instincts the day a junior high classmate informed her that only boys could be class president, a sentiment that blossomed into outrage when her gynecologist, a right-to-life proponent, refused to give her birth control as if he knew what was best for her. She began to ask herself, whose body was this? Then, when she decided to have a child, she worried that her mother's milk would be full of DDT. For her, these were not abstract questions about the role of women or the safety of food, but real-life concerns about her own body, personal freedom, and the health of the next generation. She began to educate herself about antiwar, environmental, and women's issues, seeing them as connected.

Luhrs had come to Vermont "purely by accident" in 1969 when she and her former husband were living in New York City with their small infant. There had been a record number of murders in the city that year, six hundred perhaps, and the couple wanted to move to the country. They considered upstate New York, but the decision was made for them when her husband, who worked for IBM, got transferred to Vermont. Luhrs felt a bit lost in Burlington, a rather drab and struggling city in 1969, until she "made friends among other young people, met the antiwar people, the folks working to create a food co-op, and the feminists." The new friends included Sallie Soule, who had moved back to Vermont the previous year. Soule, a Michigan native, was older than the counterculture youth in Chittenden County. She had earned her MA in history at the University of Vermont before moving to New York, where she worked for Macmillan Publishing and Eastman Kodak. In 1968, she and her husband opened Horsford Nursery in Charlotte, and she later served as Vermont commissioner of employment and training under Governor Madeleine Kunin, as well as a state legislator and senator. A feminist, Soule quickly became a role model for the younger women, creating what she dubbed "the old-girls network," to show ordinary people that wives and mothers from an older generation supported the younger people in their desire to have control over their bodies.

Meanwhile, Luhrs had joined the Vermont chapter of the Women's Political Caucus. Because the national caucus did not allow members to talk about abortion, the Vermont group changed its name to the Women's Political Lobby and talked about what they darned well pleased. She joined

Soule and others at Trinity College at a planning meeting organized by Candon and others to respond to the *Beecham* ruling. "That was where we plotted how to legalize abortion in Vermont," she recalled, describing how activist women came to the conclusion that it was they who would have to open a clinic where women could have a safe abortion rather than wait for the establishment to do so. At a subsequent meeting held in a basement on Bank Street in Burlington and attended by bankers, nurses, doctors, and lawyers, the president of Chittenden Bank offered the group a small loan, and Candon offered to find appropriate personnel. A location was chosen in Colchester.

Just as quickly as the supporters had organized, so too did opponents. Luhrs recalled a well-attended meeting on reproductive rights with Vermont legislators at which one legislator asked, "How do we know there will be enough men for the next war?" if abortion became legal. While the legislator couldn't stop the clinic from opening, voters in Colchester could, as the clinic needed their approval. Colchester had a strong Catholic presence and local priests urged parishioners to defeat the measure, but the center's supporters "were well organized, had many coffee dates with women in Colchester. Remarkably, they were open to discussion of all the issues, and we won the vote," Luhrs recalled.

Roz Payne, the Red Clover member, Black Panther archivist, and filmmaker, had moved to Richmond and became deeply involved in the center's organization. As supporters worked on final preparations, she worried that something would happen at the last moment to keep it from opening. Payne came up with the idea of volunteering to be "treated" with a blood test on the Sunday evening before opening day. "We had this completely irrational belief that if we had already started providing services, they couldn't close us down," she said, considering her blood test "a talisman" that led to the center's continued existence. Like the People's Clinic, the Women's Health Center was successful; within a year, it outgrew its location in Colchester and relocated to a larger building on North Avenue in Burlington.

At the Vermont Women's Health Center's fifteenth anniversary in 1987, Governor Kunin acknowledged the work of dozens of women who had helped the center grow and prosper while reminding the audience that self-determination was an essential element of a successful society. As she put it, "To truly be in charge of one's life is a healthy act, mentally, physically—and poetically. . . . You cannot be an equal self-sustaining human being unless you understand yourself and have some control over your destiny and over the destiny of others in a real way and not have others set barriers that limit you in any way."

Among the people recognized that day for their contributions were two women doctors who performed abortions at the clinic, Judy Tyson and Emma Ottolenghi. The two had met when Ottolenghi was teaching anatomy and women's health at the University of Vermont's medical college and Tyson was a student. As a person whose Italian-Jewish family had escaped Turin as Mussolini began deporting Jews to Nazi death camps, Ottolenghi had an instinctual grasp of the way a single right can change a person's life, such as the ability for a young, unmarried woman with few resources to have access to a safe abortion in an environment where her emotional health was also respected. In a most direct way, she said she felt no contradiction in her celebration of and commitment to life and the living and her dedication to women's reproductive rights.

Ottolenghi came to Vermont in 1972 when her husband was offered a job as a cardiologist at the medical center, a position that kept him from being drafted. The two strongly opposed the Vietnam War. She had received an undergraduate degree and medical education at McGill University. Three months after the *Beecham* ruling, she was treating women at the Vermont Women's Health Center, where she continued to practice until 1976 when she opened a private practice. For Ottolenghi, who had seen women in crisis after illegal abortions, the issue was always about free will and safety, causes that led her to Bolivia, India, Kazakhstan, and Africa after her retirement, to volunteer as a women's health-care provider and researcher.

Doctor Bernstein also worked at the women's health center, the only male on the staff. "They put up with me," he joked. Along with treating patients, he trained paraprofessionals in medical procedures, preparing them to take over some procedures when he and other doctors moved on. As a result, the Vermont Women's Health Center became one of the first clinics to employ nurse practitioners, the category of nurses who receive advanced training that prepares them to diagnose and treat conditions normally treated only by medical doctors.

"Both clinics worked to empower people, not just in terms of medical training but also in decision making," Bernstein said. "They were run collectively; decisions were made by the whole group on a consensus basis. Both in their goals and the way in which they put their goals into action, they were admirable organizations."

* * *

Along with expanding reproductive rights, many of these counterculture activists were interested in improving women's economic opportunities. The two goals—reproductive freedom and economic stability—were entwined. Luhrs was among city residents who lobbied Burlington mayor Bernie Sanders to establish a women's council, becoming its longtime director in 1985. The Sanders years were busy as he, working with others in his administration, initiated programs to support and expand the arts, increase affordable housing, and other progressive projects. As head of the Burlington Women's Council, Luhrs joined forces with Ginny Winn, an activist and proud lesbian who had been one of the cottage parents at Shrewsbury's Spring Lake Ranch, the mental health treatment center in Shrewsbury, before moving to Burlington. There, she was the outspoken director of Chittenden County Community Action, created to address chronic unemployment and underemployment in the city. Winn had compiled what she dubbed the "Boom Pie Report," a study that identified what jobs were coming into Burlington, who was getting them, and who was being left out of the city's economic growth. Her study showed a need for trade laborers, particularly carpenters, and also that single mothers were receiving the smallest slice of the economic pie. Luhrs, whose many skills include carpentry, knew that women could be trained in the carpentry trade but that stereotypes blocked their entry into the field. She created a job bank that put women with trade skills together with a list of employers that needed employees. Eventually, more than sixty women with trade skills were listed in the job bank through these joint efforts.

Sanders had also created the Community & Economic Development Office, which had a broad range of goals that included making employment opportunities more equitable. To that end, the city hired Martha Whitney, a young woman who had been doing work not ordinarily open to women —house painting, landscaping, and roofing—while also serving as an advocate for people with handicaps. Whitney designed a training program, the Women's Equal Opportunity Program, in which women were trained as carpenters, tile setters, electricians, and in other skilled trades. To further the entrance of women into this growing field of employment, the city passed an ordinance that required 10 percent of all city-funded construction jobs to be filled by women. That program eventually merged with Step Up, another program instigated by a woman who had balked at the idea that there was women's work and men's work. For Ronnie Sandler, it had started in seventh grade when she was told she had to take home economics rather than workshop simply because she was a girl. Sandler learned carpentry on the job and eventually became the first woman to join the Michigan trades union. After moving to Vermont, in the mid-1980s she created Step Up to help train women in the trades. Over the decades, Step Up evolved into Vermont Works for Women, a statewide job-training program aimed at giving women a wide range of tools for economic independence.

These programs all worked together to create opportunities for women in the trades and in leadership, especially in Chittenden County. Luhrs would argue that they have contributed to the area's economic growth, far outreaching other regions of Vermont.

"From the perspective of then to now, so much has happened, and women work in every field imaginable," Luhrs said while observing that "much, much more needs to be done," particularly in the fields of pay equity, business ownership by women, and the poverty rate for families. "There are always threats to progress. Essential to remember and never forget is that reproductive freedom is central to women's progress. A society is not truly productive and equitable unless all its members have equal opportunity to pursue their dreams and that is not possible unless all its members have the right to decisions about their bodies."

To that end, while remaining active in political and social issues affecting women, Luhrs has also long campaigned for LGBTQ rights. "Looking back, I've always been counterculture," she said, while arguing that the values of the counterculture are ones that benefit the whole culture.

* * *

In 1973, the year after the Women's Health Center was established in Burlington, a group of seven women living in Rutland County began creating a similar organization. Among them were Gail Johnson, a VISTA volunteer; Anne Sarcka, whose parents had established Spring Lake Ranch in 1932 and ran it for thirty years; the artist Susan Farrow; and Chris Anderson who had helped organize the Whipple Hollow Canning Center and the Rutland County Farmers' Market. Although she never worked at the health center, the second to open in Vermont, it was Anderson who signed the mortgage for the building the group purchased at 187 North Main Street. Perhaps Anderson expressed best the fervor and confidence of the time, a self-assurance that led people to take such risks: "We had an idea and we just did it."

The Southern Vermont Women's Health Center operated until 1988, when private doctors and Planned Parenthood took over its services. As with

The organizers and early employees at Vermont's second Women's Health Center, established in Rutland. Top row, *left to right*: Mary Cannon, Susan Katz, Patty Garber, Dawn Morse, Susan Farrow, Sas Carey, and Donna Belcher. Bottom row, *left to right*: Evelyn Westebee, unidentified, Mary O'Brien, Maureen (Mo) Dwyer, Gail Holmes.

Courtesy of Maureen Dwyer

Burlington's center, it faced challenges for financing and opposition from opponents of abortion but also received support from unlikely sources such as two wealthy women who anonymously gave sizeable donations to the center.

The stories of two women hired to work there, Maureen "Mo" Dwyer and Sas Carey, illustrate the breadth and depth of commitment the movement inspired as well as the unpredictable ways in which careers evolve. Both women operate from a spiritual place. Dwyer still embraces much of her Catholic heritage but has also studied world religions, respects messages brought through dreams and visions, accepts the idea of past lives, and that people from our pasts interact with us whether we acknowledge it or not. Carey, a Quaker, speaks of the religion's basic premise that every person is loved and guided by God and called to a special purpose or a "leading."

Much as Buddhists meditate, Quakers listen. They believe that God communicates through a stirring in one's heart, and even through dreams.

In many ways, these beliefs are interwoven in the ways that Dwyer and Carey have served others in Vermont and as far away as Vietnam and Mongolia.

Dwyer has a favorite saying, "Patients teach you a lot; the healing goes both ways." It's the lesson she learned from forty years working as an army nurse in Vietnam, in the emergency room at Rutland Hospital, as a nurse in Rutland's Women's Health Center, at the Veterans Administration Center in White River Junction, and as a nurse practitioner caring for cardiology patients at the University of Vermont Medical Center.

Perhaps it began with another woman, a nurse who had comforted Dwyer when, as a junior in high school, she suffered a ruptured appendix and a dangerous infection. "I was a very spiritual child even though the nuns were all about sin and you're going to hell. I was frightened before my surgery, and my mother was no-nonsense, with guarded emotions. That nurse took charge and made me feel safe. We said the Hail Mary together. That's when I decided I would become a nurse. That recovery was a major life event that had something to do with my destiny. My family wanted me to be a teacher but I was impressed with the compassion that nurse showed me; she didn't judge me."

While Dwyer doesn't pray with her patients, she may pray for them. More to the point, she understood that it was all right to connect with patients rather than stay aloof from their hopes and fears; that healing has three parts: body, mind, and spirit. In nursing school at St. Joseph's College in Emmitsburg, Maryland, the Daughters of Charity nuns were her professors, while the black patients, nurses, and nurse's aides she worked alongside taught other lessons, about life and death, pain and suffering, and the reality of life in America's capital city. Dwyer had grown up a dreamy child in a white community, the daughter of an Irish cop and an Italian mother, with two protective big brothers in a close community. At school, she sometimes was taunted for her thick, curly hair and above-average height. It wasn't until the late 1960s that that hair of hers became stylish, and Dwyer could sport her riotous Afro. In college, too, she became convinced that the Vietnam War was wrongheaded and could not understand why Americans were fighting the Vietnamese people.

Why then, during her junior year, did she sign up to be an army nurse, taking the chance that she might be sent to Vietnam? A small reason was the

Maureen Dwyer in Vietnam where she decided that it wasn't her job to judge who had shot whom but simply to try to keep people alive. This photo is before she let her hair grow naturally into an Afro.
Courtesy of Maureen Dwyer

financial help the army gave her toward tuition. The more important reason involved her growing understanding of the struggles that most people faced and her understanding that she had been immune from such suffering growing up. "Others were joining VISTA and the Peace Corps. I, too, wanted to be of service. All the guys I knew were being drafted. I thought, I'm a well-trained nurse. Why not? I can help people while these guys have no choice."

In November 1968 she reported to Fort Sam Houston in Texas for basic training, then to Fort Knox, Kentucky, where she cleaned and packed the "dirty" wounds that returning GIs came home with. There, she became a first lieutenant and learned to push away concerns about being sent to Vietnam by hanging out at the pool, dating, and attending the "Hairy Buffalo Parties" the medics and pilots threw where a concoction of grain alcohol and juice was so strong everyone passed out on the floor to Iron Butterfly's "In-A-Gadda-Da-Vida."

War called in mid-1969. At home, as she prepared to ship overseas, a neighborhood friend who had become a priest offered to say Mass for her safety. She recalled his words spoken with her family gathered around days before she flew to Vietnam: "Maureen is going to witness suffering in a way many people don't get to see. It will make her stronger, and though difficult, it will be life-changing."

She soon learned what truth that was. Every day, there was death and patching up, evacuating soldiers back home only to see them sent back to war. There was caring for patients at a leprosarium near the base, for children burned by napalm, for grandmothers with eye infections. There was deciding that it wasn't her job to judge who had shot whom but to try to keep people alive. A year is a long time in war. It took Dwyer three months back home, much of it spent sleeping, before she began to make her way back. After a trip cross-country, driving her new, red Datsun 240z, she settled into San Francisco where she worked for a year at San Francisco General Hospital. There the wartime lessons about treatment within "the golden hour"—the time immediately after an injury—were being applied to civilians. A year later, she finally got to experience what so many other college kids had, a back-packing trip through Europe, sporting her big Afro. She planned to return to San Francisco but, without any plan, the wandering brought her to some friends' ski lodge in Stockbridge, Vermont, and, finally, the full embrace of the counterculture.

Dwyer fell in love with life on Killington Peak where she skied all day and worked as a waitress at the Summit Lodge at night. The friends she made then are the friends she has today, a family who worked and played together, danced and listened to music, made macramé hangers, smoked pot, and ate granola. "It was a magical, carefree time," she recalled.

In 1973, when the Southern Vermont Women's Health Center opened, Dwyer answered the call for a nurse to help with examinations and abortions. There, Dr. Robert Andrews, who "really stuck his neck out for women and women's rights," was a mentor. At the same time, she was doing duty in Rutland Hospital's emergency room. In 1974, grant money became available for Vermont's first nurse-practitioner certification program. While juggling two jobs, Dwyer earned her certificate in 1975 and a master's of science degree from UVM in 1998, the year the women's center closed.

As with Vietnam, she was deeply affected by the experience of being with so many women through their abortions. "My mother taught me there's nothing I couldn't do just because I was a woman—but not all women feel empowered," she said. Remembering that nurse who helped her through a scary time, Dwyer determined to find time to listen to each patient, allowing each to express her concerns in a safe environment, an approach she subsequently found useful as she worked with other war veterans at the VA Medical Center in White River Junction from 1988 to 1992.

That year, Dwyer had the opportunity to work as the first in-patient nurse practitioner for cardiology at what is now the University of Vermont Medical Center and moved to Burlington. There, she brought the same approach to patients facing life-threatening conditions. She found time to listen. That time of listening was what she missed most after retiring in 2014, the way in which a simple word spoken softly and calmly could bring deep comfort to a patient.

Thinking back to the moment that put her on the path to service for others, Dwyer said, "We're never really alone. Our ancestors, our spirits are cheering us on, and the people you get exposed to when you need them the most."

* * *

Sas Carey believes there has been a remarkable symmetry to her life, beginning with her first years in Vermont as a young hippie mother, potter, and teacher to working at Vermont's second women's health center, to her training as a physical and spiritual healer, to her award-winning work as a documentarian and caregiver to some of the planet's last migratory people, the herdsmen and women of Mongolia. As one experience has led to the next, she recognized that her ability to sleep on the ground and travel with the Mongolian people through rough, harsh terrain and weather in her seventies would not have been possible without her early experiences as a nineteen-year-old homesteader in Vermont's Northeast Kingdom.

Carey grew up in Connecticut where her father headed the Congregational Church's world service committee. In high school, she was an exchange student in Denmark through the American Field Service, the intercultural educational exchange program. The summer after graduation, her family traveled across the United States to visit a Lakota reservation at Standing Rock. There, she met a young weaver from New Hampshire named Ken Mayberger who was part of a four-man work-camp crew building a recreation center for Lakota teenagers. Mayberger, too, had been raised a Congregationalist but had become disillusioned because of the war and was interested in becoming a Quaker.

That fall, when Carey went off to Western Connecticut State College, she and Mayberger made plans to meet at an American Friends Service work camp in Roxbury, Massachusetts. They were there when President Kennedy was assassinated, a shared experience that made them close. They became Quakers and married soon afterward. Carey was just nineteen. She joined Mayberger briefly at Keene State College where he was a student, and in May 1966 they moved together to Newark, Vermont, on land given to them by a couple they'd met at a Quaker meeting. Mayberger took an old warehouse

Sas Carey, a young potter in the Northeast Kingdom.
Courtesy of Sas Carey

apart and made a home for them. He had gone to Peru a few years earlier where he learned traditional Quechua weaving using a backstrap loom, the oldest form of loom in the world, constructed of wood, bone, and strings, entirely non-mechanized and portable. In Vermont's Northeast Kingdom, he wove fabric using the ancient Peruvian loom while Carey sewed pillows and other items for sale. Their son Kai was born at home. "Ken knew how to build a house. I knew nothing. Essentially, I went camping. We were fortunate in that our neighbors were friendly and helpful because so many people had left during the Depression. They were glad to have young people around even if they didn't appreciate the way we looked. Ken had a beard and long hair. They saw that we worked really hard, though. We built amazing gardens there," she recalled.

In 1968, they learned of a house for sale in Cornwall for $2,956, and bought and fixed it up. Carey taught second grade at the Weybridge School, worked as a potter, and took time to study weaving at the Haystack Mountain School of Crafts in Maine where she met the artist Susan Farrow, also a student there. Carey and her husband adopted their daughter Jasmine Heidi, took part in a parent's cooperative school, and pursued their crafts.

The marriage didn't last, however. Carey moved to Middlebury with the children, went to nursing school, and simultaneously began pursuing her interest in psychic healing. For her, owing to her Quaker beliefs and personal experiences, mind and body were inseparable. In the summer of 1973, Carey went to the women's health center in Rutland for an exam only to discover Farrow working there. As it turned out, the center desperately needed a counselor, and Carey needed a job. Farrow suggested that Carey apply. She did and was hired. None of this was planned, but in the process of counseling women in difficult times, Carey came to realize she had a gift in helping people heal after trauma.

In 1985, she decided to devote herself to energy healing, underwent extensive training, and opened a private practice as a holistic nurse. Through all this, she felt her openness to the Quaker idea of listening for a "leading" had been essential, especially the day a client told Carey about David Eisenberg's *Encounters with Qi*, a book that explores Chinese medicine. The client had a strong feeling that Carey should go to Mongolia. Mongolia was not on Carey's radar, although she had received invitations to travel there with the American Holistic Nursing Association. That client was convinced that Carey was meant to go there and offered to pay $5,000 for the trip in return for seven years of energy treatments.

"My feet touched the ground and I felt some incredible energy. I had no clue what it was about but definitely it was big. I knew it right away," Carey recalled about her first trip to Mongolia in 1994. At the Institute of Traditional Medicine in Mongolia's capital Ulaanbaatar, she met a doctor who practiced traditional Mongolian and European medicine "and my heart started beating like crazy. Without knowing I would say the words, I said, 'Would you take an American disciple?' This is not my way but there I was and it happened."

Carey began her internship in 1995, which led to a job with the United Nations Development Program as a health educator working with the migratory people of Mongolia. There, she became interested in the nomadic herders living a traditional lifestyle in the Gobi Desert and subsequently studied their health practices for the United Nations. Recognizing that poor dental hygiene led to other health issues, she raised money for toothbrushes and taught the herdsmen how to use them. Learning a new skill—that of documentarian—she produced several award-winning films, *Women's Song* and *Migration*, the story of the nomadic herders in northern Mongolia whose way of life is endangered.

She became convinced that the West had much to learn from Eastern medicine, became one of the first Americans to receive a Physician of Tra-

Sas Carey in Mongolia, where she has taught dental health to the itinerant herdsmen, studied traditional Mongolian medicine, and created a nonprofit to bring medical care to remote areas of the country.
Courtesy of Sas Carey

ditional Mongolian Medicine certificate, and created a school to bring that teaching to Americans, headquartered in Middlebury. She also founded Nomadicare in 2003, a nonprofit program supporting two centers where doctors from rural hospitals are trained in traditional Mongolian medicine, practices they hadn't been allowed to follow under Soviet rule.

All this has been no easy task. Mongolia is bordered by the Gobi Desert in the south and Siberia in the north. Its nomadic people use horses for transportation and live on a diet consisting primarily of meat and dairy products. She must ride a horse for eight hours to get to the herdsmen's summer settlement after a long, arduous plane and truck ride. A lactose-intolerant vegetarian, she is also terrified of horses. While with the herdsmen, she lives in a Siberian tipi and sleeps on the ground.

"It's because of Vermont that I can do this," she said, not just referring to the physical challenges. "Simplicity is accepted in Vermont. You can live simply here without being judged. That's enough, and that's a Quaker tenet. That Vermont acceptance allowed me to work in Mongolia. They're about the same. I'm just a little older than I was when I was a hippie living in the Northeast Kingdom." Then, referring to the Quaker idea of a "leading," she said, "You're on a path and then you're shown the way. It's up to you whether you take it or not."

* * *

Patricia Whalen's path has been equally unpredictable. How do you go from living in a series of communes in Vermont to serving as an international judge in the War Crimes Chamber of Bosnia and Herzegovina and helping a war-torn country develop its own legal system? Whalen would also say it began with one woman, in her case a pregnant neighbor whose beating at the hands of her husband and the subsequent miscarriage of the fetus she had been carrying introduced her to the realities of domestic violence in Vermont. She discovered a legal system ill-equipped to deal with the problems of home-grown aggression or to support a young mother fleeing an abusive spouse. From that moment as a young mother herself, Whalen developed the skills needed to change Vermont's family court, create protections for victims of domestic abuse, and then bring what she learned in the Green Mountains to places where a fragile legal system had to be resurrected.

Whalen grew up in Pennsylvania where her grandfather and father were coalminers until her father at age twenty-four decided to go to college, instilling in her an appreciation of education. After graduating from Misericordia University, a women's college run by the Sisters of Mercy, in 1970 she went to Temple University for graduate school. She became involved in street theater with black kids in North Philadelphia until the Black Panthers "came and said you can't work here anymore; you're white." Discouraged about starting over as that work had been the basis of her graduate thesis, Whalen left graduate school, got married, got pregnant, and decided to leave the city to "go back to the land." She'd been to Woodstock and enjoyed the pleasures of the time but "respected my parents too much to just live with" her boyfriend. She had a church wedding with all the required pageantry.

Her husband had planned to go to Goddard but the couple "got as far as Putney, found a place to live on a beautiful stream and that was it." She was friends with the activists at Red Clover and the communards at Total Loss

A young Patti Whalen in
Vermont, summer 1970, with
Larry Dooley, deceased.
Courtesy of Patricia Whalen

Farm and eventually moved with her husband and daughter to a collective
called Cold River in Walpole, New Hampshire, then to a communal house
in Jamaica, Vermont. There, she and a girlfriend who also had a college degree realized "We were just going through this life, bored out of our minds.
We wanted to *do* something. She wanted to be a doctor. I didn't know what
I wanted to do. We were hippies. We had no money. I waitressed at the Jamaica House and Brookside Steak House and seemed to be drifting. Then
my neighbor came asking for help. After she miscarried, he was remorseful,
tried to kill himself by shooting himself in the foot. Her life seemed so dangerous, so tenuous. I instinctively looked for a woman lawyer to help her but
I couldn't find one."

Whalen had found her purpose: she would become a woman lawyer,
choosing to attend the newly formed Vermont Law School. Toward the end
of the 1960s, several women from the Brattleboro area had gathered at the
Common Ground Restaurant to discuss creating a women's center in rooms

they rented above downtown stores. They were concerned especially about the number of rapes reported in the area and began to educate themselves on the issue and ways to respond. From these efforts, the Rape Crisis Center was founded. As it became clear that many of the women had nowhere to go if the abuser was a husband or father of their child, the center's supporters began sheltering the women in their homes as they researched how to establish a safe home. In 1974, a federal grant funded the first shelter for victims of domestic violence, the Women's Crisis Center in Brattleboro, and Burlington also opened a shelter, followed by other shelters and programs statewide. The Brattleboro shelter had been spearheaded by Julie Peterson, who later served in the Vermont House of Representatives between 1982 and 1990, as legislative liaison in the Kunin administration and chief of staff for Governor Howard Dean. Two years later, the Vermont Coalition Against Domestic Violence and a statewide Battered Women's Network were established.

Throughout this time, while still in law school, Whalen worked at the Brattleboro shelter, now called the Women's Freedom Center. "No one was talking about the issue in the mid-1970s when my neighbor was in a horrible situation; then over night everyone was talking about it. Working at the shelter really colored my law-school experience," she observed. "I was very practical, disinterested in philosophical discussions. I wanted to know the rules of access, how to get help for people. I was not interested in corporations or taxes, and graduated from law school without taking those subjects. I knew I was never going to use them."

Meanwhile, working with others who were responding to the need for protective legislation, she helped write clear, statewide protocols for police and hospital personnel involved in rape cases, as well as relief-from-abuse-order legislation, all passed by the Vermont legislature to replace "an antiquated process that just didn't work. Only a few other states had [relief-from-abuse orders] before Vermont. Now it's a quick ex-parte process, then a hearing within ten days. Prior to 1980, you could get a restraining order but it was a long and complicated process and essentially the doors were closed to battered and low-income women. We had to create a process, educate judges, lawyers, and police. It was very difficult because they were so discouraged; they would do their jobs and the abuse would happen over and over. We had to convince police it was their job to protect not to prosecute, and then we worked together to create a process for prosecution to be more effective."

After law school, Whalen received a paid fellowship through a program administered by the historically black Howard University to provide legal services to Vermont Legal Aid clients. She remembered a black attorney coming from D.C. to interview her: "He was like, 'What is this place?' I spent the whole time talking to him about poverty." She told him what she'd discovered: "We don't have diversity [in Vermont] but we have bone-chilling poverty; you just don't see it." She worked as a lawyer for Legal Aid for eleven years, from 1979 to 1990. "Working in legal services you come to realize how important the legal system is to each family. I enjoyed working with people and helping them get heard, helping them to see how they could survive a divorce. You spend a lot of time in court, but there's also talking about how to make spaghetti, how to buy a board game and have fun with your kids."

In 1990, Governor Kunin began appointing more women to the bench. When Kunin's chief of staff, Liz Bankowski, asked Whalen to consider applying for a judgeship in the family court, she noted that Whalen was the first person to say she wasn't qualified to be a judge. Bankowski considered her more than qualified, noting that Whalen had helped untangle the full array of legal conundrums involving families while working for Legal Aid. They needed *her*, she said, and told Whalen all the men she'd contacted thought *they* were qualified.

At the time, Vermont's family court system was undergoing a major reorganization. "I was really interested in being part of that. I understood that child support could make or break a family. Before family court, the most important thing the judge did was the house, the divorce, the kids; child support came last and it was usually $50 a month," Whalen recalled. Again, she helped to create legal protocols, from monetary support to custody issues, working closely with other woman justices who were passionate about the need for guidelines, including family court judges Shelley Gartner of Rutland, Trina Beck of Hartland and Burlington, who went on to found the Vermont Parent Representation Center, and Amy Davenport, who became Vermont's chief administrative judge.

In 2002, Superior Court Judge Shireen Fisher, the second woman to be appointed to the Vermont judiciary and a longtime mentor to Whalen, was asked to help the International Court of Justice based in The Hague develop treaties for international child custody, support, and abduction cases. These treaties would establish laws that would apply to families in The Hague's ninety member countries. At the time, it was diplomats who normally wrote treaties, a situation that often resulted in vague language that led to litigation where the specifics would be ironed out and, thus, clarify the law. The International Court decided to take a new tack. Realizing that vague language could cause difficulties for families, The Hague hired judges to help the diplomats draft the appropriate language. Fisher was appointed to represent the International Association of Women Justices on the committee and brought Whalen with her. The two worked for five years on the international treaties now used in cases involving divorced parents living in separate countries. "To be there in that world was amazing to me, two Vermont lawyers working together on international treaties to help families with these difficult issues, a very heady experience," Whalen recalled.

She and Fisher were effective because "Vermont judges, we're workhorses; we have the tiniest judiciary in the United States. Even as a magistrate, you have to do lots of little things. When someone needed to be arraigned, if you were there, you had to step forward; sometimes it was up to you to fix the lights or shut the windows. Vermont's not a place where judges get to have a big head."

Their work got noticed, and first Fisher and then Whalen were appointed to the War Crimes Chamber in Bosnia and Herzegovina, which had the responsibility under the Dayton Accords to try war crimes stemming from the conflict in the former Yugoslavia. Developing the War Crimes Chamber was a monumental task. In that capacity, Whalen served as an international judge presiding on trials that involved war crimes, genocide, crimes against humanity, and gender-based violence. Additionally, she oversaw judicial-education programs for the national judges and legal advisors in Bosnia and Herzegovina and subsequently served as an advisor to the court as it continued to be the busiest war crimes court in the world.

As if that weren't enough, she has helped bring Afghan women judges to Vermont for leadership and judicial training as a board member of the Rural Women's Leadership Institute of Vermont. At the time, there was no functional court system to build on in Afghanistan; the women judges needed to see a system that was relatively simple and effective to use as a model upon which to build their own system. "I thought Vermont was the perfect place for these women to have their training. We don't have the crazy dockets that large cities have, and federal judges are not always that accessible. We do things in a very basic way here and we're accessible. The women could observe court management and jury trials firsthand, meet defense counsels, prosecutors, and witnesses," she said, noting how cooperative Vermont lawyers and judges were. She and Peterson worked closely together again on the project, as they had at the crisis center.

Whalen knew the Afghan judges would be nervous coming to the United

Three Vermonters at the International Court of Justice in The Hague helping to write international laws on child custody and support issues for children of international parents living in different countries: Shireen Fisher, Marian Ely, and Patricia Whalen.
Courtesy of Patricia Whalen

States, so she developed a program whereby the women stayed with local families in small groups; she hosted several at her house. Participants spent their days visiting courts to observe how they worked. Nightly dinners revolved around different themes—women in religion, education, or medicine, among them. More than one hundred volunteers in Windham County donated meals and services to the project.

As a newcomer—flatlander, if you like, or hippie transplant—Whalen married into one of Vermont's most influential old families. Fletcher Proctor, her second husband, comes from a family that includes four governors and two Vermont Supreme Court judges, including Redfield Proctor, a Vermont governor, U.S. senator, and U.S. secretary of war. All Republicans. The two met in law school; together they have three children. Proctor is the town moderator in Westminster, an attorney, and historian with an expertise in early Vermont history.

"We really have to hand it to Vermonters because, despite our different worldviews and backgrounds, they were very welcoming to [the counter-culture kids] in a Vermont kind of way. They might have judged you but certainly gave you a fair hearing. My first husband, now deceased, had hair down to his waist, but the Ballentine family we rented from were the sweetest people in the world. I remember Mrs. Ballentine always coming by, checking in, interested and curious about us. Every step along the way, all sorts of people have helped me."

She told the story of returning from Sarajevo one February to learn that the Westminster West school board had decided to close the little town school with no public process. Rather than go home to rest, she sat down to write a complaint against the board for violating the open-meeting law and filed it in time for the next board meeting, where her complaint caused a big uproar and sent the matter to town meeting.

"The process of our town meeting was so vital," she recalled, experiencing again the earnestness people brought to the issue. "People listened all day. People spoke in favor of the small school. People talked about closing it. People talked about changing their minds. I thought, that's Vermont. In the end, the town voted overwhelmingly to keep the school and supported the budget."

Coincidentally, "One of our friends' daughter had gone to Macedonia, fallen in love, and brought the Macedonian Albanian husband home. This was his first town meeting, and he started to cry" as he observed Westminster's town meeting process. Recalling that moment and her journey from the commune to the world court to that small town meeting, she said emotionally, "I would give my life for this place, this Vermont."

* * *

Charlie and Diane Gottlieb came to Vermont in 1971 as a feminist couple, committed to sharing work and childcare. There was an intentionality to their decision making that was very un-hippie, although they thought of themselves as hippies, having experimented with drugs, participated in antiwar demonstrations, and considered moving to Canada during the Vietnam War. Yet, from a very early age, their actions were quite organized and goal-oriented; together, they had vowed to do good work helping others in the mental health field, to have a child they would raise together as a feminist, and, wherever possible, to foment change that would lead to a kinder, more inclusive world. They attributed their longevity as partners in marriage, childcare, and professionally to the fact that they shared the same goals and

Diane and Charlie Gottlieb with their infant daughter
in their first Vermont home in Lincoln.
Courtesy of Diane Gottlieb

values. To watch them communicate, filling in gaps in their individual and shared stories, one hears the harmony between them.

The couple had met as counselors at a camp for children with disabilities while both were in high school. Charlie grew up in the Bronx in a Jewish family with strong labor connections, while Diane grew up in Queens where her high school friends were red-diaper babies. On weekends, she frequented the Gaslight Café to listen to Bob Dylan and other folksingers while Charlie wasn't so much interested in studying as in drugs, sex, and rock 'n' roll. The two dated through high school but lost contact when Diane went off to the University of Wisconsin, a bedrock of the antiwar movement, and Charlie to the University of Ohio in Toledo where he helped set up a draft counseling center on campus. The couple didn't see each other for five years, but when they reunited, they found their lives had followed similar paths. "We've been together ever since," Diane said. They married in 1968.

Because Charlie had a low draft number, they thought of going to Canada, but Charlie got a job teaching sixth graders in Harlem, which qualified for a deferment. Diane went to graduate school and they began to meet with other people interested in going to the country to form a commune. Charlie had vacationed in Vermont as a kid and remembered it fondly. When Diane became pregnant, however, fathers were not allowed in Vermont delivery rooms. The move could wait, as he would not be kept from welcoming his child into the world. Their daughter Sasha was born at Mt. Sinai Hospital with Charlie the first (non-hospital staff) male allowed in the delivery room. Once Sasha was old enough to travel, and impatient with their friends' dawdling on the Vermont move, they rented a farmhouse in Lincoln, choosing the rural town because they thought it would be an easy commute between Diane's job in Shelburne and Charlie's in Middlebury. "We were so clueless about commuting during a Vermont winter," Diane said, chuckling. "Anyone driving those roads knows how naïve we were."

In 1975, four years after they moved to Vermont and found work as therapists, the couple decided to leave their jobs and temporarily take welfare and food stamps so they could form a radically different model for mental health care in Vermont. Thanks to her advanced degree, Diane had been working as a counselor at the Creamery, a private psychiatric service in Shelburne, while Charlie was an outreach worker with the Addison County Counseling Service. It was a strange situation. Diane would get up in the couple's house in the woods, put on her professional clothing, and spend the day with middle- and upper-middle-class clients and colleagues, then return home, where Charlie had spent the day counseling adolescent boys living in rural Addison County.

Convinced that their studies, training, and readings into more holistic approaches to mental health were not being put to their best use, they joined with three other therapists in founding Networks, the first collectively run mental health care center in Vermont. Networks was based on feminist ideals and the belief that a person is best made whole when his or her whole community is involved in the healing, which in turn, they believed, would improve the community's health.

Both were uncomfortable with treatment models then in vogue, ones that were based on psychodynamics with its concentration on the role of unconscious forces. They believed people were more greatly influenced by their social environment, including racial and socioeconomic factors, and were interested in how those factors affected a person's ability to make decisions and move forward. In their approach to treatment, they sought to identify and address a multitude of factors that might, for example, make a child depressed or an administrator angry. At the time, both were themselves members of women's and men's consciousness-raising groups and a coed group where people challenged one another to be honest as they sought to clarify personal goals. A male consciousness group Charlie had begun in Lincoln lasted from 1971 to 1979 and spawned other men's groups. Bernie Sanders attended twice, but was more interested in economics and politics than the subject of gender roles.

Networks proved successful, serving an interesting array of clients from people the couple knew from the communes and other counterculture connections to professionals to low-income clients referred by social-service agencies. In that, they were the beneficiaries of President Johnson's War on Poverty, which provided states with substantial grants for programs to help people in need and for training the professionals who were treating them. They introduced other therapists around the state to their holistic approach to counseling by creating courses and training modules. They soon had contracts to train state employees working with families and, because their clinic was on a bus route, low-income clients had easy access to their services.

"Our biggest life mission has been to fight against hierarchy and dominance. That was the reason we created our own organization. We couldn't do it within a university or state mental health system," Charlie explained, acknowledging that the couple indeed worked for state agencies, but with the goal of changing their treatment approaches. They were also among the first therapists to serve gay and lesbian people as this population began coming out publicly.

About the time they started Networks, they also decided to try living collectively as they had planned when they moved to Vermont. But rather than a rural setting, their collective would be urban. To that end, they bought a house in Burlington along with a mother whose daughter was the same age as theirs and a man with two older kids. Chores were divided using a work wheel, allowing the three families to split shopping, daycare, and maintenance. The collective lasted three and a half years. While there was the opportunity for shared cultural experiences, meals, and adventures, there were child-rearing and other differences that led to the collective's breakup. "We left not because of the strife, but in 1978 we decided to take our daughter and travel around the country, go to Mexico, and live life a little differently," Diane explained. During that year, Networks continued. "The staff were our friends and colleagues. We went to them and said, 'We'd like to take three to six months off and pay our share to keep the office going.' We talked to Sasha's school and told them we would do her lessons every morning." With that taken care of, off they went on their family adventure. They learned Spanish together and traveled all the way to the Baha Peninsula and back, interweaving geography, history, books, and language into daily life.

While their daughter was raised in the collective and later at home with both parents, she also spent time in playgroups and at the Ethan Allen Childcare Center, at which "all gender roles were challenged, with men running the kitchen. It was a collective experience," Charlie said. "We were one of the first people to have a child in our various social groups. We would invite people to love her and be with her so she was a very adored child," Diane added.

That said, they concede that their daughter wished they had been more focused on her. As Diane put it, "We were less attentive than Sasha has herself been as a mom, a deliberate decision she made as a mother based on how she felt as a child. We were, for lack of a better word, selfish. We brought her with us when we went places, to big parties, great parties, and we both were active in our own interests. She was raised by us and by our community, which is the way we wanted it."

There's no way to measure the long impact that the Gottliebs had on the state's social and rehabilitative services, although in their various roles they introduced a holistic way of treating mental health to hundreds of practitioners and patients.

Diane Gottlieb said it was easy enough to see the influence Vermont has had on them: "From fifteen on, I identified as counterculture. I can pick up immediately someone who grew up in the sixties and if they were part of the counterculture. There's an optimism and a sense of possibility we still have. It's why we were able to do so much, especially here in Vermont where we had many friends whose goal was to make the world a better place."

The Children of the Counterculture

"The brunt I felt as a child, moving around all the time, the chaos of life, was based on these hippie kids who had kids, who just cruised around in a vw bus and raised their kids through the goodness of strangers. Their beautiful idea of let's try this, then this, led to a lot of instability, moving, changing schools, having to make new friends over and over. But on the other hand you picked up skills from doing that, like not doing it their way. They were coming out of such rigid thinking; they were the first of their kind. [My father] was the backlash to his parents, and my brother and I are the backlash to our parents. My father was the complete kid long into adulthood." That's Nero Smeraldo, an actor and builder living in Los Angeles, talking about growing up a hippie kid in Lincoln, Middlebury, Burlington, and other Vermont communities. He has pleasant memories of deep snow and the freedom to ride his bike all day and play in the woods, the freedom to live with friends rather than move to another school for his senior year of high school when his mother moved again. He praised his mother, Joode Campbell, for the hard work of raising him and his brother Paris after her marriage to their father dissolved when the boys were quite young. Their father moved to Florida, where he briefly ran a restaurant, remarried, and had a daughter.

Despite the separation, Nero learned useful skills from him. "My father built the house in Lincoln by himself from trees from the property that he had milled. It took a full year. He was good at woodworking, sculpting, so I learned important stuff from being around that. That influence, growing up in Lincoln on the land, 120 acres on the side of a mountain with no road until we built one was incredible. We heated with woodstoves, had no running water, an outhouse. We spent the summer in a lean-to up in the woods, miles from anything. All that has stayed with me," Nero recalled. "And so too did his leaving."

His father's near disappearance from everyday life took a toll, one that many children of the counterculture experienced. As has been noted, when many of the hippie marriages broke up, it was more likely that mothers had custody of the children and that fathers moved elsewhere for work, often making new families. Meanwhile, the women, who had made close friends through their children, support groups, and common interests, tended to stay in Vermont simply because it was difficult to move with kids, especially when it meant leaving those support systems behind. And, as Vermont judge Patti Whalen observed, in the 1970s when these marriages were ending, many women did not receive adequate child support and had to work, sometimes several jobs, as Campbell did, to make ends meet. Kathy Roberts, who raised her son and daughter as a single mother after her divorce from their father, observed that the hippies were sometimes estranged from their parents because of their life choices. On top of not having a father figure full-time in their lives, the children were often not as connected to or living close to grandparents as in previous or subsequent generations.

As Nero Smeraldo put it, "Everyone I knew had parents who were divorced, and they grew up with their mothers and their mothers' friends. That was a good thing, but it's not enough. Kids need to know both parents."

While his childhood may have come in handy as an actor—one reviewer wrote of his performance in a play, "Nero Smeraldo perfectly embodies the libertine, who wants to marry Fay because marriage is the only thing he's not yet tried"—he has worked hard to create "a strong marriage. There's a lot to be said for getting married and having kids once you're done having your fun." Nero traveled around the world by himself from nineteen to twenty-two, moved to Los Angeles, where he pursued an acting career and formed ENS Builders, a contracting business. "If anything, my childhood experience allowed me to see what you don't want to pass on to your kids. The whole hippie thing, you could say *selfishness* is the uglier word to describe it."

His brother Paris was in first grade when their parents divorced: "I don't have fond memories of the back-to-the-land scenario in the woods. That's when my parents divorced, just to kind of go with it, fuck responsibility, and be a hippie. Chill out. Take some drugs. As a young child during that time, it was not a positive environment to be growing up in," he said. "Children for the most part want structure and consistency mixed in with excitement."

Paris loved Vermont, as indicated in the successful farm-to-table restaurant called Northeast Kingdom he and his wife, the artist Meg Lipke, founded in New York City and ran for more than a decade, closing in 2016. As described by *Eater* magazine, Northeast Kingdom "helped spark an eventual restaurant and bar boom around the Jefferson Avenue L stop and has since become an adored neighborhood spot. The couple doubled down on their sustainable, farm-to-table ethos by selling their upstate farm's vegetables regularly."

When the restaurant's success impeded their ability to spend enough time with the children and each other, they closed it. "We were busy seven nights a week with lots of good press, making a difference in a great gentrifying neighborhood. After ten years, even the coolness starts to wear off. Even the amazement of 'I built this place.' We thought if we're going to go, let's go out at the top of our game," Paris said. They still raise their own food, have a successful CSA and farm stand in Ghent, New York. Paris returned to work as an information analyst for a law firm.

While their farm resembles the dream Paris's parents failed at, he wanted to make it clear that "there is no comparison. That was up on the side of a mountain—very Appalachian—kids in bare feet, unbathed. I'm not interested in doing anything that has been done before. This is the swing of the pendulum. We place an emphasis on the stability of our marriage and family and honoring those kinds of thing." When the couple's first child was born, Paris told his father how differently he would live his life and why. "I said I didn't know how to be a father but I'm fully committed to doing it right. [My father] is a wonderful person but he wasn't there. I didn't have his example."

Roberts's son Lars Nielson, the Smeraldo brothers, Aaron Bolton, and Kai Mayberger were childhood friends. They, Oona Adams, Bruce Wickstrom, and Spring Cerise were all born to counterculture parents who came to Vermont to live simply, artistically, and in harmony with nature. All but Mayberger have moved out of state to find work that both sustained their families and themselves. All but Cerise are in traditional marriages; she's single.

"I didn't know any traditional families until we moved to Burlington," Lars Nielson observed. "My friends and I grew up with strong mothers as role models; they were looking out for their kids while the fathers were off in their own world. My dad's kids [from a second marriage] have no perspective on that era; their reality is from when he got his act together."

After college and graduation from UVM and serving with the Peace Corps in Africa, Nielson lived and worked in Boston before marrying his wife,

Lars Nielson (*far right*) with Nero (*left*) and Paris Smeraldo, shown here
with Paris's wife, the artist Meg Lipke. The three young men were raised
by single mothers in hippie households after their parents' marriages broke
up. Now fathers themselves, each of them said the loss of their fathers as
full-time presences in their lives led them to fully commit to their families.
None currently live in Vermont but remain close.
Photo by Lars Nielson

Laney. Laney grew up around the world as the daughter of an international
bank executive, but the family kept a house in Woodstock. The Nielsons live
with their two daughters in Plano, Texas, where he is a marketing director for
Dell, and Laney is a stay-at-home mother and children's book author.

"My strongest memories are of living out in the woods—I live in a suburb
now—being outdoors and lots of group activities, lots of kids, music, appreciation of the land, people, and relationships. And great food. My mother has
this cookbook my kids love, held together with a rubber band, all the real
food recipes. She brings it with her when she visits. I always thought of my
parents as very industrious. We might have been just getting by but everyone
was like that," he said. "When you moved, everyone helped you. They were
always fixing things, sewing buttons, fixing cars, even giving us haircuts. We
may not have had a lot of money, but it wasn't that noticeable. The focus was
on what you were doing and the community."

"Living in Texas, there's nothing here that reminds us of Vermont. We bought a whole bunch of Sabra Field prints that are all over the house. The memory of Vermont—the stillness, the church dinners and strawberry suppers, the realness of the people and the land—is still very strong. Every summer we visit our parents and take the kids to the same general store in Barnard, to the state parks, and the lake. My kids have an affinity for everything Vermont stands for."

Emily Nielson, sixteen, "love[s] Vermont, how it's so spread out, peaceful, and there's so much nature and history. It feels like a whole other world. It doesn't feel present in my world today, in Texas; it feels like the past." She's fascinated with the "more carefree, less controlled" life her father experienced and her grandmother represents. "Grandma taught me how to sew, how to use a sewing machine; she's passing on her hippie traits and music. I'm like a pacifist. I get a lot from Grandma and her hippie roots. I'm totally for Bernie Sanders."

But her father is realistic. "Like any sort of movement, there are things people can accomplish at a particular time in history. It all seemed like a good idea—the dome, the teepee, the house with the root cellar—these were a response to the rigidness of the fifties and an opportunity to say no or do things differently. It succeeded but was trumped by other factors, many of them economic. My generation discovered that there's not a huge job base in Vermont and taxes are high, so it's hard to stimulate business, and living is more costly now," Nielson said. "Not that I don't dream of going back there some day."

* * *

For Aaron Bolton, who moved "seventeen or nineteen times" in childhood, all over New England, Vermont was the "bookend" to his childhood. His parents moved there when he was three. "We spent our first months living in a tent in Lincoln, out in the woods bordering a river, quite near not a commune but certainly a large gathering of like-minded folks, a refuge almost. David and Mary, my parents, knew some of them. They had followed a family that we were close with" to Vermont but they wanted "their own space, hence the tent . . . a great old army tent, set up on a wooden platform—a deck of sorts—with a temporary kitchen, hammocks, a bathroom nearby, all the trappings of home."

From 1972 to 1978, his parents operated the popular Mary's Restaurant in Bristol, "the center of our universe. It seemed like everyone who worked at

Aaron Bolton growing up
in Lincoln, Vermont.
Courtesy of Aaron Bolton

the restaurant were friends as opposed to employees. There were frequent parties, including epic holiday bashes where it was not unusual to wake up the next morning to a Tibetan Buddhist chanting in our living room, only to have us join in, and the sweet smell of burning herbs was always in the air." Bolton and his brother roamed around town and the woods with complete freedom, "exploring back roads on our bikes and riding down the roads on the tailgate of a pickup dangling our feet over the back as they got kicked out by the road."

"My father would always say they weren't hippies, although they were. You'd be a freak before you'd use the word hippie," he joked. But in fifth grade, the family moved back to Cape Cod where his parents ran several other restaurants. Life went from "color to black-and-white then." They returned to Vermont in 1987, and Aaron lived and raised his own family there until 2014 when, in his late forties, he got a job at a national publisher located in Denver. He observed that the plusses of Denver were that it was "sunny, the economy was booming in part due to legal marijuana, a juxtaposition to Vermont where people seem to be struggling economically" and pot was still not legalized. Nonetheless, he said, "I miss Vermont every day."

* * *

Sas Carey's son, Kai Mayberger, has a different take. He identifies "with my parents' generation and lifestyle more than my own," referring to his mother's work as a potter and healer, his father's as a weaver, and his uncle's as a carpenter. From them, he inherited artistry and learned woodworking skills. In high school, he was already repairing antique furniture and working as a carpenter before enrolling at Goddard where he studied sculpture, woodworking, ecology, and shamanism. There he designed a plan for a drum-making business he founded in 1993. At White Raven Drum Works, located in a building in Bridgewater known by its silo-like entrance decorated with carved wooden trees, he builds and sells drums, flutes, and didgeridoos, each a piece of art. The flutes are carved of beech and ebony, sometimes in the shape of a bird's beak, the didgeridoos sometimes fashioned of bashofia wood from a tree he grew at his father's Florida home. In Vermont, he grows elm, ash, cherry, and maple trees for his instruments. But recognizing the realities of his homegrown profession, he also purchased and renovated a rental unit in Proctor, counting on the income as an insurance policy in slow times.

Like his friends from the hippie days, he too vowed to be a partner in child raising. He and his wife, Julia Lane, a professional cake baker among other things, arranged their work schedules around homeschooling their two sons. As a child upon whom the changes of the sixties were imposed, he has watched Vermont's evolution into a liberal place with a mix of appreciation and amusement. "I often tell visitors, when I was a kid there were no Democrats in this state and it was very conservative and that amounted to a philosophy of believing this is my property and I can do whatever I want and that's your property and you can do what you want. In some ways, that's very liberal. That's why the counterculture worked."

Nonetheless, he too felt that his parents' choices, especially their divorce, were hard on him and his sister. "The net result is that a lot of us worked really hard on choosing partners we could spend a lot of time with," he said. "I wanted to have my own kids so I wouldn't make the mistakes my parents did," he said, then added with a hint of irony, "I just made different ones."

* * *

Oona Adams, one of the children born on Total Loss Farm commune, grew up between her parents' homes. From the time she started school until she was thirteen, she lived during the week with her father so that she could attend a progressive school in Marlboro where he lived. She spent weekends with her mother, the poet Verandah Porche. Finishing her schooling at Brattleboro High, Adams was well aware of the differences between the two communities and learned to appreciate both cultures. At the commune,

"It was a wonderful childhood to have so many people around, people with interests of their own whom I could talk to, to read me bedside stories, people who carried on the daily tasks of life in a most interesting way," she said. And at Marlboro, where she also attended college, there was the influence of the music school and the arts that the town is known for. All this helped her think about the culture at large and what separates people. "My mother really thought about class and making relationships with people of many backgrounds, not letting one's aesthetic be a barrier to communications. I remember one time I was going to a rally and I was dressed in one of my teenaged outfits and she said, 'You might want to think about your personal decision about self-expression and whether that [outfit] might keep you from delivering the message you want to deliver.' That's how she was. It wasn't don't wear that; she'd never say that. But I thought about what she said and at an early age pondered who I was, and what was it I wanted to say to the world and how to talk to people. I don't know how many people were encouraged in that way to seek their own identity."

These were important skills for a woman growing up on one of Vermont's best-known communes, filled with a moving collection of writers, artists, anarchists, journalists, and others with strong opinions. Perhaps these influences led to her career as a union organizer working with the working class. After Marlboro College, she earned a master's degree in labor studies at UMass–Amherst and moved with her husband to New York City where she works for a large labor union. Adams was aware that some young people she knew were dismissive of the trades and the working class. Not she. Her first internship was with a construction union. "I found I liked them and the directness of the conversations we could have. My mom was really curious about people, and that curiosity didn't end with people she agreed with. 'If you're curious about people, it's hard to find people you can't agree with on something,' that was her default position. It really influenced me."

As a young couple living in Brooklyn, Adams and her husband have maintained Vermont roots. They purchased a little cabin next to Porche's house that is twice the size of their apartment in New York and where their daughter loves to climb trees and eat vegetables fresh off the vine. With all that, she brings an interesting perspective to the subject of the counterculture's impact on Vermont and Vermont's place in the world. "Vermont seemed like a place where people were willing to overlook the fact that the people who came there were from different backgrounds. That made a profound impression on me. My mythology is that it takes an independence and single-mindedness to be a farmer" or succeed in many other jobs in Vermont. "You've got to be adaptable because there's not enough to make a go on just one thing. You have to cobble things together. That flexibility made it easier to accept the new people. Everybody gets by doing a whole series of jobs. I admired that they taught us you can fix things on your own. Some of my favorite memories are from going to a neighboring farm and haying with the family. It would have been easy for them to not want to be around these interlopers but they were incredibly welcoming. People like Ralph Rhodes, he taught [the new] people how to farm. Besides, we had this terrible hippie food. When I visited, he had actual cake, cake from a box. It was great and he was the greatest," she said, expressing how grateful she was to have grown up with so many influences, mainstream and hippie, rural and sophisticated, the best of both worlds.

* * *

Like others raised in hippie homes, Spring Cerise loved the nonconformities of Quarry Hill while also discovering the limits of personal and group freedoms. She loved the freedom to run naked when it was warm enough and knew to put on clothes when she went to town. On the commune, every door was open to her and she could "choose to be with a friend's dad making stained glass in the basement, or down by the brook, making a fort, catching salamanders. I got to experience all different parenting styles, although they all leaned toward the generous, noncontrolling end. That can have good and bad outcomes and didn't necessarily help kids develop good boundaries. I don't have kids but I think healthy boundaries are important." Also, in the commune, there was a kind of groupthink, she said. "It was only much later that I began to feel comfortable about going against the grain."

Growing up on the commune, where her father married Libby Hall, she had the freedom of living in Magi-La and, as an adult, benefitted from Hall's generosity. She doesn't take either situation for granted—that she had a father in her life and a generous stepmother.

Today, living in the Bay Area, she's amazed that some of her friends are into polyamory—having multiple romantic partners. For her, the concept brings up feelings of abandonment. "That was my parents' dynamic. Maybe if I hadn't learned about it by having it shoved down my throat, watching my parents, I'd have more curiosity," she said. Instead, at thirty-eight, she's still looking for the right person to be with and start a family.

With Hall's support and financial help, Cerise studied abroad in Uganda, lived on a Navaho reservation, volunteered in Haiti, and realized she liked being of use. She returned to school, got her master's in nursing, worked as a nurse practitioner in a county jail, then in an urgent care unit.

There were causalities among the younger generation she can't forget. "Growing up in that environment where drugs were prevalent, so many of us kids struggle to this day with addiction, both alcohol and drugs. A lot of us have not gone into traditional careers or figured out how to get into mainstream society. I was determined to do so but I had a leg up with so much support from my stepmom," she said.

What remains for her is the memory of running naked and free through fields, the larger family she was part of. "I'm glad I got to do that, had that sense of physical freedom, no judgment. It was tribal, a time that probably will never come again."

* * *

Bruce Wickstrom grew up on the New Hamburger commune in Plainfield, one of the few still in existence in Vermont, and now lives in a rather upscale neighborhood in San Francisco where he builds even more upscale homes for people with a lot of expendable cash. "For me, it was formative," he said of his years on the commune. "When people compliment my buildings, I always credit David [Palmer]. He imbued his work ethic in me and taught me there are no shortcuts. Do it once and do it right."

In 1972, Wickstrom, his mother, Jean Lathrop, and her husband, Dick Lathrop, joined educator Mary Jane Carlson, her children, and Sam Clark at the New Hamburger commune, founded in 1967 as a back-to-the-land effort that blended activism with sustainability. Dick Lathrop left after five years and eventually Jean Lathrop married David Palmer, a union that contributed to the commune's longevity.

"He raised me," Wickstrom said. "He held us together."

The land, eighty-five acres, had cost $15,000. The farmer who owned it held the mortgage until it was paid off. It was Carlson's son Freddie who named it as a kind of joke since some of the residents were vegetarians. Initially, everyone lived in one big house but, as families grew and people wanted more privacy, they added a few small houses. They shared an old vw and a Plymouth Valiant. Everything was decided by consensus.

"My whole life was meetings, not always pleasant, as all the inner-child things came out at times," Wickstrom said. But the founders and early commune members "had real principles about not allowing egos to create hierarchy. They succeeded at that. The New Hamburger wanted to change society. It was all big-picture stuff."

"We had a lot of freedom, which was both good and bad, but it was sometimes difficult going to school in Plainfield. I remember when one of my friends started eating whole wheat bread. I was so glad. It was a rural community of farmers and hillbillies, which made it really interesting when the school bus dropped me off at a place filled with a bunch of freaks called the New Hamburger," he recalled. "But, over time, Plainfield, because of Goddard and all the other people who settled there, including everyone at New Hamburger, became an alternative place embraced by the old-timers."

"When I come back, I feel it. Central Vermont is full of really smart, evolved people. I don't think there's a lot of small communities that have the sort of energy you find there. There's a consciousness of activism that you really feel in every decision, every conversation. The people I grew up with and the people around us made it a different place. I came here with a black friend recently and she was so surprised. She said 'There's more black people in central Vermont than San Francisco,' which may say as much about San Francisco these days as it does about central Vermont," Wickstrom said.

His parents died just months apart in 2015. Legally, the house Palmer and Lathrop built, a gorgeous but simple structure of wood and stone, belongs to the collective. Wickstrom understands that. Yet he asked an important question: "What happens to the legacy, to the adult children who have an attachment to the base? How do we hang on to the community . . . or do we? In fifteen years, most of the people here are going to be eighty and older. How does it transition into the future? We talk about a temporary member house or guesthouse so the adult children can come back, so we have a place to hold on to ourselves.

"We wouldn't change the structure for anything," he said, then reflected on the people who cared for his stepfather through a long illness and the people who came from around the country for Palmer's and his mother's memorials.

"Turns out," he said, "if you have to die, a community like the New Hamburger is the place to do it."

* * *

Verandah Porche and her daughters, Emily and Oona, discovered that truth when Porche's husband, Richard Coutant, was diagnosed with pancreatic cancer and died forty-seven days later on June 7, 2015. Richard, a law partner in Bellows Falls with Governor Salmon and others, was a talented photographer and collector of antique cameras, a student of history, a Red Sox devotee, a lover of adventure and family. Throughout those weeks, the commune and the community responded, helping Verandah and Richard's sister Christopher care for him at home, installing a handrail so Richard could get up and downstairs and then a ramp for a wheelchair. If anyone connected to Packer Corner had despaired of their collective sense of purpose over the years, it quickly became apparent that when the time came, as it would for all of them, that they would be there for one another, as were their children and their neighbors, those who had lived with them and those from the surrounding community.

When it was clear that Richard would not survive, they prepared for his burial. Of course, as with Verandah and Richard's wedding, as well as Oona's to her husband Matt, the burial would be on the property, on the hillside overlooking the farm and the apple orchard Coutant had pruned just a few months previously.

It would be a green burial. Porche served on the Guilford cemetery commission and had researched the proper preparations. A friend from town surveyed the plot; a local excavator dug the grave; Verandah's sister Evelyn sewed the fine linen shroud that would cloak Richard's body; the daughters and other children of the commune, made suddenly aware of the dispassion of time, vowed continuing support for their parents and one another in the coming years. Then they prepared the trundling board upon which they would carry Richard's body to a truck that would bring him up the hill to a site from which one could look down on the whole enterprise, the orchard, the outbuildings and farmhouse, and the majestic mountains all around. Together, they covered him with Guilford soil and planted wild mountain thyme and nigella, the flower the old-timers call love in a mist, on his grave.

*And yet, I found my thoughts reaching into
the past. . . . They were searching for the sweet
uncertainties of a bygone year and for all
its chance encounters—encounters which in
the moment had seemed so haphazard and
effervescent but which with time took on
some semblance of fate.*

AMOR TOWLES,
Rules of Civility

I've been living in this book and this time for
three years, maybe longer. In truth, ever since Kathy
Roberts sent me a little book about hippies in Taos and said,
"You should write this story in Vermont," part of me has been dwelling
in that golden, confounding era. That Taos book made me feel fortunate
to have spent my young adult years in Vermont as, along with the pleasures
of self-discovery and innovation expressed in *Scrapbook of a Taos Hippie*,
there were also frightening stories about the locals' reaction to the newcomers, there in New Mexico's high desert, incidents more disturbing than anything I had heard about or experienced in Vermont's green pastures.

As I've talked endlessly with friends and strangers about the sixties and
seventies in Vermont—collecting stories, delving into the era's rich and
sometimes sobering history—I've found myself also examining my own life,
making my own apologies and explanations, longing to see my parents, crying over dead loved ones and failed dreams. In the end, what remains is immense gratitude for a time and a place that feels unreal, impossible, and yet
we know it happened.

Every story told within these pages is but a glimmer of a life, limited not
just by space and my ability to render it, but also by the complexities of the
individual stories in relation to the whole, this place we call Vermont. Ours
was not the first generation to turn our backs on a society viewed as vacuous
and deadening at best, indifferent or complicit at worst. There have been
many counterculture experiments in the wilderness and the cities, all fueled
by the belief that their proponents knew better. In this state, time and time
again, people have come seeking the comforts and challenges of the country

and life experienced in concert with the seasons and one another, only to be tempered by reality and time. Vermont has witnessed many such gatherings, from the Abenaki people—the People of the Dawn—who lived along the shores of the Missisquoi, to the Oneida Community with its own version of open marriage, to Scott and Helen Nearings' cohorts along Pikes Falls. Along the way, other alternative communities and lifestyles have flourished briefly in Vermont's verdant hills and lush valleys, including the early Mormons, Millerites, Swedenborgians, Fourierists, Garrisonians, and Transcendentalists. Among these groups, some of the causes espoused were abolition, anti-materialism, vegetarianism, and total self-reliance—concepts that the young hippies and back-to-the-landers shared. I have no doubt that new attempts at creating a utopian lifestyle in our precious and demanding state will come again, as they will to other places, near and far. That is the nature of the human.

Is the world a better place for our efforts? Who can say? The arguments for yes and no could go on forever. We look to the sky. We honor those we might have honored better and more openly, our parents. We know our remaining years on the planet are few. We plant our gardens. We love our grandchildren. We treasure our music. Our books. The small memorabilia of our lifetime, the memories we hide away or display. We recognize each other still, just as Diane Gottlieb does, anywhere we go.

Melinda Moulton said it best: we were many and our impact was substantive, but we were just a small part of a large generation in a large country in a large world. We sing the song Sandy Denny wrote and Judy Collins made ours, "Who Knows Where the Time Goes." We hope there is still time for our dream of peace to come to fruition. That is our legacy, that undying hope.

ACKNOWLEDGMENTS

To live with a writer through the throes of research, organization, frustration, success and failure, and self-doubt can be a trying experience. Chuck Clarino, who helped raise my children and has shared forty-four years with me, a fellow lover of words, has endured all of these emotions, along with computer crashes and technical snafus that sometimes made me a rather unpleasant companion. Over the past two years, as I've traveled the state interviewing people, then struggled to tell their stories in as succinct and organized fashion as I could, he has made my morning coffee, found my glasses, taken the dogs out, and otherwise been a partner in the endeavor. He has endured my obsession and distraction gracefully. My thanks, therefore, goes first to my husband for patience and devotion, for all the small and large ways he made the journey easier and believed in its worth.

My editor, Richard Pult, has also shown remarkable patience as the deadlines came and went. His faith in this project has helped me move forward again and again. Gratitude also to Cannon Labrie, Rachel Shields Ebersole, and Maria van Beuren for their careful attentions to many small and large details.

So many people have been part of this book, from the friends of many years who

The author and her husband, Chuck Clarino, in 1976.
Photo by Stephen Smith

read sections and gave useful comment, to strangers who invited me into their homes and trusted me with their stories. My gratitude to them is immeasurable. I apologize to those who gave me their time and stories, only to not find themselves in this book. Know, please, that your observations and experiences informed the text in ways that may not be apparent, but were immensely valuable.

Contemporaneous with my project, the Vermont Historical Society conducted a two-year study of the impact of the counterculture on Vermont. The society conducted numerous interviews, held public meetings, and otherwise gathered and shared the story of the hippie invasion of Vermont and its impact. Vermont journalists reported on several of the society's gatherings. That rich material, both the society's reports and the newspaper accounts, has been a valuable resource as this book unfolded. Thanks in particular to Jackie Calder, who led the society's project and ushered it into the public view throughout Vermont.

* * *

Many readers have their own memories of this time period to share and are welcome to do so or to leave comments on the book and its subject matter at http://daley .got2web.net or on Facebook at yvonnedaleybookgoingupthecountry.

APPENDIX / *Soundtrack*

Introduction
"The Power and the Glory," Phil Ochs; "Spirit in the Sky," Norman Greenbaum; "My Sweet Lord," George Harrison; "Beginnings," Chicago; "Pack Up Your Sorrows," Richard and Mimi Farina; "Thirsty Boots," Eric Andersen; "This Land Is Your Land," Woodie Guthrie; "The Times They Are A-Changin'," Bob Dylan; "Late for the Sky," Jackson Browne.

Chapter 1: The Hippie Invasion
"Going Up the Country," Canned Heat; "Groovin'," Young Rascals; "San Francisco (Be Sure to Wear Flowers in Your Hair)," Scott McKenzie; "Time Has Come Today," Chambers Brothers; "Scarborough Fair," Simon and Garfunkel; "Get Together," the Youngbloods; "Aquarius," the Fifth Dimension; "For What It's Worth," Buffalo Springfield; "Can't Find My Way Home," Blind Faith; "Fire on the Mountain," Charlie Daniels; "Into the Mystic," Van Morrison; "Seven Bridges Road," the Eagles; "Mister Tambourine Man," Bob Dylan.

Chapter 2: Life on the Commune
"Light My Fire," the Doors; "Everyday People," Sly and the Family Stone; "Touch Me," the Doors; "In-A-Gadda-Da-Vida," Iron Butterfly; "Someone to Love," Jefferson Airplane; "With a Little Help from My Friends," Joe Cocker; "Jesus Is Just All Right," the Doobie Brothers; "Our House," Crosby, Stills & Nash; "You Ain't Going Nowhere," the Byrds; "Lost in the Woods," Leon Russell; "Gimme Shelter," Rolling Stones; "Golden Slumbers," the Beatles.

Chapter 3: Higher Education
"Fresh Air," Quicksilver Messenger Service; "You Keep Me Hanging On," Vanilla Fudge; "Burn Down the Mission," Elton John; "Someday Soon," Ian and Sylvia; "Adult Education," Hall and Oates; "Old Man," Neil Young; "Strange Magic," Electric Light Orchestra; "Dr. Wu," Steely Dan; "Everybody Knows," Leonard Cohen; "My Old School," Steely Dan.

Chapter 4: Food . . . and Revolution
"Scarborough Fair," Simon and Garfunkel; "Badge," Cream; "Time of the Season," the Zombies; "Alice's Restaurant," Arlo Guthrie; "Tangerine," Led Zeppelin; "Reflections of My Life," Marmalade; "Tupelo Honey," Van Morrison; "After the Gold Rush," Neil Young; "Black Coffee in Bed," Squeeze; "Strawberry Fields," the Beatles; "Suzanne," Leonard Cohen; "Maggie's Farm," Bob Dylan.

Chapter 5: Entrepreneurship—Hippie-Style

"Money," Pink Floyd; "Your Wildest Dreams," Moody Blues; "Going to California," Led Zeppelin; "Goodbye Yellow Brick Road," Elton John; "Woodstock," Joni Mitchell; "Willin'," Little Feat; "Free Man in Paris," Joni Mitchell; "Levon," Elton John; "All Along the Watchtower," Jimi Hendrix; "A Day in the Life," the Beatles; "Joe Hill," Joan Baez.

Chapter 6: Political Transformation

"In the Year 2525," Zager and Evans; "Give Peace a Chance," John Lennon; "Ohio," Crosby, Stills, Nash & Young; "Vietnam Song," Country Joe and the Fish; "Outside of a Small Circle of Friends," Phil Ochs; "Imagine," John Lennon; "I'd Love to Change the World," Ten Years After; "Court of the Crimson King," King Crimson; "25 or 6 to 4," Chicago; "Peace Train," Cat Stevens; "White Winged Dove," Mark Spoelstra; "The Ballad of Ira Hayes," Patrick Sky; "The Lonesome Death of Hattie Carroll," Bob Dylan.

Chapter 7: Creativity

"Ripple," the Grateful Dead; "So You Want to Be a Rock and Roll Star," the Byrds; "Good Vibrations," the Beach Boys; "Dear Mr. Fantasy," Traffic; "Summer Breeze," Seals and Crofts; "Headkeeper," Dave Mason; "You've Got to Have Freedom," Uptown Funk Empire; "Forever Young," Bob Dylan; "Time in a Bottle," Jim Croce; "Miracles," Jefferson Airplane; "Changes," David Bowie; "Pride of Man," Quicksilver Messenger Service.

Chapter 8: Drugs

"A Whiter Shade of Pale," Procol Harum; "White Rabbit," Jefferson Airplane; "Hey Jude," the Beatles; "Sky Pilot," Eric Burdon; "Eight Miles High," the Byrds; "Are You Experienced," Jimi Hendrix; "Lucy in the Sky with Diamonds," the Beatles; "Purple Haze," Jimi Hendrix; "Magic Carpet Ride," Steppenwolf; "Comfortably Numb," Pink Floyd; "Kid Charlemagne," Steely Dan; "Rainy Day Women #12 & 35," Bob Dylan.

Chapter 9: Women's Work Reimagined

"Respect," Aretha Franklin; "Amelia," Joni Mitchell; "San Francisco Girls," Fever Tree; "Me and Bobby McGee," Janis Joplin; "Hold Your Head Up," Argent; "Visions of Johanna," Bob Dylan; "Shouldn't Have Took More Than You Gave," Dave Mason; "Corrina," Taj Mahal; "Suavecito," Malo; "Melissa," Allman Brothers; "Farewell, Angelina," Joan Baez; "Layla," Derek and the Dominos; "Sisters, O Sisters," Yoko Ono; "Different Drum," Stone Poneys (with Linda Ronstadt).

Chapter 10: The Children of the Counterculture

"Teach Your Children," Crosby, Stills, Nash & Young; "God Bless the Child," Blood, Sweat & Tears; "Waiting on a Friend," Rolling Stones; "Angel from Montgomery," Bonnie Raitt; "Dolphins," Fred Neil; "Circle Game," Joni Mitchell; "Wear Your Love Like Heaven," Donovan; "Cat's in the Cradle," Harry Chapin.

Epilogue

"These Days," Tom Rush; "Who Knows Where the Time Goes," Judy Collins; "Over the Rainbow," Eva Cassidy; "Urge for Going," Tom Rush; "Hallelujah," Leonard Cohen; "Life's a Long Song," Jethro Tull; "Box of Rain," the Grateful Dead; "I Shall Be Released," the Band.

SOURCES AND RESOURCES

PEOPLE

While literally several hundred people were interviewed or informally discussed the subject of this book with the author, the following individuals offered more detailed comments and information:

Charles Adams, Oona Adams, Christine Anderson, Victoria Arthur, Mary Azarian, Barrie Bailey, Richard Bernstein, Cecile Betit, Elliot Blinder, Bea Bookchin, Debbie Bookchin, Terry Bouricius, Grace Brigham, David Budbill, Ginny Callan, Sas Carey, Chris Carrington, Bill Carris, Michael Carpenter, Spring Cerise, Andy Christiansen, Dan Chodorkoff, Claire Clarino, Rod Clarke, David Cowles, Greg Cox, Jay Craven, Hamilton Davis, Peter Diamondstone, Jim Douglas, John Douglas; Maureen Dwyer, Ruth Dwyer, Steve Early, Lois Eby, Nancy Edwards, Susan Farrow, Tim Fisher, Isabella "Ladybelle" Fiske, Eldred French, Lily French, John Froines, Judy Geller, Grace Gershuny, Charlie Gottlieb, Diane Gottlieb, Peter Gould, Jenny Buell Greco, Susan Green, Jerry Greenfield, Greg Guma, Phil Hoff, Lucy Horton, Robert Houriet, Loraine Pingree Janowski, Perry Kacik, Jeff Kahn, Joey Klein, Kathleen Kolb, Martha Lasley, Susan Leader, Charles Light, Lisa Lindahl, Robin Lloyd, Peggy Luhrs, Mary Mathias, Kai Mayberger, Dick McCormack, Libby Mills, Melinda Moulton, Ray Mungo, Garrison Nelson, Emily Nielson, Lars Nielson, Barbara Nolfi, Oke, Torie Osborne, Emma Ottolenghi, Kathleen Murphy Patten, Will Patten, Roz Payne, Larry Plesant, Richard Pollak, David Ritchie, Anthony Pollina, Verandah Porche, Kathy Roberts, John Rosenblum, Bernie Sanders, Bill Schubart, Elka Schumann, Peter Schumann, Paul Sgalia, Allen Sherman, Stephen Sherrill, Nero Smeraldo, Paris Smeraldo, Andy Snyder, Ellen Snyder, John Specker, Steve Spensley, Bill Stetson, Richard Sugarman, Marcy Tanger, Steve Terry, David Tier, Wayne Turiansky, Patricia Whalen, Bruce Wickstrom, Claire Wilson, Richard Wizansky, Art Woolf, and David Zuckerman.

REFERENCES

Sources are listed by chapter in order of appearance. Sources not listed here are from personal interviews with the subjects.

Chapter 1: The Hippie Invasion

Richard Pollak, "Taking Over Vermont," *Playboy*, April 1972.
James F. Blumstein and James Phelan, "Jamestown Seventy," *Yale Review of Law and Social Action* 1, no. 1 (1971), http://digitalcommons.law.yale.edu/yrlsa/vol1/iss1/6.

Yvonne Daley, "The Hippie Legacy," *Sunday Rutland Herald/Times Argus*, October 10, 1983.

Rod Clarke, "Life at Earth People's Park," *Northland Journal*, July 2015.

Larry Plesant, "The Last American Hippy," an unpublished novel.

Vermont Census Data, Vermont Historical Society, http://vermonthistory.org /educate/online-resources/vermont-census-records#vermont-in-the-1900s.

US Census: www.census.gov.

Two court rulings, the federal *Baker v. Carr*, https://supreme.justia.com/cases/federal /us/369/186/case.html, and a Vermont case, *Mikell v, Rousseau*, https://casetext .com/case/mikell-v-rousseau, led to reapportionment. The high court had ruled in 1962 that states should reapportion legislative representation based on the 1960 census, while the Vermont case forced the reapportionment when the state body failed to do so.

Jane Lindholm, "Buddhism in Vermont," February 12, 2013, WVPR, www.vpr.net /episode/55410/buddhism-in-vermont.

Pew Research Center, "Religious Landscape Study," 2014, www.pewforum.org/ religious-landscape-study/state/vermont.

Jason Kaufman and Matthew E. Kaliner, "The Re-accomplishment of Place in 20th-Century Vermont and New Hampshire: History Repeats Itself, Until It Doesn't," *Theory and Society* 40, no. 2 (March 2011): 119–54, available at jstor.org.

Samuel Hand, Anthony Marro, and Stephen Terry, *Philip Hoff: How Red Turned Blue in the Green Mountain State*, Hanover, NH: University Press of New England, 2011.

"20 in 20: Vermont Great Moments in the 20th Century, Reapportionment of the Vermont House—1965," VermontToday.com, available at https://web.archive.org /web/20160716111027/www.vermonttoday.com/century/topstories/reapportionment .html.

Harry Thompson's obituary, *Barre-Montpelier Times Argus*, September 10, 2013, www.legacy.com/obituaries/timesargus/obituary.aspx?n=harry-a-thompson&pid= 166887855.

Tom Slayton, "In This State: Green Mountain Parkway Might Have Preserved the Mountaintops," March 25, 2012, VTDigger, http://vtdigger.org/2012/03/25.

Chapter 2: Life on the Commune

Sally Johnson, "Excesses Blamed for Demise of the Commune Movement," *New York Times*, August 3, 1998, www.nytimes.com/1998/08/03/us/excesses-blamed-for -demise-of-the-commune-movement.html.

Daniel A. Brown, "The History of the Brotherhood of the Spirit/Renaissance Community: 1968–1988," History 104 course at UMass–Amherst, https:// brotherhoodofthespiritblog.wordpress.com/people/michael-metelica.

Greg Joly, *Almost Utopia: The Residents and Radicals of Pikes Falls, Vermont*, Barre, VT: Vermont Historical Society, 2008.

Randy Kennedy, "When Meals Played the Muse," *New York Times*, February 21, 2007, www.nytimes.com/2007/02/21/dining/21soho.html.

Gloria Moure, *Gordon Matta-Clark: Works and Collected Writings*, Barcelona, Spain: Poligrafa, 2006.

The July 1974 issue of *National Geographic* contains a twenty-five-page article entitled "Vermont: A State of Mind and Mountains," featuring furniture maker and artist Peter Murray and the Mad Brook Commune.

Charles Light, "Far Out: Life On and After the Commune," www.youtube.com /watch?v=fPmmQuyhtZM.

Ray Mungo, *Total Loss Farm: A Year in the Life*, Seattle: Madrona, 1970.

Ray Mungo, *Famous Long Ago*, Boston: Beacon Press, 1970.

Verandah Porche, Marty Jezer, Raymond Mungo, Peter Gould, Richard Wizansky, and others, *Home Comfort: Stories and Scenes of Life on Total Loss Farm*, New York: Saturday Review Press, 1973.

Oral history with Euan Bear and Mary Schwartz, Vermont Historical Society, July 2, 2015, www.digitalvermont.org/vt70s/AudioFile1970s-1.

Verandah Porche, *The Body's Symmetry*, New York: Harper & Row, 1974.

Verandah Porche, "At Work Rebuilding a Castle with Mark Fenwick," *Northern Woodlands*, (Winter 2011), http://northernwoodlands.org/articles/article/at-work -with-mark-fenwick.

Reid R. Frazier, "1960s Communes in Southern Vermont," master's thesis, University of Vermont, 2002.

Robert Houriet, "Back-to-the-Land 1969: The Earthworks Commune," The Philo School of Herbal Energetics website, http://herbalenergetics.com/?p=298.

John Douglas, *Crossfire*, Newsreel, Activist Film Collective archive, available at https://web.archive.org/web/20170704040009/www.counterfire.org/news -archive/176-news-archive/99-katherine-cleaver.

John Douglas, *Strike City*, 1966, Newsreel, www.youtube.com/watch?v=6 -ZOp3mEtpQ.

You can view a clip from *People's War* and other John Douglas films, read the *New York Times* articles about the government's confiscation and subsequent release of the film, a redacted CIA document about the delegation, and other documents relative to Newsreel at www.douglaswork.com/pages/peoples-war.

A clip from with Grace Paley explaining her views on the Vietnam War and her response to meeting the Vietnamese people can be seen at www.youtube.com/ watch?v=pk2iN-rgjpo and at www.douglaswork.com/pages/milestones.

John Douglas's film on the Free Farm is available at www.youtube.com/watch?v= mWjn5vPJAlw.

Robert Kramer's obituary, *New York Times*, November 13, 1999, www.nytimes .com/1999/11/13/arts/robert-kramer-60-a-director-of-films-with-a-political-edge .html.

Bruce Taub's letter to the Franklin town librarian is posted on his website, A Man on a Walkabout, http://brucetaub.net/to-the-town-librarian.

Roz Payne's collective works on the Black Panthers is available on *What We Want, What We Believe: The Black Panther Party Library*, www.newsreel.us/DVD/information.htm.

James Drew, *A Societal History of Contemporary Democratic Media*, New York: Routledge, 2013, www.newsreel.us/DVD/information.htm.

David Van Deusen, "Green Mountain Communes: The Making of a Peoples' Vermont," January 15, 2008, Anarkismo.net, www.anarkismo.net/article/7248.

Bryan Burroughs, *Days of Rage: America's Radical Underground, the FBI, and the Forgotten Age of Revolutionary Violence*, New York: Penguin Books, 2015.

Robert Houriet, "Life and Death of a Commune Called Oz," *New York Times Sunday Magazine*, February 16, 1969, http://timesmachine.nytimes.com/timesmachine/1969/02/16/90052594.html.

Robert Houriet's interview on the *Today* show, August 21, 1971, is available at www.today.com/video/-70s-flashback-author-discusses-communes-683686979723.

Irving Fiske biography is available at Wikipedia, https://en.wikipedia.org/wiki/Irving_Fiske

Becky Armstrong, "Quarry Hill 1969–1976: An Oral History of a Time and Place," master's thesis, Dartmouth College, 1999.

Quarry Hill Creative Center's Facebook site can be found at www.facebook.com/quarryhillcreativecentervermont.

You can learn more about Adam Sherman's film, *Happiness Runs*, at www.imdb.com/title/tt1079964.

Rod Clark, "Life at Earth People's Park," *Northland Journal*, May 2015.

Chapter 3: Higher Education

Susan Green, "Faith in Goddard: A Collective Memorial for 'Little Moscow on the Hill,'" *Seven Days*, July 24, 2002,
www.sevendaysvt.com/vermont/faith-in-goddard-a-collective-memorial-for-little-moscow-on-the-hill/Content?oid=2525544.

Jesse Jarnow, "The Roots of Phish: A Psychedelic Pedigree," Cuepoint, March 22, 2016, available online at https://medium.com/cuepoint/the-roots-of-phish-a-psychedelic-pedigree-131252db0490.

William Macy, "My Little Piece of Vermont," *New York Times*, February 17, 2006, www.nytimes.com/2006/02/17/travel/escapes/my-little-piece-of-vermont.html.

Royce Pitkin's obituary, *New York Times*, May 6, 1986, www.nytimes.com/1986/05/06/obituaries/royce-stanley-pitkin-goddard-college-head.html.

Lee Webb interview with Pierre Clavel, June 30, 2005, available online at http://progressivecities.org/wp-content/uploads/2013/01/Lee-Webb-Interview-Short-version1.pdf.

George Warshow's obituary, *Barre-Montpelier Times Argus*, November 15, 2015, available online at www.legacy.com/obituaries/timesargus/obituary.aspx?pid=176545581.

Archival footage of Bread & Puppet's *Stations of the Cross* with Whole Note singing by Larry Gordon's choral group in 1972 can be viewed at http://breadandpuppet .org/50th-anniversary-2/from-the-archives/archival-footage.

An article about demonstrations at the University of Vermont are available at "Dissent on Campus," *Vermont Quarterly*, www.uvm.edu/~uvmpr/?Page=news& storyID=24025.

James Marsh biography, University of Vermont, www.uvm.edu/president /formerpresidents/marsh.html.

Alexander Twilight biography available online at www.biography.com/people /alexander-lucius-twilight-213035.

Robert Keren, Middlebury News Room, "Campus Unrest in the '60s and '70s," January 24, 2014, available online at www.middlebury.edu/newsroom/node/468467 #sthash.IvcLyW7G.dpuf.

Torie Osborn, "Sweet Vermont Vindication: Remembering Justice—Vetoing Governor Douglas Back When . . ." *Huffington Post*, April 9, 2009, www .huffingtonpost.com/torie-osborn/sweet-vermont-vindication_b_185110.html.

Marlboro College history, available online at www.marlboro.edu/about.

Windham College history, and how it transformed into Landmark College, available online at www.landmark.edu/library/landmark-college-archives/college-history /windham-college-how-landmark-came-to-occupy-the-former-windham-campus.

Chapter 4: Food . . . and Revolution

Jeff Danziger, "Vermont's Epicurean Evolution: How 1960s Hippies Took Vermont Farmhouse Cooking to Today's Artisanal Heights," July 27, 2012, VTDigger, July 27, 2012, http://vtdigger.org/2012/07/27/vermonts-epicurean-evolution-how-1960s -hippies-took-vermont-farmhouse-cooking-to-todays-artisanal-heights.

Information about Vermont's Farm to Plate effort to strengthen the agricultural economy is available at www.vtfarmtoplate.com.

Howard Weiss-Tisman, "Brattleboro Food Co-op Building Wins National Creating Community Connection Award," *Brattleboro Reformer*, June 19, 2015, www .reformer.com/stories/brattleboro-food-co-op-building-wins-national-creating -community-connection-award,307858.

Plainfield Co-op history, available online at www.plainfieldcoop.com/History.html.

Robert Houriet's oral history and early history of Northeast Organic Farming Association was recorded in 1998 at http://credo.library.umass.edu/view/full /mums461-s07-i005.

Dan Chodorkoff, Jake Guest, Roz Payne, Roger Fox, Grace Gershuny, Jim Higgins, Liz Guest, Larry Kupferman, Jaqueline Calder, "Colleges, Communes & Co-ops in the 1970s: Their Contribution to Vermont's Organic Food Movement," Excerpts from the 175th annual meeting of the Vermont

Historical Society, September 21, 2013, https://vermonthistory.org/journal/82 /VHS8202CollegesCommunes.pdf.

Data on Vermont's agriculture is found on the Vermont Department of Agriculture, Food, and Markets website at http://agriculture.vermont.gov.

Stephen Klein, "Community Canning Centers: A Project Profile in Community Economic Development," is an excellent resource for studying the various efforts supported by nonprofits and government alike in the 1970s to help people become more sustainable through gardening and canning, https://www.scribd.com /document/246182190/Community-Canning-Centers

The Northeast Organic Farming Association of Vermont website, http://nofavt.org, offers a history of the organization, profiles on member farms, information on farming and programs.

The Middlebury Food Co-op website offers not only its history, written by Charles Adams, but also information on the development of the co-op movement, http:// middlebury.coop/tag/co-op-history.

Chapter 5: Entrepreneurship—Hippie-Style

Roger R. Griffith, "What a Way to Live and Make a Living: The Lyman P. Wood Story," Charlotte, VT: Capital City Press, 1994.

The Kaufman Index, 2015 study of the best states for entrepreneurs and start-ups, www.kauffman.org/kauffman-index.

Jess McCuan, "It's Not Easy Being Green," Inc.com, Nov. 1, 2004, www.inc.com /magazine/20041101/seventh-generation.html.

"Carris Reels History—Over a Half Century of Quality Reels," www.carris.com /company/2/carris-history.

The history of the Green Mountain Spinnery can be found at https://www.spinnery .com/about-us.

Cathy Keen, "The First Jogbra Was Made by Sewing Together Two Men's Athletic Supporters," *Smithsonian*, April 13, 2015, www.smithsonianmag.com/smithsonian -institution/first-jogbra-made-sewing-together-two-mens-athletic-supporters -180954968.

Information about Main Street Landing and Melinda Moulton, available at www .mainstreetlanding.com/about/staff/melinda-moulton-ceoredveloper.

Margaret Michniewicz, "Moulton-Steele: Sustaining a Bold Vision," *Vermont Woman*, July 2005, www.vermontwoman.com/articles/2005/0705/moulton-steele .html.

Information about the Ben & Jerry's Foundation available at http:// benandjerrysfoundation.org.

"Our Non-GMOs Standards," available at www.benjerry.com/values/issues-we-care -about/support-gmo-labeling/our-non-gmo-standards.

David Gelles, "How the Social Mission of Ben & Jerry's Survived Being Gobbled

Up," *New York Times*, August 21, 2015, www.nytimes.com/2015/08/23/business/
how-ben-jerrys-social-mission-survived-being-gobbled-up.html.

Chapter 6: Political Transformation

"University of Chicago Sit-ins," Wikipedia, https://en.wikipedia.org/wiki/University
_of_Chicago_sit-ins.

Rick Perlstein, "A Political Education," *University of Chicago Magazine*, January/
February 2015, http://mag.uchicago.edu/law-policy-society/political-education.

Frederick H. Gardner, "William H. Meyer: The Campaign," *Harvard Crimson*,
November 1, 1960, www.thecrimson.com/article/1960/11/1/william-h-meyer
-pvermonts-three-electoral.

Tim Murphy, "How Bernie Sanders Learned to Be a Real Politician," *Mother Jones*,
May 26, 2015, www.motherjones.com/politics/2015/05/young-bernie-sanders
-liberty-union-vermont.

Greg Guma, *The People's Republic: Vermont and the Sanders Revolution*, Shelburne,
VT: New England Press, 1989, offers an interesting perspective of the progressive
movement through journalistic articles and personal reflection.

Richard Sugarman profile, University of Vermont, https://www.uvm.edu/~religion
/?Page=sugarman.php.

David Fahrenthold, "How the NRA Helped Get Bernie Sanders Elected,"
Washington Post, July 19, 2015, www.washingtonpost.com/politics/how-the-nra
-helped-put-bernie-sanders-in-congress/2015/07/19/ed1be26c-2bfe-11e5-bd33-
395c05608059_story.html.

David Moberg, "How Bernie Sanders Put Socialism to Work in Burlington: A Profile
from 1983," *In These Times*, http://inthesetimes.com/article/18806/this-1983-profile
-of-bernie-sanders-shows-how-his-success-in-burlington-mir.

Data on Vermont's Progressive Party: Vermont Progressive Party website, http://
progressiveparty.org/elected-progressives.

Darcy G. Richardson, *Bernie: A Lifelong Crusade against Wall Street & Wealth*,
Sevierville Publishing, 2015.

Tamara Keith, "Leaving Brooklyn, Bernie Sanders Found Home in Vermont," NPR,
June 20, 2015, www.npr.org/sections/itsallpolitics/2015/06/20/415747576/leaving
-brooklyn-bernie-sanders-found-home-in-vermont.

Bernie Sanders, with Huck Gutman, *Outsider in the White House*, New York:
Verso Press, 2015.

Mark Davis, "Bernie Sanders Recorded a Folk Album. No Punchline Required,"
Seven Days, September 17, 2014, an entertaining article and recording of Sanders
singing "This Land is Your Land," www.sevendaysvt.com/OffMessage
/archives/2014/09/17/bernie-sanders-recorded-a-folk-album-no-punchline
-required.

Carey Goldberg, "Vermont Residents Split Over Civil Unions," *New York Times*,

September 3, 2000, www.nytimes.com/2000/09/03/us/vermont-residents-split-over-civil-unions-law.html.

Jim Douglas's autobiography, *The Vermont Way*, New Haven, VT: Common Ground Communications, 2014, offers interesting insights into Vermont's recent political history.

Chapter 7: Creativity

Catharine Wright and Nancy Means Wright, *Vermonters at Their Craft*, Shelburne, VT: New England Press, 1987.

To see Kathleen Kolb's paintings and read more about the artist, go to www.kathleenkolb.com.

Judith Weinraub, "From Anti-War Activist to Committed Filmmaker," *Washington Post*, May 8, 1994, www.washingtonpost.com/archive/lifestyle/style/1994/05/08/from-anti-war-activist-to-committed-filmmaker/ecd4bf5a-b004-4fdf-9c5f-119254b42254.

Judy Tzu-Chun Wu, "June 2013: Vietnam Revisited: Forty Years after the Paris Peace Accord," *Origins*, June 2013, https://origins.osu.edu/milestones/june-2013-vietnam-revisited-forty-years-after-paris-peace-accord.

Andrew Ruseth, "Six Feet of the 1960s and '70s: Patty Mucha—Once Mrs. Oldenburg—on Her Archives and New Memoir," *Observer*, January 16, 2012, http://observer.com/2012/01/patty-mucha-oldenburg-on-her-archives-01162012.

Kenward Elmslie's biography, Poetry Foundation website, www.poetryfoundation.org/poets/kenward-elmslie.

Patricia Minichiello, "Gayleen Aiken: Folk Artist's Work Lives On in Home State," *Rutland Herald*, March 17, 2016,www.rutlandherald.com/articles/gayleen-aiken-folk-artists-work-lives-on-in-home-state.

A list and review of Jay Craven's movies is available on the IMDb website at www.imdb.com/name/nm0186610.

Mary Azarian's work and history is available at her website, www.maryazarian.com.

Information about musician John Specker can be found on Old Time Archive, a repository of articles and film clips about Old Time Music, https://oldtimeparty.wordpress.com/category/john-specker.

Videos of John Specker and his daughters performing are available at https://oldtimeparty.wordpress.com/category/john-specker.

Nikolai Fox's cinema portrait of George Ainley from the documentary *Music for the Sky*, 2011, is available at https://vimeo.com/23588966.

The history of Susan Leader Pottery and examples of her folk-art-inspired pottery can be seen at www.vermont.com/business/susanleaderpottery.

Bill Schubart's website, http://schubart.com, is a repository of his commentaries about Vermont, synopses of his many books, and reviews of his work.

A wonderful video of Steve Spensley singing and playing is available on YouTube at www.youtube.com/watch?v=AI2F2gghAWo.

Thomas Mitchell's obituary, April 26, 2006, can be viewed at www.legacy.com
   /obituaries/bennington/obituary.aspx?n=thomas-w-mitchell&pid=17544715.
Although the Patrick Farrow Gallery closed after his death, his work can be viewed at
   the gallery site, located at http://patrickfarrow.com/gallery_miniatures.html.
John Bell, *Puppets, Masks and Performing Objects*, Cambridge, MA: MIT Press,
   2001.

Chapter 8: Drugs

Jay Stevens, *Storming Heaven: LSD and the American Dream*, New York: Harper &
   Row, 1987.
Hamilton Davis, *Mocking Justice: America's Biggest Drug Scandal*, New York: Crown
   Publishers, 1978.
Bob Boyd, "Legacy of a 'Super Cop' Turned Bad," *Burlington Free Press*, January 3,
   2015,
www.burlingtonfreepress.com/story/news/local/2015/01/03/legacy-asuper-cop-turned
   -bad/21230427.
Jane Mayer, "Pat Leahy Recalls a Sting," *New Yorker*, October 15, 2001, www
   .newyorker.com/magazine/2001/10/15/pat-leahy-recalls-a-sting.
Mike Harris, "Pardons an Attempt to Right Wrongs for 71 Vermonters," *Washington
   Post*, January 6, 1977.
John Knifer, "Drug Raid Leader Jailed for Vermont Frame-ups," *New York Times*,
   August 2, 1976, www.nytimes.com/1976/08/02/archives/new-jersey-pages-drug-raid
   -leader-jailed-for-vermont-frameups.html.
Tom Slayton, "Justice, Finally, Did Come to the Aid of Lawrence's Victims," *Rutland
   Herald/Sunday Times Argus*, May 30, 1976.
Aaron Smith, "Vermont Lawmakers Try Again for Marijuana Legislation," CNN,
   June 20, 2017, http://money.cnn.com/2017/06/20/news/vermont-marijuana
   -legalization-special-session/index.html.

Chapter 9: Women's Work Reimagined

Look, "50 Pages on the American Woman," January 11, 1966.
Sister Elizabeth Candon's obituary, *Burlington Free Press*, February 3, 2012, www
   .legacy.com/obituaries/burlingtonfreepress/obituary.aspx?pid=155751120
Sallie Soule, Vermont Historical Society, http://vermonthistory.org/research/vermont
   -women-s-history/database/soule-sallie.
Change the Story, 2017 Status Report: Vermont Women and Leadership, http://
   changethestoryvt.org/2017-status-report-vermont-women-and-leadership.
Vermont Commission on Status of Women, http://women.vermont.gov/who_we
   _are.
Change the Story VT, http://changethestoryvt.org.
Robert Houriet, *Getting Back Together*, New York: Putnam Group, 1971.
Susan Green, "Vermont Remains a Hippie Epicenter," *Burlington Free Press*, July 24,

2015, www.burlingtonfreepress.com/story/news/local/vermont/2015/07/24/vermont
-remains-hippie-epicenter/30564907.

Community Health Centers of Burlington history, www.chcb.org/about.

Bruce Bistrian, et al., edited by Stuart A. Copans, *The Home Health Handbook:
A Preliminary Guide to Self-Help and Rural Medicine*, Burlington, VT: La Pauvre
Press, 1971.

Jackie Calder and Amanda Gustin, "History Space, 'Hippies, Freaks and Radicals,'"
April 1, 2017, *Burlington Free Press*, www.burlingtonfreepress.com/story
/news/2017/04/01/history-space-hippies-freaks-radicals/99910072.

Community Health Centers of Vermont, www.chcb.org/about.

Megan James, "Prepared for Arrival: Comparing Vermont's Hospital Birthing
Centers," *Kids VT*, April 29, 2014, www.kidsvt.com/vermont/prepared-for-arrival
-comparing-vermonts-hospital-birthing-centers.

Raven Lang, *Birth Book*, Cupertino, CA: Genesis Press, 1972.

Vermont Midwives Association, www.vermontmidwivesassociation.org.

Thurmond Knight website, www.violinviolacello.com.

Cindy Bittinger, "We Won't Go Back," *Vermont Woman*, February/March 2014,
www.vermontwoman.com/articles/2014/0214/abortionhistory/wontgoback.html.

Beecham v. Leahy, 287 A.2d 836 (1972).

Steve Zind, "Sister Elizabeth Candon, Longtime Educator, Is Dead at 90," VPR,
February 2, 2012, www.vpr.net/news_detail/93277/sister-elizabeth-candon
-longtime-educator-dead-at-90.

Vermont Folklife Center, oral history, Sallie Soule, March 3, 2016, www
.vermontfolklifecenter.org.

David Goodman, "Emma's Lifelong Mission to Better Women's Health," *Stowe
Today*, October 10, 2007, www.stowetoday.com/waterbury/archives/emma-s
-lifelong-mission-to-better-women-s-health/article_1d441b51–453d-5cbb-b8f0
-8576f3d96f6b.html.

Susan Green, "Losing Winn: A Burlington Activist Dies the Way She Lived—
Fighting Poverty," *Seven Days*, June 5, 2002, www.sevendaysvt.com/vermont/
losing-winn-a-burlington-activist-dies-the-way-she-livedfighting-poverty/Content
?oid=2547646.

Peter Dreier and Pierre Clavel, "What Kind of Mayor Was Bernie Sanders," *Nation*,
June 2, 2015, www.thenation.com/article/bernies-burlington-city-sustainable
-future.

Bernie Sanders interview with Martha Whitney, November 13, 1987, can be viewed on
YouTube at www.youtube.com/watch?v=m7Z4dlM2uTs.

Vermont Works for Women, www.vtworksforwomen.org/about/our-team/ronnie
-sandler.

David Eisenberg, *Encounters with Qi*, New York: W. W. Norton & Co., 1995.

See the trailer of Gobi Women's Song on YouTube at www.youtube.com/watch?v=
LGAgaGYfrvo.

Nomadicare website, http://nomadicare.org.

Vermont Historical Society, profile of Patricia Whalen, http://vermonthistory.org
    /research/vermont-women-s-history/database/whalen-patricia.

"Vermont Family Court opens for business," *Burlington Free Press*, October 2, 1990.

"Pioneering Women Judges on International Courts," International Association of
    Women Judges website, https://iawj-womenjudges.org/hon-patricia-whalen.

Networks, Inc., www.networksvt.org.

Oral history interview with Diane and Charlie Gottlieb, Aug. 17, 2015, Digital
    Vermont: A Project of the Vermont Historical Society, http://digitalvermont.org
    /vt70s/AudioFile1970s-4.

Vermont Historical Society annual meeting, "Freaks, Radicals and Hippies:
    Counterculture in 1970s Vermont," September 10, 2016, http://vermonthistory
    .org/visit/events-calendar/annual-meeting-conference#2016-freaks-radicals-and
    -hippies-counterculture-in-1970s-vermont.

Chapter 10: The Children of the Counterculture

Michele Clark, "Oh Death, Where Is Thy Sting?" The Wake Up to Dying Project,
    May 6, 2015, www.wakeuptodyingproject.org/2015/05/06/oh-death-where-is-thy
    -sting-2.

David Palmer's obituary, *Barre-Montpelier Times Argus*, June 5, 2013, www.legacy
    .com/obituaries/timesargus/obituary.aspx?pid=165156493.

Jean Lathrop's obituary, *Barre-Montpelier Times Argus*, August 31, 2015, www.legacy
    .com/obituaries/timesargus/obituary.aspx?pid=175689188.

RECOMMENDED READING

Brown, Edward Espe. *The Tassajara Bread Book*. Boulder, CO: Shambhala, 1977.

Callan, Ginny. *Horn of the Moon Cookbook*. New York: Harper & Row, 1987.

Daloz, Kate. *We Are as Gods: Back to the Land in the 1970s on the Quest for a New
    America*. New York: Public Affairs, 2016.

Davis, Adelle. *Let's Have Healthy Children*. New York: Harcourt Brace Jovanovich,
    1972.

Farrell, James J. *The Spirit of the Sixties: The Making of Postwar Radicalism*.
    New York: Routledge, 1977.

Fels, Tom. *Buying the Farm: Peace and Love on a Sixties Commune*. Amherst:
    University of Massachusetts Press, 2012.

Gershuny Grace. *Organic Revolutionary*. Barnet, VT: Joe's Book Press, 2016.

Gibbons, Euell. *Stalking the Wild Asparagus*. New York: David McKay, 1973.

Gould, Peter. *Horse Drawn Yogurt: Stories from Total Loss Farm*. Brattleboro, VT:
    Green Writers Press, 2017.

Hersey, John. *Hiroshima*. New York: Alfred A. Knopf, 1946.

Hewitt, Jean. *New York Times Natural Foods Cookbook*. New York: Avon Books, 1972.

Lappé, Frances Moore. *Diet for a Small Planet*. New York: Ballantine Books, 1971.

Michener, James A. *Kent State: What Happened and Why*. New York: Random House, 1971.

Schumacher, E. F. *Small Is Beautiful: Economics as if People Mattered*. New York: Harper & Row, 1975.

Stern, Jane and Michael. *Sixties People*. New York: Alfred A. Knopf, 1990.

Talbot, David. *Season of the Witch*. New York: Free Press, 2011.

Wavy Gravy, *The Hog Farm and Friends*. New York: Links Books, 1974.

INDEX

Page numbers in italics indicate illustrations.